Public Administration in India

Public administration in India is often synonymous with the role and performance of the Indian Administrative Service (IAS). In this volume, Maheshwari stresses the indispensability of the civil service in a democratic polity like India and the decisive role it plays in assisting with the social and economic development of the country.

While paying special attention to the selection and training of civil servants, staffing of the top management in government, the differences between the all-India and central services, promotions, conditions of service, and the issue of accountability, the book also analyses growing corruption in the bureaucracy and the question of ethics and morality. In addition, it looks at the elaborate and competitive recruitment process of the Union Public Service Commission of India.

Public Administration in India

The Higher Civil Service

S.R. MAHESHWARI

OXFORD
UNIVERSITY PRESS

OXFORD
UNIVERSITY PRESS

Oxford University Press is a department of the University of Oxford.
It furthers the University's objective of excellence in research, scholarship,
and education by publishing worldwide. Oxford is a registered trademark of
Oxford University Press in the UK and in certain other countries.

Published in India by

Oxford University Press
22 Workspace, 2nd Floor, 1/22 Asaf Ali Road, New Delhi 110002, India

© Oxford University Press 2005

The moral rights of the author have been asserted.

First Edition published in 2005
Oxford India Paperbacks 2006
Eighth impression 2015

ISBN-13 (print edition): 978-0-19-568376-9
ISBN-10 (print edition): 0-19-568376-5

ISBN-13 (eBook): 978-0-19-908783-9
ISBN-10 (eBook): 0-19-908783-0

Printed in India by Repro India Limited

To the sacred memory of my parents

Muniraj Mundra
1 November 1897–22 November 1971

कार्तिक पूर्णिमा सं. 1954—मार्ग शीर्ष पचमी सं. 2028

and
Kalavati Devi Mundra
20 September 1900–5 September 1968

आश्विन कष्ण सं. 1956—भाद्रशुक्ल चर्तुदशी सं. 2025

Contents

Preface

In the course of my professional career I have authored more than 50 books, nearly half in the discipline of political science, others in public administration. Four books are focused mainly on civil service, one each on the higher civil service of Britain, Japan, and France, the fourth one being *Major Civil Service Systems in the World*. This has made me the target of criticism. The criticism is rightly made. The criticism is that while I have written on other civil services, I have singularly neglected my own country's higher civil service. The omission is corrected now. I have great pleasure in placing *Public Administration in India: The Higher Civil Service* in the hands of readers. The present book has been in the making for a long time but the effort has been characterized by pauses, interruptions, and periods of inactivity. The work has now been completed. I am indebted to many for the successful completion of the work and I thank all of them warmly. I was allowed access to the proceedings of the provincial premiers' conference held in 1946 and the book represents an authentic account of what transpired at that momentous time in India's political history.

I would like to thank the Ford Foundation for the support it has extended in the completion of this study. If the present book is able to see the light of the day, the credit for this rightly goes to Bimla, my 'best' half.

January 2005   S.R.M.
New Delhi

CHAPTER 1

The Role and Importance of the Higher Civil Service

Civil service is the executive agency or action arm of the state and as such is engaged in implementing its policies and decisions. In addition, it is the accredited adviser of the political executive advising it on policy making, its advice based on professionalism. Ministers are career politicians and broadly know about the needs and interests of the people, but lack the detailed and specialized knowledge necessary for policy formulation in today's complex environment. This is made available by the civil service.

What is the likely role and importance of the civil service in context of the declared policy of the government towards liberalization, free market, and globalization? This is a natural query in India and the civil service has always been viewed as the trusted solution to all kinds of problems facing the country. Civil society was not developed to make people depend on the government to undertake all functions necessary to promote their well-being. This was the prevalent perception both during the colonial period and after Independence. It was in the 1980s that the country began to feel uncomfortable with its public bureaucracy. The growing feeling was that the solution itself was a problem, thus necessitating a search for alternatives. In 1991, India formally announced its new economic policy of liberalization and free market economy. This declaration was hailed as marking a retreat of the State. The space being vacated by the State is to be occupied by a free market and civil society, especially non-governmental organizations. New approaches now finding favour with the government are public choice and new public management (NPM). The report of the Fifth Central Pay Commission (1997) emerges as the first authentic text of the new face of India's public administration, including the civil service.

One must hasten to add that these changes, momentous as they certainly are, change the role of the civil service but certainly not its importance. Under the declared policy of economic liberalization, the private sector would surely grow, which would then be required to be monitored and controlled. India has already set up bodies like the Securities Exchange Board of India (SEBI), Telecom Regulatory Authority of India (TRAI), Disinvestment Commission, Competition Commission, and many others. The regulatory bureaucracy must cultivate new skills, traits, orientations, and predispositions. What can be said, therefore, is that the precise role of the civil service would certainly undergo a change, without affecting its importance and place in society. Nor can the civil service withdraw from its customary direct interventionist role towards over 30 per cent of the country's population reported to be living below the poverty line.

Ministers are laymen while civil servants serving them are politically neutral, impersonal, and professional. These roles add up to their traditionally high image in Indian society. Above all, higher civil servants are viewed as 'successful' persons in society and young graduates regard them as career models. They constitute the primary reference group in Indian society—a society in which the State has always occupied an extraordinarily exalted place and those who serve under it are easily set apart from the rest. Empires have risen and fallen, but the central place of the State in society has not diminished. The historical process in India kept the State amply endowed, but Independence leading to a sovereign, independent nation-state in the modern world in 1947 directed the civil service to assume far larger functions. The Indian State is engaged in tasks the nature, range, and magnitude of which would be daunting to even the most highly developed nations of the world. The colonial economy which it has inherited remains at the best times difficult to manage and extremely stubborn to accommodating processes of development. Considering that India chose until the 1990s a 'mixed' pattern of economic development with an important role for the public sector, public responsibility goes further than if it were a purely capitalist economy. The State in the republic of India is an activist one, evincing active interest in economic uplift, social reform, and cultural renaissance. Since it is India's declared policy to promote development in economic, social, cultural, and other spheres simultaneously—and not sequentially—the challenges are all the greater. And this array of functions is in addition to the traditional role of maintenance.

The nature and variety of challenges that a developing democracy encounters constitute the ideal background for analysing the role and place of its civil service. The expectations from it are bewilderingly large. In India, it is not even possible to catalogue all the functions that fall to the lot of the civil service. These remain, always, more undefined than defined. And in times of crises, these functions expand incredibly. We may recall what the Indian Statutory Commission, headed by Sir John Simon (popularly known as the Simon Commission), wrote in the 1930s:

In a country of small cultivators, no accumulated resources and little experience in organisation, except along the limited and traditional lines of the village community, private enterprise cannot undertake new and costly experiments. The task of bringing within reach of such a society the benefits of the administrative experience and the applied science of the West was possible for one agency only—Government; no other had the necessary knowledge or machinery. Thus the civil service of India, which in origin was little more than a revenue-collecting agency, gradually took upon itself a very wide range of duties. As the work became specialised, new services had to be created to carry it on, and in this way there grew up departments dealing with public health, education, forestry, agriculture, irrigation, archaeology, and many more. India looks to government to do many things which in the West are done by private enterprises.[1]

In short, civil service has always occupied a place of great honour in India.

The range and variety of tasks which public functionaries have to perform are immense. A member of the higher civil service may today be administering law and order but later would be given responsibility, say, in rural development, industrial development, etc. He goes on deputation to an organization where the work may be novel and challenging. He even goes abroad for a spell. Many of the jobs that he handles are totally beyond the reach or comprehension of any private sector organization, howsoever large. Some of his tasks would be peculiar to public administration, such as handling a disaster situation. Often, he handles crises that may mean life or death for thousands of people.

This variety of tasks gives the functionary job satisfaction and job enrichment. What is more, he directly serves the people and the State, and a consciousness that he is not working for profit and profit alone imparts a higher purpose, a nobler meaning to life. The satisfaction in administering rural development programmes is not of the same kind and level as, say, in selling toothpaste or soap. This adds to the elitism of the civil service in India, and is evidenced by a high level of competition for the service.

The social usefulness of a civil servant does not necessarily end on his superannuation from active service. Higher civil servants continue to be appointed as governors, members of commissions and committees or are given other jobs after retirement. The knowledge that there is no final sunset for a civil servant increases the attractiveness of civil service in

society. Where civil service commands such great honour it is bound to be
the dream of the brightest young graduates to enter it. Public employment
itself becomes the gateway to social recognition, and as such bright
university graduates are motivated to join the government. The attractiveness of civil service is of a high level in a developing country because—
among others—of the feeling of solidarity which it engenders among its
members. Recruitment means that one joins a select club, and members
will help each other in a wide variety of matters. A member may count on
his service colleagues wherever he may be. While an ordinary citizen will
have to stay in a hotel when he visits a new place, a civil servant, even
when on a private visit to a far-off place, may have little difficulty in
getting subsidized accommodation. (This is apart from the ease with
which a higher civil servant may make his own official programmes!)

There is a general view that civil services in a developing country are
not well paid—as compared to the private sector. This is a very loose kind
of observation. First, it depends on which private sector we have in mind.
There are very good pay masters in the corporate sector, but their numbers
are limited. Besides, salary from profits and salary from the tax-payer's
money are on a different footing and cannot, in all fairness, be equated.
Above all, the private sector can pay only in terms of money. Members of
the higher civil service enjoy a status and influence in society which is
beyond the imagination of the private sector. They get preferential treatment in an economy of shortages and scarcities.

In short, in a country like India, the civil service is an institution of
critical relevance to society. The social status which the higher service
enjoys is the top of the ladder. It continues to be the most attractive avenue
of employment even though the country's expanding private sector has
begun to attract a share of the nation's talent.

The credit for coining the term 'civil service' goes to India. The East
India Company (1600–1858) called its employees 'servants'. The servants
who were working on the 'civil side' in contrast to those employed for
military, including naval duties, were called 'civil servants'. The term was
formally adopted in the year 1785. The Oxford English Dictionary defines
the term as 'the permanent professional branches of state administration
excluding military and judicial branches and elected politicians'. Another
contending term is 'public service': it is much more expressive of the
loyalty centre of the group and is in consonance with the prevalent
democratic ethos of a modern society. The P.S. Sarkaria Commission on
Centre-State Relations (1983–7) has also shown its preference for 'public
servants', and not 'civil servants' on the grounds that the former expression

'emphasises the point that they are servants of the people and not of the members of the government'.[2] Two terms, 'civil service' and 'public service', must not confuse the reader. While every civil servant is a public servant, the converse is not always true. Members of the military or judicial wing of the state are not civil servants but are all public servants. The present work employs the term 'civil service' loosely and freely to refer to the employees of the state in its civil side of governance. The term 'civil service' is deeply entrenched in Indian public administration and is preferred as the title of the present work.

The higher civil service of a country necessarily plays a more or less decisive role in shaping its ultimate destiny. This is particularly true in the case of developing societies like India, where it has been viewed as a central institution since time immemorial. This is not because of its overwhelming numbers. Quantitatively speaking, the higher civil service constitutes hardly five per cent of the total strength of nearly four million employees in the Government of India. Members of the higher civil service as a rule occupy all strategic positions in all the sectors of the government, and thus directly participate in public policy-making. Their decisions influence the lives and happiness of all sections of society. They execute laws and implement policies and decisions of the government. In a democracy, policy-making is the prerogative of the politician, even though the civil service assists. In India, the politician arrived much later on the administrative scene, and as such the civil service was engaged in both policy-making and policy-implementation for a long time. The politician made his advent in administration only after the introduction of the Montford Reforms in 1919. Even at that time, the politician's role was in part of the provincial administration, with over-riding powers vested in the colonial governor. In the rest of the administration, the primacy of the Indian Civil Service prevailed. It is thus safe to assert that the politician in India has occupied a position of unquestioned primacy and leadership only after Independence.

In 1994, the Government of India employed 39 lakh people, of whom five per cent were in class I and II, the sphere of the higher civil service. In terms of numbers, the higher civil servants were not more than 1.91 lakh. A sizable number of them were recently recruited and are still in the junior and middle level positions, which means that there are far fewer higher civil servants. The three all-India services comprise nearly 11,000 officers, their service-wise break-up being 5336 in the Indian Administrative Service, 3519 in the Indian Police Service, and 2721 in the Indian Forest Service. Of these, many are at the junior levels and yet to work their way up. What is being emphasized is that the higher civil service is not a very large component, quantitatively speaking. Yet, they provide the much-needed leadership to the entire administration.

NOTES

1. Report of the Indian Statutory Commission, vol. I. Survey, emd. 3568, 1930, pp. 263–4.

2. Report of the Commission on Centre–State Relations, Part-I, New Delhi: Government of India, 1988, p. 219.

CHAPTER 2

The Environment of the Civil Service in India

The environment in which the civil service of a country functions is, in many respects, unique in itself and imparts to it a distinctive characteristic and shape. The environment within which public administration, including the civil service operates is a conditioning factor. Civil service, particularly when viewed as an activity, cannot escape being influenced by its immediate environment. It was Fred W. Riggs who first drew attention to the continuing interaction between bureaucracy and the environment within which it functions, though John Gauss had earlier referred to the interactive relationship between the two. Riggs employed the term 'ecology'. 'Environment' and 'ecology' are generally used as synonyms. The dictionary defines 'environment' as: 'that which environs; surrounding; specifically the aggregate of all the external conditions and influences affecting the life and development of an organism, etc.'; and 'ecology' as: 'biology dealing with the mutual relations between organisms and their environment'. In 'environment', the relational aspect between an entity and its environment is implicit, in 'ecology' this aspect is made explicit. Ecology is more deterministic whereas environment is subject to human engineering. Because it can be manipulated, environment is much more dynamic than ecology.

TYPES OF ENVIRONMENT

Environment may be physical or human. Physical environment is a matter of geography, which directly and persistently affects the working conditions in public administration, thereby affecting morale and motivation. A rural posting in India entails varying levels of deprivation, because of poor infrastructural facilities. Deserts and mountainous areas, with their thin and scattered population, pose a variety of problems in respect of administration, and civil servants show marked reluctance in accepting rural postings, especially in geographically difficult regions. The human environment entails several dimensions such as socio-cultural, psychological, economic, political, administrative, etc. Public administration being the art and science of human relations, the human inputs emanating from the environment influence people at work in various ways.

SOCIO-CULTURAL DIMENSION

Indian society is a stratified one, both vertically and horizontally. Hindus are divided into four major castes and each caste has numerous sub-castes. This has in its turn influenced the stratification process among Muslims and Christians too. Although the caste system is gradually shedding its traditional role under the impact of universal suffrage, it evokes new meanings and serves other purposes: it has quickly emerged as a rallying point, a mobilizational device for political ends, and at times manipulating even civil servants.

Horizontally, Indian society is divided along regional, linguistic, and religious lines and these cast varying degrees of influence on the civil service. Weberianism would expect civil servants to be objective and impersonal in their administrative behaviour, but they are continually exposed to forces drawing sustenance from caste, community, religion, region, language, etc., and it is difficult not to succumb to these forces and demands. For instance, the culturally induced craving for a male child affects family planning programmes. The high cultural value generally attached to twenty-four carat gold has made the Gold Control Order, first issued by the government in the mid-1960s to reduce the content of pure gold in ornaments, a virtual dead letter. Also, the postal rule that nothing other than letters and cards be enclosed in postal envelopes remains virtually suspended, when sisters mail rakhis to brothers in envelopes.

The impact of the socio-cultural environment on the theory and practice of government is felt in other ways as well. Society in India still remains feudal and many of the country's public officials come from this feudal stock. The expectations of the society they are expected to serve are also feudal. At the same time, democracy is embedded in the modern state in India. This introduces contradictions and conflicts of varying magnitude in the structure and patterns of interaction in society. There is also the matter of hierarchy, which provides a basic principle of administration. But where society itself is hierarchical, as in India, hierarchy tends to make public functionaries extra timid and inhibits them in tendering professional counsel to their superiors. The feudal culture of society thus reinforces the worst aspects of hierarchy while at the same time suppressing its better attributes. Because of the incongruity between the civil service—based as it is on the rule of law, constitutionalism, and democracy—and the operative societal norms, public officials are often exposed to an additional range of stresses and strains. Formally, public officials are objective and impartial, but society expects them to safeguard the interests of their kith and kin. They are exhorted to be achievement-oriented, but society's culture being ascriptive, they are expected to keep clan and community in mind.

ECONOMIC DIMENSION

Overall, poverty, unemployment, and general scarcity are among the chief features of the Indian economy; some of them being the direct outcome of the economic policies and strategies of development followed over the decades. It is also true that the rapidly growing population has partly wiped out the economic gains achieved by the country since the advent of planning in 1950. Poverty, unemployment, and shortages lead to a kind of equilibrium—rather 'disequilibrium'—between the citizens and the bureaucracy. Poverty makes people meek and pliant in their interaction with public servants. Acute unemployment results in intense pressure for government jobs and consequently overstaffing in government offices. Shortage, compounded by government interference, breeds pressures for supply and consequent corruption. There are, for example, more rail reservation seekers than seats available on a particular day, so people bribe the officials concerned to get accommodated. Shortage of electricity forces consumers to grease the palms of electricity staff to get connections. Whether it is housing, transport, fuel, school admissions, jobs, medical facilities or even food, shortages are the order of the day. Since the civil servant controls the distribution of essential articles, the system is subjected to heavy pressures. The considerable discretionary authority vested in the bureaucracy paves the way for corruption and political interference. Public servants are also seen to evince undue interest in what are called 'wet' posts—and politicians seek to manipulate them to extract the maximum advantage for themselves. More pernicious is the phenomenon where, for a consideration, the public servant allows the public to cheat the government in a plethora of fields—whether it is in revenue administration, theft of electricity, doctoring of meters, putting up false medical claims, encroachments on public land, or the administration of civil order and criminal justice.

POLITICAL DIMENSION

In a parliamentary democracy, the executive is responsible to the legislature where the political opposition plays its role, sometimes effectively. The judiciary is independent and the press is free and vigilant. People are politically conscious and have not hesitated in voting out of power a party that failed to meet their aspirations and thus alienated them. Political succession in India has always been constitutional and peaceful, when either the incumbent chief executive passed away or his party lost the election.

But there is a downside also. In the parliamentary system of government, the political executive being continually accountable to the elected legislature makes the ministers vulnerable to individual legislators' demands, even when they are unreasonable, leading to the problem of political interference in the work of the civil service. The single-party dominance system, a central feature of Indian polity for the last four decades (except for brief periods), tends to bring under stress the political neutrality of the civil service and compromises its objectivity and impartiality.

As governments at the central and state levels are elected every five years on the basis of adult franchise, a definite shift of power is rapidly taking place from the higher strata of society to the lower strata. The emerging political leadership is more concerned with ends, and means are increasingly losing their traditional relevance. The present political culture is also reward or benefit-oriented; and in the process national interest is given short shrift. The ethos dominating the contemporary political scene in India is one without norms, and the politics of the country is tending to become more and more unprincipled. The contemporary political culture inevitably impinges upon the country's bureaucracy, the intensity of the impact increasing as one goes down to state and lower levels. As a result, populism has come to characterize policy making, with its inevitable impact on public administration. Indian planning is often criticized for being over-ambitious, which also explains why the implementation of our programmes is unimpressive. Reservation of jobs is more and more common, which at times affects the play of merit in public administration.

PSYCHOLOGICAL DIMENSION

Perceptions are another dimension of environment. Perceptions are mutually supportive. They tend to travel in clusters and thus form syndromes. The public personnel in India, to give an illustration, are often a dissatisfied lot. Similarly, society perceives civil servants as obstacles who are there only to harass the citizen. As a basically insecure individual, a civil servant prefers to be on the right side of his boss. The result is weak socialization in the fundamental values of the Constitution such as socialism, constitutionalism, rule of law, limited government, etc.

To sum up, the civil service is inevitably influenced by the ecology within which it necessarily operates. The relationship may not be deterministic, but its influence is far-reaching. It is only over a period of time that ecology may itself undergo a change as a result of the interplay of several forces.

THE CONSTITUTION OF INDIA AND THE CIVIL SERVICE

Constitutions generally make an implicit distinction between government and administration, in the sense that they deal with the former but observe absolute silence about the country's public administration, including its civil service. Walter Bagehot (1826–77), in his celebrated work entitled *The English Constitution*, uttered not a word about public servants. The constitution of India is unique in the sense that it, unlike other constitutions, discusses public administration, including the civil service, in a somewhat detailed way. Part XIV of the Constitution is devoted to 'services under the union and the states'. It guarantees security of tenure to public servants. It recognizes the all-India services and even lays down the procedure for creation of new ones. It talks about public recruitment, conditions of service and the recruitment agency, namely the public service commissions. Many commentators of India's civil service think that such constitutional provisions confer excessive security of service on civil servants, which is dysfunctional.

In addition, the constitution of India is an elaborate document; it even discusses matters which are purely administrative in nature, making the supreme document of the land an administrative handbook also. The Constitution's concern for such matters shows that its framers did not wish to take chances and leave unlimited discretion to the executive. In other words, a detailed concern of the Constitution for administrative matters has an effect of fettering the freedom of the executive of the day.

SOCIO-ECONOMIC BACKGROUND OF HIGHER
CIVIL SERVANTS

A study of the higher civil service is not supposed to be complete without an examination of the socio-economic background of those who comprise it and conduct administration. The purpose of such a probe is to find out how far the country's civil service is representative of the various cross-sections of society. The idea underlying the concept of a representative civil service is that no single 'society' exists in a country; instead what is called society is a coalition of several publics, the defining belief being that those who live differently think differently. Here it can be boldly asserted. India's higher civil service is not representative in its social composition.

The higher civil service comes predominantly from the country's middle class, which at present ranges between 20 and 25 per cent of the total population. India's middle class is still a minority, which makes the civil service all the more unrepresentative of society. It comes from families following modern professions, but with exceptions. Medical doctors do not always produce doctor-children. Neither do lawyers. A large number of parents of successful candidates are teachers: in India, teachers do not evince much inclination to produce teacher-children! Nor is the spatial spread of the higher bureaucracy adequate. The country today claims nearly 300 universities and institutions of higher learning, but most of the successful candidates to the higher civil service hail from a limited number of universities—Delhi (University of Delhi and Jawaharlal Nehru University), Rajasthan, Chandigarh, Allahabad, Bhubaneshwar, Patna, and Osmania. Allahabad and Madras universities used to be the principal source of recruitment to the now-defunct ICS, but in modern India their hegemonic role has passed into the hands of the two universities in Delhi. The IITs are also showing considerable interest in the higher administrative services, giving little thought to the resultant wastage of professional engineers. Facilities required for making the requisite preparations for the competitive examination are abundant in Delhi, which makes aspiring students flock to the national capital. The road to Mussoorie (the location of Lal Bahadur Shastri National Academy of Administration) is said to lie via Delhi, so goes a saying.

Graduation is the minimum educational qualification demanded of eligible candidates, but most are post-graduates. In India, the job market is tight, and post-graduate degrees are achieved in order to strengthen employment chances. Some even possess a doctorate degree as well as work experience. This is because the upper age of entry in the civil service is 30 in India. The practice in India is to pursue education uninterruptedly.

It is normal for a student to pursue post-graduation immediately after obtaining his bachelor's degree. He may even obtain his doctorate while below thirty. Jobs in the country are scarce and over-qualification is a mechanism to ensure one's career. Most members of the administrative service possess a degree in humanities or social sciences, though this is not mandatory. Since the 1980s those with engineering, information technology, and other professional qualifications have been getting into the higher service. The formal knowledge base of the successful members of the higher civil service is thus expanding. It is not required that one should be examined in subjects chosen for the final degree. What happens is that certain subjects are perceived to be more mark-fetching in the competitive examination and even science graduates are seen to prefer subjects like public administration, geography, sociology, and history. The adopted subjects serve mainly a utilitarian value and do not have a high survival rate: the candidates forget their subjects as quickly as they have learnt them.

Women are getting into the IAS, though only about 10 per cent of the total membership of the service. Their annual intake is increasing though very slowly and not keeping pace with the increasing higher education among them. Women in the IAS hail from professional families living in larger cities with strong family orientations, and there is nothing to distinguish them by way of economic, social or educational backgrounds from men.

What may be in the nature of corrective measures to broaden the social and spatial base of the civil service, the state in India has adopted the policy of positive discrimination, known as the reservation system, for Scheduled Castes (SCs), Scheduled Tribes (STs) and backward classes. Scheduled Castes have 15 per cent of the jobs in the higher civil service reserved for them, and Scheduled Tribes 7.5 per cent. This has been their proportion in the total population. Twenty-seven per cent of jobs are reserved for backward classes (called Other Backward Classes—OBCs) also since 1993, although the Scheduled Castes and Scheduled Tribes have enjoyed the benefits since the commencement of the present Constitution. The earlier years of the Republic did not get enough candidates from these disadvantaged sections of society and thus their quotas were not fully filled. But with the spread of education among them, all the reserved posts are presently being filled, as is shown in the following table.[1]

But a difficulty is still sometimes felt while filling jobs requiring technical and professional qualifications. Pressure is exercised to include more and more castes as beneficiaries of the reservation policy, and powerful pro-reservation lobbies have sprung up all over the administrative space. Reservation for SCs and STs is introduced in promotions also, although no

Service	SCs		STs		OBCs	
	Vacancies	Selected candidates	Vacancies	Selected candidates	Vacancies	Selected candidates
Indian Administrative Service	10	10	5	5	15	15
Indian Police Service	5	5	2	2	10	10

such advantages are conferred on the OBCs. They are also given concessions like relaxation of the upper age limit, unlimited number of chances, exemption from payment of examination fee, etc.

A second set of measures to provide access to government jobs is to permit the aspiring candidates to write the competitive examination in Hindi and other regional languages of India. Since the 1970s, the subject papers can be answered in Hindi and other regional languages. Those who answer in Hindi constitute 10 to 12 per cent and their number is nearly static. These candidates are presently handicapped by a general dearth of standard text-books on the subject and other literature, necessary for success.

Before concluding the present discussion, it is appropriate to raise a question. Do the people show empathy for the social group or class they emerge from? Civil service is a profession and those who join it are expected to serve everyone in society even-handedly and without showing any partiality or favouritism. Does Kingsley's thesis uphold in practice? Is it not a fact that the cause of the proletariat has, in practice, been spearheaded by persons hailing from the higher classes and castes of society? Is not the 'social origin' theory too deterministic, and not upheld empirically? The core issue before the civil service is to make it professional and ethical.

Civil service in India, originally designed by the colonial masters for the performance of regulatory functions in a dependent country, was almost lock, stock and barrel, taken over by independent India and is utilized for tasks of state-building and development. What is more, parliamentary democracy and federalism, the key features of the Constitution, provide the basic framework within which it is called upon to function. Its activities and responsibilities have expanded spectacularly in all directions, more so in promotional and developmental fields. Not only have the functions increased, they have become more complex, with society itself becoming increasingly diversified. In the process, new skills and specialities have been inducted into the civil service. In-service training of public personnel is given more emphasis. Modem management aids and techniques are being introduced increasingly in administration, particularly in the area of development.

India has a federal polity, but its civil service, one must note, is a highly integrated one, a feature that has been reinforced under successive Five Year Plans as well as by the earlier single party dominance system, especially under the leadership of prime ministers like Jawaharlal Nehru and Indira Gandhi. An integrated administration has obvious uses, its foremost merit being its capability to counter centrifugal forces that are always at work in a country which was a colony till recently; and to keep intact the chain of command vital for swift action. The Constitution itself sought to foster a sense of unity by making the lower level of government dependent on the higher one for finance, as also for many other provisions. These mechanisms have brought up problems. Indian administration is a centralized one, and the concentration of authority at the top tends to sap the initiative and drive of personnel working in the field. Also, the Centre-strengthening federal formula enshrined in the Constitution has come increasingly under criticism and today, state governments are making a demand for greater autonomy.

In view of the challenges faced and tasks ahead, a substantial transformation of the civil service capabilities in all sectors and levels of activity seems urgent, which is also realized by the national political leadership. Many civil service reform committees have, for instance, examined issues like the following:

1. How should the various processes of civil service administration such as recruitment, training, placement, performance appraisal, promotion, salary-fixing, etc., be improved?
2. What should be the staffing policies in the government, particularly at senior levels?
3. How could better coordination be secured between various organized services?
4. How should the grievances of public personnel be redressed?
5. How should corruption be controlled in public administration?
6. How should citizens' grievances be redressed?
7. How should waste and extravagance in the civil service be controlled?
8. How can the civil service be made accountable?

As a result, the civil service in India has absorbed many changes, but the apparent conflict between the needs of development in all spheres of life and the colonial attributes of an overly cautious bureaucracy seems unsolved. Inadequacies of the civil service have come to light with increasing vividness in the course of implementation of various schemes and programmes in the field of development. The machinery of the administrator lacks the speed and flexibility necessary. Though its magnitude naturally varies from department to department, there is considerable over-staffing, which acts as a drag on efficiency. Besides, work ethics generally, is not high. According to civil service gossip, nearly 25 per cent of employees in the government are believed to be superfluous. But the perception of the government as a kind of social security system prevents meaningful action. Procedures of work are antiquated, and more often than not, the edict of the *babu* (clerical personnel) prevails because of unwillingness and inertia on the part of higher level functionaries to apply their minds to matters coming up before them for a decision. The civil service is still patterned after the colonial requirements and its reorganization is overdue. Corruption is rather rampant despite vigilance agencies which have been set up to deal with the problem. What is more, there appears to be an acceptance of corruption in the belief that it is a worldwide phenomenon. Citizen-orientation on the part of the bureaucracy is weak and peoples' grievances generally remain unaddressed though many public organizations have a late proclaimed citizens' charters. A demand for an ombudsman has been pending for long, but the ruling élite is lukewarm towards it. Ombudsmen, called *Lokayuktas*, have been set up by most state governments, but the functionary is generally kept idle, without much work.

While these and some other problems are of a serious nature, at least some of them are the result—though unintended—of development itself. Some of the earlier solutions have, over a period of time, themselves become problems, putting the civil service under stress. To give an example, the state of backwardness of certain sections of society was sought to be solved, among others, by the device of reservation of government posts for their members. Though over three decades of implementing this positive discrimination has benefited them, it has also created certain vested interests in the system and produced a backlash. Today, there have emerged powerful lobbies of reservationists and anti-reservationists arrayed against each other, and much of the civil servant's time and energy is spent on sorting out such problems. What is emphasized here is that the civil servant is presently engaged in devising solutions to what are basically second generation problems.

One must also note that the civil service is the accredited instrument of development in India, though the adoption of economic liberalization since the 1990s has been changing its role and place. It has to its credit many achievements, the most impressive ones being the unabridged practice of democracy and sustained promotion of developmental activities. Its competence to respond to challenges is enormous, as has been demonstrated repeatedly. Indeed, the crisis managing capacity of the Indian civil service is apparently infinite.

NOTES

1. Annual Report of the Ministry of Personnel, 2002–3, p. 118.

CHAPTER 3

The Higher Civil Service during British Rule

The present civil service system in India had its origin in the arrangement developed by the East India Company, although its work has changed drastically. Employees of the East India Company were called civil servants but they were all traders, their job being mercantile in nature. Writers were thus entirely commercial. They had even 'to weigh tea, count bales, and measure muslins'. The traders' role was gradually replaced by responsibilities. It was not till the beginning of the nineteenth century that a governor-general found himself compelled to state publicly that commercial knowledge was no longer necessary: 'Not only,' he said, 'is mercantile knowledge unnecessary, but Indian civil servants invested with the powers of magistracy are bound by an oath to abstain from every commercial pursuit.' Then on 18 August 1800, Lord Wellesley (1748–1805) wrote: 'To dispense justice to millions of people of various languages, manners, usages and religions; to administer a vast and complicated system of revenue throughout districts equal in extent to some of the most considerable kingdoms in Europe; to maintain civil order in one of the most populous and litigious regions of the world; to discharge the functions of magistrates, judges, ambassadors, and governors of provinces; these are now the duties of the large proportion of the civil servants of the Company.'[1]

The East India Company, to recap, was a trading company, at least to begin with, and its employees, called civil servants, were traders, arranged in the following four grades—president, merchant, factor, and writer, in descending order. The first appointment was at the level of a writer: the writer would move to other levels in course of time. Writers were entirely commercial. In 1765, the East India Company acquired administrative duties also. Lord Cornwallis (1786–93), the Governor-General of India, reorganized the civil service. Civil servants were not to engage in trade or receive presents. They, moreover, were paid a handsome salary and the principal administrative posts were, as a rule, held by European officers. The mode of recruitment of civil servants was patronage vesting in the Directors of the East India Company. The higher civil service was known as the Covenanted Civil Service. The service was so called from the covenant which its members had to execute with the Company. A covenant was a contract which spelled out the obligations and prerogatives of the civil servants. A covenant is reproduced at the end of the chapter. Indians, if they were lucky to find patrons could at best find entry into the uncovenanted service, which was of a lower order.

In 1853, the British Government decided to do away with patronage in favour of an open competitive examination as the mode of public recruitment. The first open competitive examination was held in London in 1855. Earlier, in 1836, it had been decided to introduce English as India's official language, and to provide formally for its instruction in the country. This measure proved to be of historic significance for India. Indians began to learn English to prepare for a secure career, and the growing number of English-educated youth expectedly led to a demand for employment of Indians in civil service. Queen Victoria, the reigning sovereign, when she proclaimed in 1858 the British Crown's direct assumption of rule over India from the hands of the East India Company, assured complete equality between Indians and Europeans. This included matters of public recruitment as well. The royal assurance, however, remained virtually a dead letter. To undertake the long voyage to London, the centre of the examination, was not easy or practical for most Indians. What is more, racial considerations also coloured public recruitment. The first-ever Indian—Satyendra Nath Tagore—was able to enter the Covenanted Civil Service as late as in 1864—nine years after the commencement of the competitive examination.

INDIAN CIVIL SERVICE

Any attempt to present an account, howsoever modest, of the history of the civil service in India must necessarily accord a place of pride to the Indian Civil Service. If India was the jewel in the British Crown, the ICS kept this jewel polished, shining, and bright. Rushbrook Williams was not far off the point when he asserted: 'No other service was better officered.'

On exactly when the Indian Civil Service was born, there is little unanimity. Some trace its birth to the year 1600, when the East India Company received its charter from Queen Elizabeth and the Company started recruiting 'factors' for its 'factories' in India. Philip Woodruff, pseudonym of Philip Mason, himself a member of the ICS, ascribes the birth of this service to the year 1769, when its members began to perform functions so characteristic of it and inseparable from its nomenclature. In his inimitable *The Men Who Ruled India*, he writes:

If there is any one point other than Elizabeth's charter to the Company at which the Indian Civil Service may be said to have begun, it is now [year 1769]. The members of the service were to become used to tasks more than human, but perhaps never were men asked to perform such feats as are set out in Verelist's instructions to his supervisors! It must be mentioned that in 1769, English officials were appointed as supervisors in the whole of Bengal and Bihar.[2]

On the other hand, one may as well ascribe the origin of the service to the year 1853, when merit as judged through an open competitive examination was made the basis of recruitment, thereby creating a level of efficiency which became a synonym for the ICS. The Macaulay Committee Report provided the philosophy and base for the Indian Civil Service.

STATUTORY CIVIL SERVICE

In 1879, a separate civil service, called the Statutory Civil Service, was created, with its own distinctive features—to provide avenues of public employment to Indians. Nomination to the service—for posting within the province exclusively—was made by the provincial government, subject to the approval of the Secretary of State for India. To attract Indians to the service, one-sixth of the covenanted posts were transferred to it.

THE AITCHISON COMMISSION AND CIVIL SERVICES

To meet the growing demand of educated Indians for public employment, the government set up, in 1886, a committee designated as the Public Service Commission, under the chairmanship of Sir C.U. Aitchison. The Aitchison Report published in 1887 recommended the admission of Indians, subject to their being fit, into the covenanted service. It did not, however, favour the holding of competitive examinations in India. In the commission's view, this was not violative of Queen Victoria's royal proclamation. The basic objective of the British Government's public recruitment policy in India, it said, was to secure a public administration that was conducted on principles and by methods in harmony with the norms and standards of Western civilization. The competitive examination was, moreover, to bear a distinctively English character and was to be a test of English qualifications. England, therefore, was alone appropriate as the centre of the examination. Also, Western education in India was not equally or widely developed, both spatially and socially. Above all, little purpose would be served when the intake was not to exceed six or so: on the contrary, it would rather create 'a large disappointed and thereby probably discontented class which would cause embarrassment to the government'.

The Aitchison Commission wanted the covenanted service to become a *corps d'elite*, by membership limited to what was absolutely necessary to fill the chief administrative positions of the government and such a number of smaller positions as was to ensure a complete course of training for junior civilians. Another service, the Provincial Civil Service, was to occupy the administrative posts released by the covenanted service. The commission observed:

In the present circumstances of the country, the claims of natives of India to higher and more extensive employment in the public service and the admission of competent natives of each province of India to a due proportion of the posts heretofore reserved for the Covenanted Civil Service, can be best provided for by reducing the strength of the Covenanted Civil Service and transferring a corresponding number of appointments to a local service to be separately recruited in each province of India.[3]

Accordingly, the Provincial Civil Service, or the PCS, was created in 1892, when the government announced action on the report. This service was entirely locally recruited and 'inferior' to the ICS in power and status.

To make the PCS attractive to Indians, the commission, as already mentioned, suggested deletion of a considerable number of posts hitherto reserved for the covenanted service and making them available to members of the PCS. At the same time, a novel device of 'Listed Posts' was created to raise the stature of the latter service. 'Listed Posts' were posts hived off from the list of posts reserved for the covenanted service, which had been included in the schedule of the Indian Civil Service Act of 1861, to be filled from amongst the members of the PCS on the basis of merit. At the same time, the post belonged to the covenanted civil service cadre, and not to the PCS. The provision of 'Listed Posts' was discontinued with the commencement of the Constitution of independent India in 1950.

The commission, in short, recommended a three-tiered civil service. The covenanted service, to be called the Imperial Civil Service of India was to be at the top. Below it came the Provincial Civil Service. There would of course be a third service comprising the lower administrative appointments above the ministerial grades, and this might appropriately be called the 'Subordinate Civil Service'.[4] The civil service of the country , accordingly, came to be divided into three categories in 1892—Indian Civil Service. (The term preferred by the Secretary of State for India was Civil Service of India in place of Imperial Civil Service.) This term 'Civil Service of India' was notified also but the term which gained currency was Indian Civil Service. But the officially notified term was the Civil Service of India (See L.S.S.O. Malley, *The Indian Civil Service 1601–1930*, London: John Murray, 1931, p. 85), Provincial Civil Service, and the Subordinate Civil Service. The Indian Statutory Service was abolished, with its superior posts being reabsorbed into the ICS.

The closing years of the nineteenth century saw many changes in the country, the more prominent being its political unification, the centralization of its government, and the gradual assumption by it of new functions. In this process, new services were bound to be created and the existing ones strengthened. In 1892, the Indian Service of Engineers (Irrigation, Roads, and Buildings Branches) and the Indian Veterinary Service were created; in 1897, the Indian Medical Service was constituted; and in 1905–7, three new services, namely the Imperial Police (1905), the Indian Education Service (1906), and the Indian Agricultural Service (1907) were added to the list.

THE BRITISH DECLARATION OF 1917

The First Great War (1914–18) substantially changed the international equilibrium, particularly on the ideological plane, which affected India's political destiny directly. As part of this change, the British declaration of 20 August 1917 held out the promise of a 'responsible government' in India, opening a new chapter in the public services of the country. Clarifying the goal of its mission in India, the British Government in London said in the declaration:

The policy of His Majesty's Government with which the Government of India are in complete accord is that of increasing association of Indians in every branch of the administration and the gradual development of self governing institutions with a view to the progressive realisation of responsible government in India as an integral part of the British Empire.

THE GOVERNMENT OF INDIA ACT, 1919

The Government of India Act, 1919 spelt out the intent of this declaration in greater detail. It introduced, for the first time in 1921, responsible government in a limited sphere at the provincial level through the device of 'transferred' subjects put under popular control. As a consequence, the central government ceased to be the exclusive government of the country. While not departing from the existing unitary set up, the responsibility between the Centre and the provinces was vertically divided, the latter acquiring a sphere of functions defined by the Act itself.

To protect the superior civil services from possible political harassment, the Act of 1919 provided specific safeguards. For instance, no officer could be dismissed from service by an authority subordinate to that by which he was appointed.[5] Also, his pay and allowances could not be altered to his disadvantage, nor could the term and conditions of service. His salary was not subject to vote in the legislature. In other words, a system of governmental protection was given to the members of the all-India services even when working in the sphere of transferred subjects and thus under the politician-minister.

The provinces were equipped with an independent sphere of administration in subjects like education, agriculture, medical, health, local government, roads and buildings, animal husbandry, cooperative societies, etc. The country's public administration was thus horizontally divided into central administration and provincial administration. Since the provincial governments were to administer these subjects independently of the central government, it was expected that the workload of the central government would decline. But this did not happen. The central government now had to deal with matters that the provinces referred to it for advice or action, and the volume of work involved was not inconsiderable. Moreover, as the transferred subject in the provinces came under the control and direction of elected representatives of the people and as the latter were, expectedly, committed to the general welfare, public expenditure on 'nation-building' departments like agriculture, public education, women's education, public health, cooperatives, etc. began to increase as part of the ideology of the national movement. The war effort created its own momentum and load of work. The League of Nations and the International Labour Organization, of which India was a member, also created new work for the Government of India. To meet the demand for personnel, the technical departments in the provincial governments recruited more and more expertise in nation-building activities.

As it was, the Provincial Civil Service was already in existence since 1892. The Act of 1919 gave greater autonomy to the provinces in the matter. Also, the provincial civil services came to be known by the name of their respective provinces, such as the U.P. Civil Service and the Bengal Civil Service. In 1925, the Subordinate Civil Service was redesignated as the Junior Civil Service, under the provincial government.

THE ALL-INDIA SERVICE

There were, in addition to the central services and the provincial services, a set of services known as 'all-India service'. The term 'all-India services' was first coined by the Committee on Division of Functions (1918) under M.E. Gauntlett. The Gauntlett Committee observed: 'For the purpose of dealing with the subject we accept classification ... viz., Indian (which we shall call all-India services), provincial and subordinate'.[6] The all-India services were recruited and controlled by the Secretary of State for India (hence they were also known as the Secretary of State's Services). On the eve of the Government of India Act, 1919, the following all-India services existed:

1. The Indian Civil Service
2. The Indian Police Service
3. The Indian Forest Service
4. The Indian Educational Service
5. The Indian Agricultural Service
6. The Indian Civil Veterinary Service
7. The Indian Forest Engineering Service
8. The Indian Medical Service (Civil)
9. The Indian Service of Engineers

When the Act of 1919 came into force, the Indian Civil Service, the Indian Police Service, the Irrigation Branch of the Indian Service of Engineers, the whole cadre of the Indian Service of Engineers in Assam, and the Indian Forest and the Indian Forest Engineering Service except in the provinces of Burma and Bombay operated in the field 'reserved' for the Centre, and they survived the implementation of the Act. But those which fell in the 'transferred' fields, such as the Indian Educational Service, the Indian Agricultural Service, the Indian Veterinary Service, the Indian Forest and Forest Engineering Services in Burma and Bombay, the Indian Medical Service (Civil) and the Buildings Branch of the Indian Service of Engineers, were discontinued. The existing members of the relevant all-India services continued to enjoy the usual privileges and facilities of all-India services.

Thus the Act of 1919 brought to an end the golden age of the all-India services. The Indian Civil Service and the Indian Police Service, the two security services, were however, retained in the face of strong Indian protests. Also retained was the Indian Medical Service (Civil), which was meant to cater to the medical requirements of the European civil servants. Nationalism in India was always sceptical of the all-India services, and at that stage of political development was strongly in favour of provincialization of the services. The need for the country to retain these services is a belated, post-Independence discovery of Indian nationalism, and that too not by the entire political spectrum. In the provincialization of the service both the declared British policy and the Indian nationalist demand coalesced.

The British were formally committed to a process of Indianization of services within the framework of India as an integral part of the British empire, and making a beginning in the provinces was considered safe. The timetable of Indianization was first suggested by the Islington Commission on the Public Services in India (1912–15), which fixed the ratio of Indians in the superior civil services in the country. In 1919, the Government announced its decision on the Islington Report; and the process of Indianization became operative. The Lee Commission on the Superior Civil Services in India (1924) which came next, raised the scale and recommended a 50:50 cadre to be produced in the ICS in about 15 years, all to be recruited directly. For the IPS, too, the cadre was to be 50:50. All the Europeans and 30 Indians were to be recruited directly, the remaining 20 Indians to be promoted from the provincial service. In this way, the IPS was integrated with its provincial level partner. The provincial services, it was expected, would be entirely manned by Indians.

Provincialization of services, accompanied by the emergence of responsible government in the field of transferred subjects, brought the civil servants in the provinces and the politicians closer to each other, exposing this arrangement to all the pitfalls inherent in it. The upshot of the thrust towards provincialization of the services was that the hold of the Secretary of State for India over the superior services got loosened in the process. The gainers were the Government of India and, to a far greater extent, the provinces.

After World War I (1914–18), which inevitably led to an expansion of the central as well as provincial services, the functions of the State began to increase in range, scale, and complexity. In the years to come, to cope with the increased functions, many new services, both central and provincial, were established. Expectedly, the greatest increase occurred in provincial administration. At the same time, the combined forces of both democracy and development strengthened departmentalism in public administration, creating in the process, the problem of coordination at the field level. Consequent on the emergence of the politician-minister assertive of his control over the departmental hierarchy and of the specialists with their ego of professional expertise, the district collector's writ could not be taken to run very smoothly.

Such developments could not but unnerve the European members—and the Indian Civil Service began to lose its attraction to the bright graduates in Great Britain. Indianization of the service made the security of tenure uncertain for the European incumbents. The description at the time by Lloyd George, the British prime minister, of the ICS as 'the steel-frame', did little to remove the uncertainty. Enhancing the uncertainty was the mass political movement led by the Indian National Congress, with Mahatma Gandhi at its head. The all-India services were becoming politically unacceptable and coming under public criticism. Many members of the service resigned and left India, the number increasing from 200 in 1922 to 433 by 1927. Also, the brighter university graduates were somewhat hesitant to offer their services to India, with the result that the number of seats reserved for the Europeans were not being filled up. To lure them to the civil service in India, some innovations outside the field of a written test were devised. An element of racialism also crept in, with the British civilians perceiving a threat to their career from the Indians entering the civil service. They organized themselves into an association—and so did the Indians.

To curb political patronage, as well as to maintain reasonably high standards of recruitment in public services, the Act of 1919 had provided for a public service commission. The Lee Commission (1924) urged action on this constitutional provision 'without delay', regarding it as 'one of the cardinal features of our report and as forming an integral part of the whole structure of our proposals for the future of the (civil) services'.[7] The Central Public Service Commission was, accordingly set up in 1926, with Sir Rose Barker, a senior member of the Home Civil Service, as its chairman, this choice being dictated by a desire to fashion the commission after the traditions of the British Civil Service Commission. Public service commissions were later set up in the provinces as well.

In the 1920s, the civil service in India stood classified into the following:

1. All India Services
2. Central Civil Services
3. Provincial Services
4. Subordinate Services

The members of the all-India services owed their appointment to the Secretary of State for India, who alone could terminate their services. The central civil services came under the control of the Government of India and were generally recruited by it.[8] The provincial services fell under the appointing authority of the provinces. The subordinate services comprised minor administrative, executive, and ministerial posts, to which appointments were made by the provincial government concerned or an authority subordinate to it.

THE GOVERNMENT OF INDIA ACT, 1935

The Constitution of 1919 was avowedly a temporary one, paving the way for the ultimate goal of a responsible government in India within the British empire. The next Constitution, the Government of India Act, 1935, had a long gestation period, with inputs from the Indian Statutory Commission, the All Parties Conference (though it was not set up by the Government), the Round Table Conferences, and the Joint Parliamentary Committee of the British Parliament. The Act visualized a federal form of government with the provinces enjoying an autonomous sphere of functions. A parliamentary form of government was set up at the provincial level in which the executive was made accountable, within certain bounds, to the legislature. This had far-reaching consequences on the structure of public administration, including the civil service in the country. Though the contemplated federation never formally came into effect, the provision made it necessary to find out whether the country's traditional integrated administrative system needed to be recast.

Historically and operationally, Indian public administration at every level, right from the top to the village level, has always been a coherent unity. Even when the federalizing process first began under the Act of 1919 (though formally not so designated), this integrated nature was not touched. The secretariat of the Government of India did not have a separate civil service of its own: as a rule, it drew its policy-making and supervisory personnel from the provinces and the field services. In the light of the Act of 1935 with its feature of federalism, the Maxwell Committee on Organisation and Procedure (1937) discussed in great detail whether the civil service needed to be bifurcated. In the end, it recommended that the existing tenure staffing of the central secretariat should continue. The committee held that a permanent civil service of the central government would have hardly any direct touch with the everyday reality of India. Officers dealing with subjects of concern to the central secretariat would be poorly equipped to decide matters unless they had direct experience of working in the provinces, for it was at this level that the effect of their policy decisions would be felt. A rotating civil service would therefore provide a valuable link between the central and provincial governments. The state government personnel would also benefit from the insight into the outlook, method and even difficulties of the central government, which a system of periodic interchange would provide.[9] The traditional method of staffing of the central secretariat, thus, continued.

The British component in the ICS was to be one-half the Joint Committee; the report of which formed the basis of the Act of 1935, had put it on record: 'We are convinced that India for a long time to come will not be able to dispense with a strong British element in the services' (para 273). Part of the Indian half was to be recruited by examination in India and the rest by examination in Britain. The British officer element, however, showed a disinclination to join the Indian component. The examination in Britain was meant for selection both for the Home and Indian Civil Services. In the order of their place on the merit list, the candidates had the option to choose either Home Service or service in India. In 1936, the vacancies for the ICS were 20 and for the Home Service 33. In the joint examination, British candidates secured the first 20 places, not one of whom accepted the ICS. And of the 12 British candidates who were not high enough for Home Service, but high enough for the ICS, 10 opted out of service.[10]

The Act of 1935 provided for the setting up of public service commissions at both the federal and provincial levels. There was to be a federal public service commission at the central level and a provincial public service commission, closely patterned after the federal one, for each province. The new modes of public service commissions came into being on 1 April 1937, when the Act of 1935 came into force. Some provinces, however, decided to pool their resources to launch joint commissions. Thus Bihar, Central Provinces, and Orissa established a joint public service commission located at Ranchi.[11] Punjab and North-West Frontier Province had a joint public service commission which functioned till 30 September 1947. Similarly, Bombay and Sindh jointly formed the Bombay Sindh Public Service Commission, which functioned till July 1947.

Another change had taken place earlier, on account of the growing specialized needs, particularly of the economic departments in the wake of the Ottawa Agreement on Imperial Preference and the setting up of the Reserve Bank of India (1935). Officers obtained on a tenure basis and from a non-specialized service could not meet the needs. Accordingly in 1937, a Finance-Commerce pool was constituted. Though recruited mainly from the ICS, the pool had a sprinkling of officers from other eligible central services such as the Indian Audit and Accounts Service, Customs Service, Income Tax Service and Military Accounts Service. The pool had a strength of 47. With the pressures of the war, the pool, which was originally designed for the finance and commerce departments only, began to be used for appointment to other departments as well. The door was opened, though grudgingly, to some central services through the Commerce-Industry Pool. Also, its application was waived for some officers already in the Secretariat.

Before the Constitution of 1935 could fully take effect. World War II broke out. With India becoming an important centre for the Allies for military operations in the East, there was a frantic demand for personnel to attend to the scale of activities that had grown to near-explosive proportions. The Secretariat was expanded, and appointment of additional personnel surged. The centre was indenting for a much larger number of officers from the provinces and was loath to revert them to their home province at the end of their tenure. At all the levels of governance, the machinery of administration expanded, the sudden additional demand for public personnel being met by relaxing the usual standards of recruitment. The tenure of wartime recruits was to be temporary, to tide over the exigency of wartime requirements. Meanwhile, the Congress ministries resigned on ideological grounds, leaving governance in the hands of the career bureaucracy.

The Quit India movement launched by the Congress party brought about another change of scene in public recruitment. Recruitment to the all-India services was stopped from July 1942 because of the volatile situation. In 1947, when India won independence after partition of the country along religious lines, the public personnel were given, as part of the partition plan, the option of service in either of the newly created countries or retirement with generous pensions.

On the eve of Independence, the civil service at the centre consisted of the following:

1. All-India Services
2. Central Services—Class I
3. Central Services—Class II
4. Subordinate Service[12]
5. Inferior Service[13]

The Central Services (Class I) were the following:

1. Indian Audit and Accounts Service
2. Central Engineering Service
3. Central Electrical Engineering Service
4. Imperial Customs Service
5. Superior Telegraph Engineering and Wireless Branches of the Indian Posts and Telegraphs Department
6. Indian Posts and Telegraph Service

7. Geological Survey of India
8. Indian Meteorological Service
9. Mines Department
10. Archaeological Department
11. Zoological Survey of India
12. Indian Ecclesiastical Establishment
13. Medical Research Department (including Indian Medical Service)
14. Central Revenues Chemical Service
15. Bengal Pilot Service
16. Income-Tax Service
17. Mercantile Marine Training Ship Service
18. Imperial Secretariat Service
19. General Central Service
20. Railway Inspectorate Service
21. Indian Railway Service of Engineers
22. Transportation (Traffic) and Commercial Departments
23. Indian Railway Accounts Service

INDIANIZATION OF THE SERVICES

It is inherent in colonialism to man the strategic positions by nationals of the ruling country. A colonial public service could not therefore completely do away with the European elements in it. Nevertheless, after the competitive examinations were opened to Indians, despite the disability implicit in long expensive travel to London, Indians, particularly the offspring of the literary classes of Calcutta, Madras, and Bombay, took the chance and began to trickle into service. At the same time, educated Indian opinion was supporting the simultaneous holding of the competitive examination in India. When the Indian National Congress was founded in 1885, a resolution was passed in its first session itself to the effect that the Indian Civil Service examination should be held simultaneously in England and in India. This demand was reiterated time and again but in vain.

The turning point came with the Montagu-Chelmsford Report. Departing from the line taken earlier by both the Aitchison Commission (1886) and the Islington Commission (1916), the report recommended that 'For all the public services, for which there is recruitment in England open to Europeans and Indians alike, there must be a system of appointment in India'.[14] The traditional system of recruitment to the higher two civil public services, to be made only in Britain, needed to be supplemented 'by fixing a definite percentage of recruitment to be made in India'.[15]

In pursuance of this recommendation, for the first time in 1922, the competitive examination to the ICS was held in India. The papers set for the competitive examination were, however, different from those set for the London examination, though the examination was conducted by the British Civil Service Commission. For conducting the examination, the secretary of the commission came to Allahabad, the venue of the competitive examination, to supervise the arrangement

The British policy of Indianization would alter the racial composition of the higher civil service (see Table 3.1). The bright British graduates were not finding a career in civil service as attractive as before. The ICS was eventually to consist half of Europeans and half of Indians under the scheme outlined by the Royal Commission on the Superior Civil Services in India (Lee Commission). Around the mid-1920s, the all-India services included some 3000 posts, of which only some 1300 British officers including the doctors of the military service were to remain in the service in India. In the two security services, namely the ICS and the Indian Police Service, Europeans were to hold no more than 900 posts. The ICS was eventually to consist half of Europeans and half of Indians—675 each. Of this number, less than 400 officers were to fill posts of major responsibility, such as heads of districts, sessions judges, political officers and the like in a country with more than 300 million people, the remainder of the officers holding responsible posts or even away on long periods of training.

Table 3.1
Composition of Indian Civil Service

Year	Total no. of selected candidates	No. of Indians	Percentage
1894	60	6	10
1895	66	1	1.51
1896	58	3	5.17
1897	62	3	4.83
1898	64	7	10.93
1899	53	3	5.66
1900	52	2	3.85
1901	43	2	4.65
1902	55	3	5.45
1903	51	3	5.88
1904	52	3	5.77
1905	48	4	8.33
1906	60	3	5

Year	Total no. of selected candidates	No. of Indians	Percentage
1907	57	4	7.02
1908	50	.3	6
1909	52	1	1.92
1910	60	1	1.66
1911	53	3	5.66
1912	47	7	14.89
1913	44	2	4.32
1914	53	7	13.20
1915	14	3	21.43
1916	9	5	55.55
1917	6	4	66.66
1918	9	9	100
1919	101	39	3.86
1920	50	6	10.20
1921	55	25	40.54
1922	33	24	70.27
1923	36	25	41.66
1924	18	15	83.33
1925 & 26[16]	50	29	58
1926	56	27	48.2
1927 & 28	73	36	49.3/50
1928 & 29	72	36	50
1929 & 30	66	31	46.97
1930 & 31	68	43	63.28
1931 & 32	45	22	47.82
1932 & 33	37	23	62.16
1933 & 34	44	27	61.11
1934 & 35	35	22	62.85

Source: File No. 43/36-Ests. 1936, Home Department, Establishment Section, Government of India.

Members of the ICS—1032 in 1919 and 1029 in 1938—comprised about 0.001 per cent of the total number of public servants in India who, according to the 1931 census, numbered one million in a population of 353 million.[17] Thus, Great Britain was ruling India through a civil service of 1000–1100 members, of which nearly half were Englishmen. The administration of colonial rule in India rested in the hands of Indians working under this small ruling elite of Englishmen.

The ICS was truly an all-India service. Its members used to man the judicial posts in India. The foreign and political service of the Government of India as a rule used to draw its officers from this service. It is not a small wonder in the history of administration that so few people were able to administer so many in India. The other mentionable profile of the ICS was that nearly half of its membership worked in the districts (that is, in the field) in India, making it truly a camp service. About one-quarter of them worked at the provincial headquarters. Only 11 per cent of the total membership worked for the Government of India, making the Indian Civil Service virtually a state service.

India's innate culture, embedded in its high level of intellectualism reinforced by conscious colonial policy, however slow and halting, of promoting the employment of natives ensured an availability of educated, more or less experienced manpower in the country, which stood India in good stead in 1947 at the time of Independence. The literary classes in India were the first to take advantage of the educational facilities being created by the colonial power, and their supply was in a way always in excess of the demand.

Table 3.2
Communal Composition of the ICS on I January 1936

	Number	Percentage
Europeans	618	60.53
Hindus	294	28.79
Muslims	65	6.37
Indian Christians	25	2.45
Domiciled Europeans and Anglo-Indians	2	0.19
Sikhs	6	0.59
Depressed Classes	I	0.10
Parsis	9	0.88
Other Communities	I	0.10

Source: File No. 180/1/36-Ess (5), Home Dept. Establishment (5), Govt. of India, Statement I.

It also needs to be pointed out that the demand for Indianization of services in the political context of the day was to produce reactions, not all of which were wholesome to nation-making and national integration. As the country's politics was becoming growingly communal, the process of Indianization could not escape further fragmentation. A demand for separate representation based on religion began to be made by the Indian

Muslim League. These demands were becoming more and more insistent in the 1930s. In 1934, the Government of India passed a resolution fixing 25 per cent of posts in the civil service to be directly recruited for the Muslims. As such the communal representation in the civil service began to increase. The communal composition of the ICS in January 1936 is given in Table 3.2. Table 3.3 gives the Muslims' representation in the services on the eve of Independence. It may, however, be noted that posts filled by promotion and posts requiring technical qualifications were kept excluded from the communal rules.

Table 3.3
Muslims' Representation in the Services in 1945

Name of service	Proportion of Muslims
ICS	20.23
Central Services (Class I)	16.05
Central Services (Class II)	18.32
Subordinate Services	21.66
Superior Railway Services	15.21
Subordinate Railway Services	20.04
All Services together	20.67

Source: Government of India, Home Dept, Establishment (Special Section File 23/1/46–Ests(S).

Covenant of the Writers Signed in 1756

A.B.........will not directly or indirectly take, accept or receive or agree to take, accept or receive any Gift, Reward, Gratuity, Allowance, Compensation, Sums of Money whatsoever from any Persons or Person, of whom he, the said A.B. shall by himself or any agent for him, buy or barter any Goods, Merchandize, Treasure or Effects for or upon account of the said Company [or from those to whom he sells] ... And upon condition that the said A.B. shall in all things perform his Covenants and Agreements with the said Company and to encourage him so to do. It is further covenanted and agreed by and between the said Parties to these Presents, that it shall and may be lawful to and for the said A.B. and the Company doth accordingly license the said A.B. during the 5 years, commencing as aforesaid, freely to trade and traffick for his own account only, from Port to Port in India, or elsewhere, within the Limits aforesaid, [i.e. between the Cape of Good Hope and the Straits of Magellan] but not to or from any Place without the same, [further that servants having injured Natives may be judged and punished by the Company].

And the said A.B. doth ... agree that he ... will not carry on ... Trade either from Europe to the East Indies or to any Place within the said Company's limits ... or from the East Indies etc. to Europe ... nor shall carry on, use or be concerned in any Trade or Traffick whatsoever but such as is expressly allowed ... by the true Intent and Meaning of these Presents.

COPY OF THE COVENANT EXECUTED BY MEMBERS OF
THE COVENANTED CIVIL SERVICE

This indenture made the ... day of ... in the year of our Lord 1891, between ... hereinafter called the covenantor, of the first part; ... hereinafter called the surety, of the second part: and the Secretary of State in Council of third part. Whereas the Secretary of State in Council has appointed the covenantor to serve Her Majesty as a member of the Civil Service of India in the Presidency of Fort William in Bengal, in the East Indies (with the option to the Government of India at any time and from time to time to require him to serve elsewhere in India), such service to continue during the pleasure of Her Majesty, her Heirs and Successors, to be signified under the hand of the Secretary of State for India, but with liberty for the said covenantor to resign the said service, with the permission of the said Secretary of State in Council or of the Governor-General of India in Council. And whereas by reason of the said Covenantor's minority the said surety hath agreed to become a party to and execute these presents as a surety for the due performance of the covenants hereinafter contained on the part of the said covenantor. Now this Indenture witnesseth, and the said covenantor and the said surety do and each of them doth hereby severally covenant and agree with and to the Secretary of State in Council, in manner and form following; that is to say— 1st. That while he the said covenantor shall be employed in the said service he will faithfully, honestly, and diligently do all such things as shall be lawfully committed to his charge by or on the part of the Secretary of State in Council or of the Government of India, or execution of his duty.

2nd. That he will perform and obey all such general rules and regulations of the Secretary of State in Council and of the said service as shall be in force in relation to all things to be committed to his charge or to be done by him, or to any rank, office or station in which he shall act, and will observe and obey all such orders relating to himself or his conduct as he shall receive from the Secretary of State in Council, or the Government of India, or any person who shall have lawful authority to command him.

3rd. That he will regularly and justly keep all accounts touching his transactions for the Government in India, and will preserve and keep all such documents, chattels, and realty as shall be committed to his charge, or as it shall be his duty to preserve and keep, and shall not wilfully obliterate, cancel or injure, nor permit to be obliterated, cancelled, or injured, any documents, chattels, or realty belonging to Her Majesty or in the custody of any person or persons on account of the Government, and will deliver all such documents, chattels, and realty as shall be in his custody or power to any person to whom he ought to deliver the same. And on demand made by or on behalf of the Secretary of State in Council, or of the Government of India, will deliver to such person or persons as shall be authorised to demand the same, all documents whatsoever touching any of the affairs or

From Bengal Secretariat Records, by kind permssion of the Government of Bengal.

concerns of the Government, or anything in which he shall have been engaged as a servant in the Civil Service of India: such delivery to be made without obliteration or concealment of any part of the books, papers, or writings to be delivered up, and notwithstanding that they may not be the property of Her Majesty or that there may be any entry or entries relating to his own affairs or those of any other person or any other reason whatever.

4th. That he shall not make use of or apply the property of Her Majesty which he may have for any purposes other than those for which he ought to use and apply it in the course of his said service, save and except such furniture, goods and chattels as he may be justly entitled to the use of for his own proper accommodation.

5th. That he shall not nor will divulge, disclose or make known any matter relating to the affairs or concerns of the Government in India, or relating to any matter or thing in which he may act or be concerned or which may come to his knowledge in the course of his said service which may require secrecy, and which ought to be kept secret (save and except as his duty may require), unless he shall be authorised or required to disclose and make known the same by the Secretary of State in Council or the Government in India, or some other person or persons having competent authority for that purpose.

6th. That he shall not at any time, directly or indirectly, ask, demand, accept, or receive any sum of money, or security for money, or other valuable thing or service whatsoever, or any promise or engagement by way of present, gift or gratuity, from any person or persons with whom or on whose behalf he shall, on the part of the Government in India, have any dealings or transactions, business or concern whatsoever, or from any person or persons from whom, by law or any orders or regulations of the Secretary of State in Council or of any of the branches of the Government of India, he is or shall be restrained from demanding or receiving any sum of money or other valuable thing as a gift or present, or under colour thereof.

7th. That he shall not nor will by himself, or in partnership with any other person or persons, either as principal, factor or agent, directly or indirectly engage, carry on, or be concerned in any trade, dealings or transactions whatsoever.

8th. That he shall not nor will at any time return to Europe, nor remove from or leave the Presidency, within which he shall be serving, without the previous permission of the Governor-General of India in Council in writing: and previously to any such return or removal he shall pay, satisfy, and perform all such debts, sums of money, duties, and engagements as he shall owe or be liable to perform to Her Majesty or to the Government in India, or any branch or department of the same.

9th. That he shall and will forthwith upon his arrival at the said Presidency, and from time to time, so long as he shall continue in the service of Her Majesty, make such payments as, under the rules and regulations which shall be in force within the said Presidency of Fort William in Bengal, shall become due or payable by him on account of the provision for his own pension or for pensions to his wife, or children or shall at the option of the Secretary of State in Council of the Governor-General of India in Council, allow the amount of such subscriptions to be deducted out of the money due or payable by the Government to him.

In witness whereof, the said covenantor, the said surety, and ... being two members of the Council of India, have hereunto set their hands and seals, the day and year first above written.

Signed, sealed, and delivered by the above-named covenantor in the presence of — signed (seal)

Signed and sealed, and delivered by the above-named surety in the presence of — signed (seal)

Signed and sealed, and delivered by the above-named two members of the Council of India in the presence of — signed (seal)

NOTES

1. Frederick Charles Danvers and others: *Memorial of Old Haileybury College*, Westminster: Archibald Constable and Company, 1894, p. 31.
2. Philip, Mason, *The Men Who Ruled India*, vol. 1, London: Jonathan Cape, 1963, pp. 120–1
3. Report of the Public Service Commission, 1886–7, p. 68.
4. Report of the Public Service Commission, 1886–7, p. 70.
5. Section 96-B of the Government of India Act, 1919.
6. Report of the Committee on Division of Functions, 1918, para 70.
7. Report of the Royal Commission on the Superior Civil Services in India, London: H.M.S.O., 1924, p. 16.
8. Some central services continued to be recruited by the Secretary of State for India. An example is the Imperial Customs Service.
9. Report of the Committee on Organisation and Procedure, 1937, pp. 19–20.
10. Government of India, Home Department (Establishment) F. 21/4/36–Ests., 1936.
11. On 1 June 1948, Central Provinces seceded from this body to form its own public service commission in April 1949; Orissa, too, opted out to form its own PSC.
12. The Subordinate Services comprised clerks, assistants, stenographers, typists, etc.
13. The Inferior Service included record sorters, jamadars, daffadars, daftaries, peons, farashes, chowkidars, etc.
14. Report on Indian Constitutional Reforms, Calcutta: Superintendent, Government Printing, 198, 9. 201.
15. Ibid.
16. Since 1925, the total recruitment made in the London examination of one year and the examination and nominations in India in the succeeding year have been taken together as forming one recruitment year.
17. David C. Potter, *India's Political Administrators 1991–1983*, Oxford: Clarendon Press, 1986, p. 21.

CHAPTER 4

The Higher Civil Service
since Independence

The politician made his advent in administration only after the introduction of the Montford Reforms in 1919. Under the colonial raj, the predominant concern of the public administration in India had been regulatory and maintenance. Whatever developmental and promotional work was undertaken was certainly not part of the central thrust of governance. Also, as a matter of deliberate policy, strategically sensitive positions in the government were entrusted to British officers; they alone could be trusted to ensure a rule which respected metropolitan interests over everything else.

Independence did not bring about any violent break with the past, notwithstanding the unfortunate partition of the country, which inflicted untold hardship on millions of people. An element directly contributing to the strong continuity with the past was the civil service. Though there was an exodus of large numbers of European and Muslim officers, causing depletion of cadres in the administrative hierarchies, when the transfer of power took place in 1947, Indian public personnel with 12 to 25 years' experience were available in reasonably large numbers—in over three quarters of their pre-war strength. It was fortunate that since the mid-1920s, direct recruitment of high quality had been made in India not only to the Indian Civil Service, but also to the central services as well as the civil services of some provinces. This created a small but significant reserve of high quality personnel, which could be drawn upon to meet the challenges of nation-making, state-building, and development.

Maintenance of statistical information on public administration including the civil services had broken down during World War II, and as such one cannot readily adduce the figures of central government employees in 1947, the year of India's Independence. In 1939, the total number of members of the public services in the central government was 0.8 million, which rose to 1.2 million in 1951. Of this number, 3958 occupied leadership and supervisory positions in 1939; the number rose to 11,017 in 1951.[1]

During the freedom struggle, the nationalist leadership had been strongly critical of the colonial civil service. It left no one in doubt that one of its priorities as soon as governance passed into Indian hands would be reform of the civil service. In 1936, Jawaharlal Nehru wrote:

Of one thing I am quite sure, that no new order can be built up in India so long as the spirit of the Indian Civil Service pervades our administration and our public service. That spirit of authoritarianism is the ally of imperialism, and it cannot coexist with freedom. It will either succeed in crushing freedom or will be swept away itself. Only with one type of State it is likely to fit in, and that is the fascist type. Therefore it seems to me quite essential that the Indian Civil Service and similar services must disappear completely, as such, before we can start real work on a new order. Individual members of these services, if they are willing and competent for the new job, will be welcome, but only on new conditions. It is quite inconceivable that they will get the absurdly high salaries and allowances that are paid to them today. The new India must be served by earnest, efficient workers who have an ardent faith in the cause they serve and are bent on achievement, and who work for the joy and glory of it, and not for the attraction of high salaries. The money motive must be reduced to a minimum.[2]

Even after becoming prime minister in the Interim Central Government in 1946, Nehru observed at the Meerut session of the Indian National Congress:

The [civil] services were fossilised in their mental outlook. They were wedded to bygone and obsolete methods and refused to move with the times .... It remains to be seen how long we can function in these circumstances. The experience of the past three or four months has shown us that the conduct and attitude of the officers have not changed.[3]

Nehru was not the only critic of the civil service: Mahatma Gandhi once dismissed it as 'ruinously expensive'.

ALL-INDIA SERVICES

During the British rule in India, the institution of an all-India service was consistently opposed by the nationalist leadership. In a somewhat para-doxical reversal of attitude, however, when the Secretary of State for India announced in 1946, the British Government's decision not to make future recruitment to the all-India services, the Indian leadership suddenly began to solicit their continuation and activated itself to retain these services. As a result, two all-India services were created—Indian Administrative Service and Indian Police Service, and the Constitution itself contained a provision for the establishment of new ones.

The partition of the country along religious lines changed the political scenario completely and the Provincial Premiers' Resolution of 1946 became the charter for the Indian Administrative Service (IAS) and the Indian Police Service (IPS), successors, respectively, to the Indian Civil Service and the Indian Police. The first competitive examination for recruitment to the IAS was held in July 1947. Personnel selected earlier for the ICS but not actually appointed in that service were also diverted to the IAS. By the middle of 1948, officers selected on the basis of their war records were also appointed to the IAS.

Why was the public administration, including its civil service with such a low track record in the nationalist books, not overhauled when the opportunity presented itself in 1947? This is a puzzle of modern Indian administrative history, and no conclusive or easy answer can be given—or accepted either. A possible explanation for this change of attitude lies in the smooth manner in which India won its independence. Once Great Britain decided, after the end of World War II, to leave India, a constitutional process was firmly set in motion to complete the process. This process of making India independent was called 'transfer of power', characterized by the closest and fullest adherence to constitutionalism and legality, and further facilitated by an abundant presence of goodwill on both sides. Everything was done in accordance with laws, rules, and regulations. The conduct of the civil service smoothed the transition of power and must have endeared itself to the topmost leadership. At any rate, the pressure of work demanded that a newly independent country required the optimal use of the administrative machinery: its reform could await the return of more salubrious times.

The new government's pragmatic outlook was in evidence even when functioning as the Interim Government. Jawaharlal Nehru, as prime minister, initiated negotiations with London on guarantees given to the former Secretary of State for India's Services. India, on its own, had agreed to respect the existing rights of all members of these services, whether European or Indian, if they were willing to continue and were retained by the successor government. Members of the all-India services were also given a joint guarantee by the central and provincial governments protecting their existing rights and terms and conditions of service.

Whether it was wise or not of the nationalist leadership to leave unchanged the inherited administrative system is debatable. While the decision not to make any radical change certainly allowed the new political leadership to take full advantage of the old system, an opportunity of revamping the country's civil service to suit new goals and aspirations was missed. Systemic administrative reform is easier to carry out at a time of intense political change than in calmer times, and the period following independence was an opportune one for such an exercise. But one thing more. Nehru had lifelong regrets over this pragmatic compromise on the reform of the civil service. Shortly before his death, he is said to have confided as to what was his greatest failure: 'I could not change the administration. It is still a colonial administration'.[4]

THE CONSTITUTION AND THE CIVIL SERVICES

With the exit of the British from India in 1947, the highly restricted objectives of governance ceased to be either valid or sufficient in themselves. The new constitution of India, promulgated in 1950, rested on the following three axes:

1. From a remotely governed country, India would emerge as a democracy of the parliamentary type, based on a system of periodic elections held on adult franchise.

2. India was a union of states, the Constitution making both the Centre and the constituent states autonomous in their respective areas of operation. This implied autonomous civil services also.

3. Irrespective of levels or political complexions, the government in the country was irrevocably committed to the Directive Principles of State Policy enshrined in the Constitution itself, which direct it actively to work for the economic and social well-being of the people. This brought about a philosophical change in the role and place of government, including the civil services, in Indian society.

A remarkable feature of the Constitution is its manifest administrative elaborations and concerns. It established public services commissions at the Centre and in the states and devoted several of its articles to the public services. It referred to the all-India services and even prescribed the procedure for formation of new ones. The Constitution provides safeguards to the civil services—safeguards which became the characteristic features of all the constitutional arrangements covering the civil services enacted since 1919. The Constitution guarantees security of service to the public servants by laying down that no one was to be removed from service by an authority lower than one by whom he was appointed. Powers of public recruitment and disciplinary action are vested in the President of

India. Many critics allege that the Constitution confers excessive security on the civil servants. In the year 2002, the Supreme Court of India held the Government's right to compulsorily retire a public servant if his conduct becomes untenable to public interest or obstructs the efficiency of public service. The Supreme Court of India emphasized that it cannot be disputed that the deadwood needs to be removed to maintain efficiency in the service. For redressing the grievances of mandarins, administrative tribunals are set up at the Centre and in the states. The provision for such bodies was made in the Constitution in the early 1980s through an amendment process. Parliament has been authorized to set up all-India services.

CREATION OF NEW ALL-INDIA SERVICES

Pre-independence India had as many as nine all-India services. The central government in post-independence India also has been making conspicuous efforts to create new ones. The constitutional feasibility of creating new all-India services itself is a temptation for the central government to create more such services. The demand for them has often arisen from other sources as well. For instance, these services have been viewed (see the States Reorganization Commission 1953–5) as a check on the separatist trends in the country, posing thereby a threat to national integrity.

In the 1960s, social turmoil in many parts of the country was steadily increasing. To formulate an effective strategy of action to curb this trend the government convened, in August 1961, a Chief Ministers' Conference. Among other recommendations, the conference proposed the creation of three new all-India services, namely:

1. The Indian Service of Engineers (Irrigation, Power, Building, and Roads)
2. The Indian Forest Service
3. The Indian Medical and Health Service

The Centre initiated the necessary constitutional action on this recommendation in the winter session of Parliament. On 6 December 1961, the Rajya Sabha (the Upper House) approved the proposal.[5] (It may be noted that a resolution by the upper chamber is constitutionally obligatory for the creation of all-India services.) The Lok Sabha passed the necessary legislation on 6 September 1963, which involved an amendment of the All India Services Act, 1951. Section 2A was inserted in the Act, making provision for these three new services. Official orders were also promptly issued announcing the constitution of the Indian Medical and Health

Service; and basic rules regarding recruitment and cadre management were notified in the *Gazette of India*. The statement of Lal Bahadur Shastri, then Home Minister, when introducing the proposal in the Rajya Sabha is pertinent here as indicative of the thinking of the central government on the matter. Dwelling upon the many advantages which would accrue from the formation of the services, the minister said that an all-India service would ensure a uniform and high standard of recruitment and training of officers. It introduced mobility amongst the officers between the state and the Centre. The experience he gathered was of value to him when he moved to the other level for work.[6]

The Centre's initiative in constituting the three new all-India services, however, was taken without due regard to the state governments' susceptibilities. Jammu-Kashmir, Karnataka, Maharashtra, Punjab, Tamil Nadu, and West Bengal fiercely opposed the proposed medical and health service, which compelled the Centre to hold the constitution of the service in abeyance. The formation of the Indian Service of Engineers was opposed by Assam, Jammu & Kashmir, Himachal Pradesh, Kerala, Tamil Nadu, and West Bengal. Many of these states had earlier agreed to these two services in principle, but the non-Congress governments which came to power in the election of 1966–7 in many states reversed the earlier decision. Even some Congress-ruled states were opposed to the proposal.

On 26 March 1965, the Minister of State for Home, Jaisukhlal Hathi, moved a resolution in the Rajya Sabha for the creation of two more all-India services, namely the Indian Agricultural Service and the Indian Educational Service (General Education, Technical Education).[7] Hathi reiterated the arguments which Lal Bahadur Shastri had adduced four years earlier. The resolution had a smooth passage in the Rajya Sabha on 30 March 1965, in view of the majority of the Congress party in the House. The Government introduced the All India Services (Amendment) Bill, 1965 in the winter session of 1965 of Parliament, but the bill lapsed as the Lok Sabha was dissolved.[8] Meanwhile, the Indian Forest Service was formally constituted on 1 July 1966, with officers selected from the state forest services. The first examination for direct recruitment to the service was conducted by the Union Public Service Commission in September 1967.[9]

The general election of 1967 drastically changed the political complexion of India, with the hitherto ruling party, the Congress, suffering defeat in nine of the then 17 states and having a much reduced majority at the Centre as well. The non-Congress government—and some Congress governments as well—signified their disapproval of the central government's scheme, and the central government had to bow before their opinion, as may be discerned from the following comment in the Home Ministry's Annual Report for 1968–9:

After the general election a few state governments modified their stand on the formation of All India Services in general and some state governments, on further consideration, did not agree to participate in the Indian Education Service ... . It has been decided that for the present the All India Services Act, 1951 need not be further amended.[10]

The Indian Forest Service had already been formed on 1 July 1966, but the others were stalled. In reply to the central government's order constituting the Indian Medical and Health Service, issued on 1 February 1969, Tamil Nadu (DMK-ruled), Mysore (Congress), Assam (Congress), Maharashtra (Congress), and Jammu & Kashmir (National Conference) withdrew their participation in the scheme, while Punjab and West Bengal were 'considering this question afresh'.[11] The central government confessed in 1970: 'While action was being taken to collect the necessary information from the state governments to make the initial selection from amongst the State Medical Service Officers some of the State Governments have had second thoughts about participating in the scheme ...'. It concluded: 'In view of the fact that as many as seven states have either declined to participate in the service or are reconsidering their earlier stand the Government of India is re-examining the whole matter.[12]

Finally, in 1977, the union government decided to drop the proposal altogether. Also dropped at the same time was the proposal for the Indian Service of Engineers, after Assam, Jammu & Kashmir, Tamil Nadu, West Bengal, and Himachal Pradesh conveyed to the Centre their resolve not to participate in the service.[13] The plan for an Indian Educational Service and an Indian Agricultural Service was abandoned soon after the fourth general election (1967) itself, as 'some state governments revised their stand on the need for these services'.[14]

Although the Medical and Health and Engineers services could not be the All India Service Act, 1951 had in 1963 been amended to provide for the constitution of these two services, besides the Forest Service. When the Janata Party came to power at the Centre in 1977, it took up the proposal for setting up these services, but dropped it in view of the resistance of several state governments. The Congress (I) party, coming to power at the Centre in 1980, revived the move.[15]

Other bodies to go into the question of all-India services were the Commission on Centre-State Relations, commonly known as the Sarkaria Commission (1988), in the context of Centre-State relations, and the Fifth Central Pay Commission (1997). The first commission recommended further strengthening of all-India services, with greater emphasis on selection, training, placement, etc., and on more regular consultation between the Centre and the states on matters relating to their management. It recommended the creation of all-India services in the fields of engineering, medicine and education, and even supported constituting such services in other sectors like agriculture, cooperation, industry, etc.[16] The Fifth Central Pay Commission too recommended the strengthening of the all-India services.

Matters, however, remain as they were. Resistance from the states is persistent and intense, the vehemence of their articulation depending on factors such as the political weight of the state concerned, the status of the state-level chief executive, etc. The Centre's argument in favour of all-India services is administrative efficiency and insulation from local political interferences. But accredited tools and agencies of Indian federalism also provide the Centre with a silent but very effective tool of manipulation and pressure, which the government at the Centre has not shied away from using for its short-term partisan ends. This being the track record, the country would do better to drop any idea of creating new all-India services and rather concentrate on allowing the existing all-India services to function along purely professional lines. Such an action would permit these services to evolve, in course of time, a distinct identity of their own and become an institution which would be sought after by society for its own thorough professionalism.

CENTRAL SERVICES

In 1950, the Constitution came into force, irrevocably pledging the nation to the ideals enshrined in the Preamble, the Directive Principles of State Policy, and the Fundamental Rights. The era of systematic socio-economic planning began in the 1950s, and the First Five-Year Plan was put under way. The Government had necessarily to take up new or additional responsibility in social, economic or cultural fields, which necessitated the creation of new organizations and expansion of the existing ones. The challenges of nation-making and state-building had to be met by the State, and in the process administrative machinery and personnel too expanded.

As has already been seen, three all-India services were created in post-independence India. To meet the needs of the times, another higher public service was created, called the central services. Within a decade of independence, many new central services came into existence, notable among them being the Central Secretariat Service, the Central Health Service, the Central Legal Service and the Central Information Service. These were soon joined by the Indian Economic Service and the Indian Statistical Service. By 1971, thirty organized services came into existence. The number increased to 49 in 1984 and 59 in 1995—a consequence of assumption of new functions by the State, according to the Fourth Central Pay Commission (1986). At present their number stands at 66, the complete list being given below. It may be noted that the all-India services are common to both levels of government—the central as also the state governments—but the central services are exclusive to the central government.

It is customary to classify positions in public administration in (i) duties or position classification, and (ii) rank classification, also known, respectively, as rank-in-the-job system and rank-in-the-man system. The USA has adopted the first method while India practises the rank-in-the-man system. A closer comparison of the two categories shows that the basic principles underlying position classification are the same as those underlying the rank classification. Indeed, the basic principles are universal in character and form the basis of any organizational structuring in designing its hierarchy.

HIGHER CIVIL SERVICE IN INDIA IN 2005

All-India Services

1. Indian Administrative Service
2. Indian Police Service
3. Indian Forest Service

Central Services (Non-Technical)

1. Indian Audit and Accounts Service
2. Indian Trade Service
3. Indian P&T Accounts & Finance Service
4. Indian Postal Service
5. Indian Defence Accounts Service
6. Indian Defence Estates Service
7. Indian Ordinance Factories Service
8. Indian Foreign Service
9. Indian Civil Accounts Service
10. Indian Customs & Central Excise Service
11. Indian Revenue Service
12. Indian Information Service
13. Indian Railway Accounts Service
14. Indian Railway Personnel Service
15. Indian Railway Traffic Service

16. Railway Protection Force .
17. Central Secretariat Service
18. Railway Board Secretariat Service
19. Armed Forces Headquarters Civil Service
20. Custom Appraisers Service
21. General Central Service

Central Services (Technical)

1. Indian Inspection Service
2. Indian Supply Service
3. Indian Telecommunication Service
4. P&T Building Works Service (Architectural, Electrical & Civil Wing)
5. Border Roads Engineering Service
6. Indian Naval Armament Service
7. Military Engineering Service
8. Central Power Engineering Service
9. Indian Broadcasting Service (Engineering)
10. Indian Railway Service of Electrical Engineers
11. Indian Railway Service of Engineers
12. Indian Railway Service of Mechanical Engineers
13. Indian Railway Services of Signal & Telecom Engineering
14. Indian Railway Stores Service
15. Central Engineering Service (Roads)
16. Central Architects Service (CPWD)
17. Central Electrical & Mechanical Engineering Service (CPWD)
18. Central Engineering Service (CPWD)
19. Central Water Engineering Service
20. Overseas Communication Service
21. Central Health Service
22. Indian Railway Medical Service
23. Indian Ordinance Factory's Health Service
24. Central Reserve Police Health Service
25. Border Security Force Health Service
26. Indian Tibetan Border Security Police Health Service
27. Indian Economic Service
28. Indian Statistical Service
29. Indian Legal Service
30. Indian Cost Accounts Service
31. Defence Research and Development Service
32. Defence Aeronautical Quality Assurance Service
33. Defence Quality Assurance Service

34. Central Company Law Service
35. Survey of Indian Service
36. Geological Survey of India Service
37. Indian Meteorological Service
38. Central Labour Service
39. Indian Broadcasting Service (Programme)
40. Indian Broadcasting Service (Engineering)
41. Indian Salt Service

Other Services

1. Central Reserve Police Force
2. Border Security Force
3. Indo-Tibetan Border Police
4. Central Industrial Security Force

THE CENTRAL SECRETARIAT SERVICE

Reorganization of the Central Secretariat Service was one of the earliest measures which the Government of independent India initiated. The redesigned service consisted of four grades in descending order—undersecretary, superintendent, assistant superintendent, and assistant. In the Imperial Secretariat Service the highest one could aspire to reach was the post of assistant secretary, one notch below the under-secretary. The new service, designed with a much higher reach, allowed for upward mobility from the clerical level, as well as direct recruitment for first-line supervisors in the Central Secretariat. Considering that officers of the Central Secretariat Service had to have high administrative ability, their recruitment process had to be relatively stiff and competitive, and their training of a high standard. The Central Secretariat Service is recruited from the combined civil services examination conducted by the Union Public Service Commission. It has been the country's administrative philosophy that those engaged in policy-making must possess direct and first-hand experience of field, that is state level administration. An essential feature of the Central Secretariat Service therefore has been to systematically expose its members to a minimum period of work in the field, to enable them to acquire practical experience of executive administration. When the scheme for the Central Secretariat Services was being finalized, a provision was accordingly made for 'training deputation' under state governments. Members of the service were to be sent out on deputation to state governments to work in the district administration for not less than two years, the additional expenses being borne by the central government. The first batch was sent for this training around 1952. In view of the importance attached to this deputation, the Central Secretariat has as a rule avoided giving itself a corps of permanent officers, and not been keen on the constitution of a permanent officer class in the form of the Central Secretariat Service. The state level deputation of the members of the Central Secretariat Service has fallen into disuse since a long time, and needs to be revived.

SIZE OF THE SERVICES

The number of the central services—64 as of 2003—may look large, but many services are small in size. The Indian Salt Service, for example, has a total membership of 11. The Central Legal Service has 70 posts within its cadre. Only twenty-nine services have a cadre strength of more than 500. The Indian Economic Service and the Indian Statistical Service have 600 and 560 members respectively. All the engineering services taken together have a strength of about 10,000. In other words, engineering personnel constitute 15 per cent of the higher public servants (group A) in India, whereas the non-technical central services personnel recruited through the combined civil service examination number 9000 which is 13.4 per cent of the higher civil servants.

Table 4.1
Indian Administrative Service Authorised Strength

Year 1951		Year 1987	
Assam	42	Assam	186
		Nagaland	44
Bihar	96	Bihar	356
Bombay	110	Maharashtra	318
		Gujarat	195
Madhya Pradesh	73	Madhya Pradesh	361
Vindhya Pradesh	24		
Madhya Pradesh	36		
Madras	151	Tamil Nadu	288
Hyderabad	72	Andhra Pradesh	312
Orissa	71	Orissa	199
Punjab	48	Punjab	180
PEPSU	21	Haryana	179
Uttar Pradesh	190	Uttar Pradesh	500
West Bengal	98	West Bengal	281

Thus the IAS, the premier leadership service of the land, had an authorized strength of 1188 in 1951, which rose to 5047 in 1984.[17] Table 4.1 provides the authorized strength, state-wise, of the IAS for 1951, when the planning process first began in India, and for 1987. The seven five-year plans plus a couple of annual plans which were more or less successfully completed since the 1950s, have led to a vast increase in the number of personnel. Many states of 1951 no longer exist in their original size or even nomenclature, having undergone boundary changes in 1955, 1960, 1961, 1966, 1971, and 1975, but the table still is an indicator of the changed situation.

CLASSIFICATION OF THE CIVIL SERVICE

Various modes are adopted to classify the civil service in India. Civil service is commonly classified into gazetted posts and non-gazetted posts—a practice which dates back to the early colonial period. The holders of the higher services are gazetted officers, while low-ranking personnel are the non-gazetted officials. The higher post holders are called gazetted because their appointment, transfer, promotion, retirement, etc. are announced in the official gazette in a notification issued by the government. This practice began in the year 1793, when the government of Fort William in Bengal brought out its official gazette. The Government of India published its own gazettes from January 1864. Another way of classifying the civil service is into four classes—class I, class II, class III and class IV, now changed to group I, group II, group III and group IV, after the report (1973) of the Third Central Pay Commission. This classification corresponded to differences in the responsibility of the work performed and the qualifications required, with class or group I being the highest and class IV being the lowest. Class I and class II constitute the officer class, while those in class III and class IV are known as officials. The last two categories were known as inferior and subordinate services but were designated as class III and class IV by the First Central Pay Commission (1947). The members of class I and class II are gazetted officers while class III and IV posts are non-gazetted ones. The all-India services are all in class I while the central services are put both in class I and II. These two services in class I and class II are involved in policy-making and supervising responsibility. Class III is the support service while unskilled workers are put in class IV.

It may be noted that though in 1994 the central level civil service was 3.76 million strong, personnel in managerial cadres numbered only 68,000. Of these, as many as 31,825 were in the central services, which comes to 1.8 per cent of the total number. This number included personnel of

Table 4.2
Size of the Civil Service

	1957	Percentage of the total	1971	Percentage of the total	1984	Percentage of the total	1994	Percentage of the total
Class I	10,400	0.6	34,100	1.2	68,000	1.8	90,000	2.2
Class II	19,300	1.1	46,100	1.6	80,000	2.1	148,000	3.3
Class III	728,800	42.0	1,545,00	52.1	2,286,800	48.0	290,000	66.8
Class IV	978,400	56.3	1,337,500	45.1	1,330,900	35.4	1,168,600	27.2
Total	1,736,900	100.0	2,962,700	100.0	3,765,700	100.0	1,696,600	100.0

Source: Second, Third, Fourth, and Fifth Pay Commissions.

technical services also, the bulk of whom were engaged in jobs of an executive nature and thus were not directly engaged in policy-making. Of the rest, many were rather new in the service and were in junior positions. In 1994, the managerial cadres in the Government of India numbered 229,000, constituting 5.6 per cent of the total government employees. A large number of them were too junior. This means that about 30,000-40,000 personnel or so could be said to constitute India's managerial class, directly performing public-policy making and reviewing functions. They occupy leadership positions in the government and their decisions impinge on large numbers of people with varying degrees of gravity. Of the 68,000 higher civil servants, as many as 31,825 were in services other than the three all-India services. In 1984, the IAS had an authorized strength of 5047, the IPS 2679 and the Indian Forest Service 2006 whereas in 1994, the authorized membership of these services stood at 5336, 3519, and 2721 respectively.

THE CHANGING CONCERNS OF CIVIL SERVICES

The dominant concern of the political leadership in newly independent India was to rehabilitate the battered civil service of the land and to tone up its operational efficiency. This exercise was essential to ensure that the country's public administration was fit for the emerging challenges of state-building and development. Filling up the vacancies left by the European and the Muslim officers who opted to serve Pakistan was a major task that could not be postponed. Decisions were quickly taken to constitute two new all-India services and to get them going. The earliest concern in regard to the civil service was thus principally structural—to launch new services, to undertake fresh public recruitment to them, to formulate and standardize rules and regulations relating to them, etc. This was also the period when India launched its First Five-Year Plan, which made public administration its instrument of execution.

A shift of priority was discerned while the Second Five-Year Plan (1956–61) was in progress. The emphasis of the plan was on industry, self-reliance, and self-sufficiency. Ironically, however, the strategy of industrialization led to the spawning of a vast network of regulatory administration, the government seeking to develop and regulate private industries through a control mechanism in the form of permits and licences. The emerging interface between industrialists and the governmental leadership, including the civil service, was not without its perils. Growing corruption in public administration became a prominent phenomenon in the 1960s, so much so that the controversial chief minister of Punjab, Sardar Pratap Singh Kairon, was publicly criticized for indulging in corrupt practices. Nehru's political stature had also declined in the wake of India's defeat by the Chinese in the 1962 armed conflict. Two committees were appointed by a reluctant Nehru to look into corruption—the S.R. Das Commission to look into charges of corruption against Kairon, and the other by Parliament under the chairmanship of K. Santhanam, to examine corruption in the public administration and suggest action. The reports of both the commissions only confirmed the popular misgivings. Over the decades, the system has become more blasé as regards corruption. The public wailing and breast-beating over corruption that characterized earlier times gave way to its pathetic acceptance as an inevitable and integral part of the contemporary lifestyle. Corruption in public life therefore ceased to be the dominant theme for public debate and discussion, but it was growing.

Since the 1970s, the priority of the policy-makers has shifted to citizen satisfaction in administration. An examination of the annual reports of the country's central personnel agency, namely, the Ministry (earlier, Department) of Personnel discloses that for some time the policy-makers are giving more thought to redressal of citizen grievances. To this end, decentralization in the country's administration is recommended and the need for 'responsive administration' is emphasized. Citizens' charters are being proclaimed. There is at the same time, a growing emphasis on the introduction of what may be called modern management in the country's civil services. Since 1984, in-service training of middle and senior level personnel has emerged as the single most significant feature of the central personnel agency. In-service training for the IAS has been made compulsory, and every member including even the cabinet secretary must attend a prescribed training programme every year. Knowledge of artificial intelligence is also widely insisted upon.

Since the 1980s, one may well notice yet another trend in the civil service of the land at all levels of governance. Merit as the basis of public recruitment is gaining less and less support, and the wind is blowing in favour of recruitment based on a quota system. Social justice is increasingly solicited and a demand is even being made to introduce it in private administration also.

Since the 1990s a paradigm-shift in the role of civil service has taken place in India. The shift is from direct doing or rowing to steering. India is presently committed to a free market economy, which calls for cultivation of new skills and competence in the country's mandarins. The role of the civil service has as a result changed—it has not suffered a diminution. This may be illustrated. India no longer enjoys a monopoly over the production and distribution of telecom services. But the public administration of the country feels obliged to establish a telecom regulatory authority of India (TRAI) to regulate the behaviour of the private sector in the field of telecommunication. There is thus a shift of the role of the civil service under the changed ideology supportive of liberalization. To conclude, the work of the civil service under a free market economy has become more varied and diverse, with new challenges, thus raising demands for new skills.

NOTES

1. R.A. Gopalaswami, *The Machinery of Government: Improvement of Efficiency*, New Delhi: Government of India, Ministry of Home Affairs, 1952, p. 3.

2. Jawaharlal Nehru, *An Autobiography*, London: The Bodley Head, 1955, p. 455.

3. The Indian Annual Register, July–December 1946, vol. II, Calcutta: The Annual Register Office, pp. 289–90.

4. Quoted in David C. Potter, *India's Political Administrators 1919–1983*, Oxford: Clarendon Press, 1986, p. 2.

5. Rajya Sabha, *Parliamentary Debates*, Vol. XXXVl. No. 7, 5 December 1961, Col. 1149.

6. Ministry of Home Affairs: *Report 1961–62*, p. 4.

7. Parliamentary Debates: Rajya Sabha

8. Ministry of Home Affairs: *Annual Report, 1965–66*, p. 1.

9. Ministry of Home Affairs: *Annual Report, 1967–68*. p. 1.

10. Ibid., pp. 2–3.

11. Ministry of Home Affairs: *Annual Report, 1969–70*, p. 3.

12. Department of Personnel, Cabinet Secretariat: Report 1970–71, p. 4.

13. Ibid., p. 5.

14. Department of Personnel: *Report 1969–70*, p. 4.

15. Department of Personnel and Administrative Reforms: *Annual Report 1981–82*, p. 38.

16. The Report of the Commission on Centre-State Relations, Part I, pp. 219–31.

17. Annual Report, Ministry of Home Affairs, 1951–2 and Fourth Central Pay Commission Report, p. 52.

CHAPTER 5

The Central Personnel Agency

Management of matters relating to its personnel is in itself a heavy responsibility on the government. Persons have to be recruited, trained, and deployed in public service. The development of their potential has to be planned in the light of their demonstrated aptitudes and jobs given to them where their potential could be optimally utilized. They have also to be adequately compensated. The terms and conditions of service should be satisfactory and planned in a way to make civil service attractive to bright young men and women in society. And when the employee retires from service, the employer assumes responsibility for his respectable maintenance even after superannuation.

In other words, all personnel functions like recruitment, training, placement, performance appraisal and promotion, compensation, employer-employee relations, etc. need continuous and careful attention. As modern governments inevitably employ a large number of persons, and these persons are very intelligent and sensitive, recruited as they are on considerations of merit, especially at the higher levels, professional handling of personnel matters is essential.

Colonial India had no single central personnel agency at any time. A division in the Home Department in the Government of India performed the personnel functions. But recruitment and control of the top level civil service remained vested in the Secretary of State for India, who was part of the British Government and functioned in London ever since his establishment in the year 1858. Even after the constitutional reforms of 1919, when the measure of metropolitan involvement and control in the colony was undergoing changes, the control of the Secretary of State for India never completely vanished until 1947 when this office went into oblivion.

In 1924, the Central Public Service Commission was set up and constitutionally empowered to recruit higher public servants for India. The British Civil Service Commission also continued simultaneous recruitment of superior services in London. This dual mode continued until 1943, when the wartime conditions disrupted the holding of the competitive examination in London.

With Independence, the Public Service Commission, already in existence, continued to be responsible for recruitment of higher public services. The Ministry of Home Affairs had a division on Public Services which, as the nomenclature indicates, dealt with personnel matters. With independence, the functions of the Secretary of State for India in this regard also devolved upon it. In personnel matters, the Home Ministry and the Finance Ministry worked very closely with each other.

The Home Ministry has been India's central personnel agency, responsible for the central and all-India services, though it had nothing directly to do with the state civil services. While the day-to-day administration of individual services remained vested in the individual ministry concerned, the Home Ministry was generally in charge of personnel matters. The ministry had necessarily to work in close cooperation, with the Ministry of Finance, for many civil service matters inevitably have a financial bearing.

Among matters falling within the province of the Ministry of Home Affairs were determining the method of recruitment and conditions of service of general application to the entire civil service and the interpretation of existing orders of general application relating to such recruitment or conditions of service. The ministry dealt with general questions (other than those with a financial bearing) including conduct rules relating to all-India services and central civil services (excluding civil services under the control of the Ministry of Railways and the Department of Atomic Energy). The ministry was the administering and controlling authority for a number of services like the IAS, IPS, the Central Secretariat Service, the Indian Economic Service, the Indian Statistical Service, and for laying down their service conditions with or without financial bearing. It was not incumbent that the Home Ministry be consulted in regard to conditions of other services, such as pay scales, fixation of pay, grant of increments, special pay, deputation allowance, compensatory, and other allowances. Nevertheless, since the Home Ministry possessed expertise in service matters and directly controlled a number of key services, it was consulted to ensure that similar guiding principles were followed for all the services in general matters and service conditions. Thus, while the ultimate responsibility in these matters rested with the Finance Ministry, the Home Ministry took into account the repercussions of these service conditions on the general functioning of the services. The line of demarcation therefore could at best be roughly defined as follows: the function of the Ministry of Finance was to consider the financial implications of these matters; that of the Ministry of Home Affairs was to take into account their effect, on the efficient functioning of the services in general.

The need for an agency entrusted with personnel functions in the central government had been felt for quite some time, particularly in the context of the rapid expansion of the civil service since independence. The Estimates Committee of the Third Lok Sabha 1963 recommended that the

... ever-expanding role of the Government in a welfare State with its natural concomitant of a large civil service, calls for effective personnel control through a single agency. In the opinion of the Estimates Committee, the present position regarding the administration of public services involving dual control by the Ministry of Home Affairs from the point of view of 'effects on the efficient functioning on the services in general' and by the Ministry of Finance from the point of view of 'financial implications' is not conducive to their efficient management.[1]

The Administrative Reforms Commission, set up in 1966, too, urged the government to set up a separate Department of Personnel to be placed directly under the Prime Minister to serve as a nodal agency for the personnel functions of the government. It emphasized: it is necessary to set up a central personnel agency. A central agency with overall responsibility in all important matters and manned largely by specialists will obviously be able to devote concerted attention to the formulation of new polices, set new standards and raise the quality of administration.[2]

All over the world, governments of the time were in favour of central personnel agencies. The Fulton Committee on the Civil Service, set up in Great Britain in 1966, made a similar recommendation in its report published in 1968. United Nations experts in public administration also saw in the setting up of a central personnel agency a big leap towards a modern personnel system.

In keeping with the times, the central government accepted the recommendation of the Administrative Reforms Commission. Accordingly, the Department of Personnel was set up in August 1970 and placed within the Cabinet Secretariat. The department took over functions performed hitherto by the 'services wing' of the Ministry of Home Affairs.

Though the Department of Personnel functioned directly under the political chief executive, the Prime Minister, its day-to-day management was entrusted to a minister of state in the Ministry of Home Affairs. This is the standard formula—a central personnel agency directly under the head of government though a junior minister is appointed for day-to-day running. In February 1973, the Department of Administrative Reforms, hitherto located in the Ministry of Home Affairs, was transferred to the Department of Personnel and Administrative Reforms, which however, did not prove a very satisfactory arrangement. The way the department functioned indicated that it was a move towards centralization in personnel management in India, and an ambitious Prime Minister, especially in a developing society, could use the new power to promote his own personal position to the detriment of overall efficiency; and this is exactly what happened. When matters relating to civil service were handled in the Ministry of Home Affairs, there were certain checks and balances ensuring fairness. Even otherwise, it is administratively desirable to locate matters like personnel at a level one point below the chief executive: this arrangement provides for an appeal to the head of government against the decisions of the personnel agency and thus ensures more rationality in decision-making. All these considerations became inoperative when the department was put directly under the Prime Minister. The Indian experience of management of civil service during the period of internal emergency (1975–7) was none too happy, and taking a cue from it, the Janata government, which came to power in 1977, in the same year transferred the department back to the Ministry of Home Affairs.

MINISTRY OF PERSONNEL, PUBLIC GRIEVANCES AND PENSIONS

In March 1985, the department was converted into the Ministry of Personnel, Public Grievances and Pensions and comprised the departments of: (i) Personnel and Training, (ii) Administrative Reforms and Public Grievances, and (iii) Pension and Pensioners' Welfare.

The ministry is the nodal personnel and administrative reforms agency in India. On its personnel side, the ministry formulates policies relating to recruitment, training, promotion, employer-employee relations, service conditions, etc., in the civil service. Staff welfare, discipline, and moral in the civil service and integrity in administration form part of its portfolio. It manages the all-India services and certain other central services and formulates training policies and programmes in the field of public administration. It deals with reservation matters relating to the Scheduled Castes and Scheduled Tribes. The Department of Administrative Reforms formulates policy relating to administrative reforms, and, in addition, formulates policy and coordinates issues relating to (i) redressal of public grievances in general and (ii) grievances relating to central government agencies in particular. The Department of Pension and Pensioners' Welfare is responsible for policy and the coordination of matters relating to retirement benefits to central government employees.

The ministry deals with all administrative matters relating to the Union Public Service Commission, Central Vigilance Commission, Staff Selection Commission, Central Bureau of Investigation, Administrative Tribunals and the Indian Institute of Public Administration, It also manages the Lal Bahadur Shastri National Academy of Administration (Mussoorie) and the Institute of Secretariat Training and Management, New Delhi.

The ministry functions under the overall charge of the Prime Minister, who is assisted by a Minister of State. It had a deputy minister in the past. Its administrative head is the Secretary (Personnel) who is a career civil servant, usually a member of the IAS. The junior and middle level positions in the ministry are filled by personnel drawn from a number of services. The senior policy-making posts are mostly occupied by members of the IAS, in the same pattern as followed in other ministries and departments. Other services find fault with such a staffing pattern on the grounds that it biases recruitment in favour of a particular service. The incumbents do not come to the ministry with any specialization. Whatever specialization they pick up is acquired on the job. On completion of their stipulated term, they are transferred out and new officers join. The junior staff do receive some training in one of the state-run training institutions, but their morale is not too high owing to a lack of recognition of whatever expertise they accumulate and to an absence of opportunities for advancement.

Having a separate Ministry of Personnel certainly facilitates undivided attention to public personnel matters by an agency unburdened with other tasks. But the arrangement is attended by a risk. When the 'public services' matters were part of another ministry, there was a check on them from disinterested quarters. The Ministry of Finance was also somewhat actively involved in the management of public services, at least in regard to numbers and efficiency. In all societies, civil servants constitute an influential though silent group and their clout in a developing democracy is formidable. In India, there is a fear, not entirely without substance, that a separate Ministry of Personnel has emerged as a powerful lobby for the bureaucrats, and the Ministry of Finance, which is professionally expected to safeguard the tax-payers' interest, has been sidelined. Ideally, the Ministry of Finance must check the creation of new posts in the civil service and filling of vacant positions. Also, the cadre controlling authorities are potentially weak and ill-prepared, and it is the duty of the ministry of personnel to strengthen them and improve their information base.

A saving grace may be that India does not have a monolithic personnel agency, charged with all personnel functions. As has already been seen in a previous chapter, recruitment of public personnel is entrusted to a separate multi-member body, the Public Service Commission, which is set up by the Constitution itself and made independent of the executive to enable it to operate objectively and impartially. This is discussed in the chapter that follows.

CADRE MANAGEMENT

Cadre management is an important problem faced in the modern civil service. As is common, civil servants are ordinarily placed in organized services, the arrangement having been in existence in India since the year 1674. Each civil servant has certain hopes, expectations, and entitlements in the civil service, and his morale would be high when these are attended to in accordance with set rules of procedures. Cadre management includes career planning, under which the civil servants are given a wide range of administrative experiences to consciously prepare them for successively higher positions. This entails a proper rotation system of posting, deputation, and training. Cadre management confronts both the sets of services in India—the central civil services and the all-India services. But it is much more complicated in the case of the latter. The Indian Administrative Service is a single service from one angle but is divided into 28 state cadres, each state managing its cadre according to its own requirements and perceptions even though these governing practices have been codified and standardized to a large extent. Cadre management becomes an active concern for a service. Take the case of the IAS.

The question of cadre management was discussed at the Provincial Premiers' Conference in 1946, and the decision taken then was to leave this matter to the discretion of the provinces. Sardar Vallabhbhai Patel, the Home Member, suggested that 'the provincial governments were to work out the number and nature of posts for which officers of the All India Administrative Service were required and they were to communicate this information to the central government. The central government would decide its own requirements and after receiving the provincial governments' proposals work out the details of the cadre.[3] The 'Draft Scheme for the formation of an All India Administrative Service' prepared in 1947 observed: 'The strength including both the number and character of posts of the All India Administrative Service shall be as specified in Schedule II.'[4] The schedule, referred to in the draft scheme, however, was prepared later; and by that time the country's political climate had undergone a qualitative change, having turned enormously favourable to the Centre. The autonomy promised at the Provincial Premiers Conference was not carried forward in equivalent measure and was instead made to suffer successive abridgements. The independence of the country changed the entire complexion of the polity and the deliberations of the premiers' conference had to be reconciled with the newly emerging compulsions of nation-making and state-building.

The blueprint which finally emerged provided that all senior positions in the provincial governments were required to be manned by IAS officers, the basis of determination being the administrative component of a particular post: if the administrative content of a job is more and the technical content less, it is classified in the IAS; posts of technical nature need to go to the relevant state service. The principle governing the fixation of cadre strength laid down for the IAS was that all superior posts in the administrative department of and above the rank of district officer, that is, district collectors, commissioners, members of the Board of Revenue, secretaries, deputy secretaries; and, in addition, a proportion of miscellaneous posts including heads of department were as a rule to be occupied by officers belonging to the IAS. The fixation of cadre is done under the IAS (Cadre) Rules, 1954, which provides that there shall be constituted for each state an IAS cadre[5] and the strength and composition of each of the cadres shall be determined by the central government in consultation with the state governments concerned;[6] Provision is also made to re-examine, at an interval of every three years, the strength and composition of each such cadre in consultation with the state government and may make such alterations therein as it deems fit.[7]

The authorized cadre strength of a state is fixed by taking into account the following elements:

(1) Senior duty posts under the state government;

(2) Central deputation reserve at the rate of 40 per cent of (1) above;

(3) Posts filled by promotion of State Civil Service ('PCS') officers at the rate of $33^1/_3$ per cent of (l) and (2) above;

(4) Posts to be filled by direct recruitment of (1) and (2) minus (3) above;

(5) Deputation reserve at the rate of 22.5 per cent of (4) above;

(6) Leave reserve at the rate of 5.62 per cent of (4) above;

(7) Junior posts at the rate of 23.17 per cent of (4) above;

(8) Training reserve at the rate of 11.91 per cent of (4) above.

In 1951, the total membership of the IAS was 1168 which shot up to over 5000 at the end of the twentieth century, marking a more than fourfold increase in the size of this service in this period although attempts have been made to prune its size. The annual rate of expansion has been over 13 per cent, which is quite impressive. It is certainly true that the activities of the state have increased in range and scale, more impressively at the district level, warranting an increase in the number of public personnel, including the size of the IAS. But even after making due allowance for this, the number at present is much larger than it should be, which may be accounted for by a variety of factors. Patronage, both at political and senior administrative levels, is a powerful reason behind the increase. In the expectation of getting a larger promotion quota for the state civil service, a large number of posts got created and encadred in the IAS. It has also happened that though some states for historical reasons suspect the IAS, their actions serve to benefit this service: when some jobs are considered to be important enough, these get offered to the members of this service alone, leading to an increase in its membership. Nor must one forget that while nearly 85 to 90 per cent of the jobs encadred into IAS are in the states, the promotional avenues for its members in the state are extremely limited, which also offers an inducement to create jobs at higher levels.

EX-CADRE POST

A state government has generally only one post carrying a salary of the Secretary to government at the Centre. Where a Board of Revenue is in existence, such posts may be two or, at the most, three, which is an absolutely inadequate number when compared to the number of such senior posts at the Centre. A big state like Uttar Pradesh with the cadre strength of over 500 has only two senior posts—President of Board of Revenue and Chief Secretary. The posts in the IAS cadre, as we know, carry centrally prescribed salaries, and the state government has no power to alter their emoluments unilaterally. Nor should one forget that politics is becoming less and less restrained, and it is no longer a convention to appoint the seniormost civil servant as Chief Secretary.[8] What therefore happens is that a state government does not hesitate to bypass a few senior civil servants and appoint, say, the fourth one to the coveted post of Chief Secretary, political acceptability having emerged as critical to such an appointment. This is a fairly common practice in states like Madhya Pradesh and Tamil Nadu. At the same time, partly to assuage the hurt feelings of the superseded officers, the state government generally ap-points them outside the cadre and declares such posts as equivalent to that of the chief secretary. This is the spillover of the politics of scarcity, and if reform in cadre management is not initiated, 'ex-cadreism' is likely to be viewed as a functional necessity by the state-level political leadership, however disliked it may be by the central government. But for a device like ex-cadreism, the senior officers would have either stagnated in the state hierarchy or migrated to the central government.

NON-IAS PRESSURE ON IAS JOBS

Alongside the tendency to create ex-cadre posts and appoint IAS officers to them runs a parallel inclination to appoint non-IAS officers to cadre posts. Such appointments confer status on the incumbents as well as raise their salary (their substantive posts do not carry these scales), even if these are temporary gains. Like ex-cadreism, such appointments are acts of political patronage and the practice continues unabated despite its disapproval by the central government. This problem is particularly widespread in states like Bihar, Haryana, Punjab, Kerala, Tamil Nadu, West Bengal, etc.

There does not thus appear to be any standard criteria in regard to the fixation of cadre strength in the states. No relationship exists between cadre strength and the states' area, population and budgetary outlay even granting that a certain fixed strength of staff has to be maintained irrespective of these factors. One also notices an unevenness in the promotion prospects of IAS cadres of different states.

The foregoing makes it clear that cadre management is presently defective and should be viewed with concern. A review of the IAS cadres is urgent and the deficiencies in the cadre management in the states pointed out in the present work must be removed. A reasonable proportion must be maintained between the high-level posts and the cadre strength of the IAS. It is no less necessary that the individual state governments undertake a cadre review of their own state civil service (PCS) to stop its thoughtless proliferation. Such a comprehensive review should be undertaken of all the services. One cannot do better than let R.P. Noronha, a senior member of the ICS, speak:

We (members of the Indian Civil Service) deteriorated later. But that is how we were in 1947. ... One never heard the phrase 'He can't do very much, he's ill, you know.' If an ICS officer was ill, he was in hospital and on leave, not dragging out his illness on government time. If he was on duty, then he was doing his duty, not talking about it ... I have spoken about a dedicated sense of duty being one of the attributes of the service. Refusal to do something mainly because it serves one's own interests should logically flow from such a sense of duty. It did in the past. Upgrading a post because you—or your wife's cousin—would get it was unthinkable; it was the good of the administration that counted, not your own. For example, in Madhya Pradesh, the post of Chief Secretary carried the same scale as that of Commissioner, and the Chief Secretary was literally and financially *primus inter pares*. There was a lot of sense in the arrangement. For one thing, the government could select a relatively junior officer as Chief Secretary without causing heartburn. For another, the Chief Secretary, being nothing more than a selected Commissioner, and sometimes junior to many of them, had to carry the Commissioners with him instead of riding them; he had to discover in himself qualities over and above an ability to note on files. At that time the post was equated with that of Joint Secretary to the Government of India, and was on a fixed pay of Rs. 3,000 per month. After the reorganisation of states, efforts began to upgrade the post to that of Additional Secretary (Rs. 3,500). The boss (H.S. Kamath), who was then Chief Secretary, resisted but ultimately the upgrading was done. Then, in 1969 or 1970, the Chief Secretary got another lift. The reason-since Chief Secretaries got only Rs. 3,500 while Secretaries to the Government of India got Rs. 4,000, there was a flight of Chief Secretaries to the Centre. As no officer serving in a state can go to the Centre without the consent of his parent government, the validity of the argument escapes me.

This kind of upgrading was bad enough. What was worse was the multiplication of senior scale supertime posts. Like flood waters the proposals seeped through or outflanked the dams you erected against them. Take the states and the Centre, compile a comparative list of senior scale and supertime posts every five years, and you will discover a rate of growth which would do credit to any Planning Commission. Parkinson only discovered his famous law—it was the services that put it into being. In doing so they inadvertently established a corollary which should be brought to Mr. Parkinson's notice. The greater the degree of overstaffing, the less the work done. We do not need any more administrative reforms commissions; all that is required is to slash the number of senior posts in the country by half, and then let the remaining half get on with the job. They will do it far more efficiently.

Let me anticipate a very legitimate question. What did I do to prevent the evils I have described? Frankly, I tried and I failed. Like the ministers.[9]

NOTES

1. Lok Sabha: *Ninety-Third Report of the Estimates Committe, (Third Lok Sabha),* 1966, pp. 18–19.

2. Administrative Reforms Commission: *Report on the Machinery of the Government of India and its Procedure of Work,* Delhi: Manager of Publication, 1968, p. 71.

3. Government of India, Home Department Ests (R) F. 45/3/46-Ests-(R), para 23.

4. Government of India, Ministry of Home Affairs, Ests (R) Section-F. 174/47/Ests-(R), Appendix I.

5. Rule 3 .

6. Sub-rule (1) of Rule 4.

7. Sub-rule (2) of Rule 4.

8. A state like UP. had no such convention and did not necessarily appoint the seniormost civil servant as the Chief Secretary.

9. R.P. Noronha, *A Tale Told by an Idiot,* New Delhi: Vikas, 1976, pp. 62.

CHAPTER 6

Recruitment

Recruitment is a critically sensitive process in a personnel system for the quality of the original timber ultimately determines the level of efficiency and success of an organization. Other processes in the personnel system like training and placement can be effective only on persons who possess the potential for growth and development: no amount of training and a system of rotation of jobs can change a donkey into a horse. Other processes of personnel administration are repeated from time to time, recruitment is a once-and-for-all process for a large number of persons: they join an organization at an early age of their life and treat it as their lifelong career, getting separated from the organization only on retirement.

Several modes are employed by organizations to recruit personnel. One is the appraisal of bio-data submitted by the applying candidates. Sometimes, the candidates seeking employment provide suitable 'references' to the employer who then seeks the views and opinions from the referees about the candidate to make the final selection. Interview is another mode of recruitment: here, the candidate is invited for a free face-to-face chat with the employer who seeks to assess the candidate's fitness for the job. Other modes of filling posts are direct recruitment, promotion, deputation, transfer, re-employment, and short-term contract. The most important mode is direct recruitment, which is the theme of the present chapter. India follows the traditional system of recruitment through a competitive written examination followed by an interview.

The higher civil service in India comprises the all-India services and the central services. All-India services are common to both levels of government in India; they are recruited and initially trained by the Government of India but allotted to one or the other state of the Union. The Government of India meets its requirements by borrowing its required manpower from each state: the officers come to the Centre on deputation, and on completion of the term they revert to their state and a fresh wave of officers come; the rhythmic inflow and outflow of officers continues under the well-known tenure system of staffing.

In addition to the bi-level all-India services, the Government of India has established the central services, numbering 66 at present, trained by the Government of India and under its exclusive control; they are not shared with the states. The central services claim a long history and were first created by the colonial rulers even though they were not consciously so called. When India became formally federal under the present Constitution, the designation 'central services' began to be used. The Indian Audit and Accounts Service, the Central Engineering Service, etc. are among the central services created during colonial times.

The central services were 30 in 1971, which increased to 49 in 1984. In 2003, their number stood at 66. Their number is thus increasing in view of the expanding need of the times. Establishment of a central service depends on the executive decision of the government.

In addition to the central services, in which most central government posts fall, there are isolated civil posts created outside the established civil services. There are posts which do not belong to any organized service: they are clubbed together and constitute the General Central Service, membership of which is extremely heterogeneous because all isolated, apparently unrelated posts are deemed to belong to the General Central Service.

Like the all-India services, the central services are recruited by the central recruiting agency, namely the Union Public Service Commission; the members of the non-technical central services as well as those in the Indian Administrative Service and the Indian Police Service are recruited through a combined competitive examination held by the UPSC. The eligible candidates must possess a bachelor's degree in any branch of knowledge and must be between 21 and 30 years of age. The examination is a two-phase arrangement: the preliminary test and the main examination. The first test is of the nature of a weeding-out test, acting virtually as a gate-keeper, keeping out of the fray those who do not possess the minimum competence as reflected in their failure to get certain minimum marks. The preliminary test comprises two papers—general studies and a specialized paper to be selected by a candidate out of a long list of subjects taught in the universities. A candidate is not obliged to study any new subject. This is consciously planned. He has to take the competitive examination soon after leaving college. The number of vacancies are limited and while many try their luck, only a few of them succeed. Those who fail to make a mark cannot complain that they wasted their valuable years in trying to get a job in vain. Nor can they justifiably complain that they had to read new subjects and thus make special preparations with no return. As already stated, candidates failing to secure a minimum number of marks are declared 'failed' and thus not allowed to go to the main arena, that is, the main examination. The real test begins with the mains, held 4–5 months after the preliminary test. The candidate has to take a combination of both compulsory and optional subjects. The compulsory subjects common to all candidates is designed to test capacity for effective thinking, sense of form, and power of clear and lucid expression. The optional paper tests the intellectual ability and scholastic attainment of the candidates, the formal standard being of BA Honours level. The examination is stiff and a large number of applicants fail. Those who are declared 'successful' are required to appear for an interview conducted by the UPSC, which assesses a candidate's personal qualities including some intellectual qualities which a written examination cannot reveal.

Marks are awarded in each examination, including the oral one. These are added up, and the final list of successful candidates is made public, the exact number depending on the vacancies announced by the UPSC earlier. Before the final list is announced, two more formalities have to be completed—police verification of the character of the candidate, and a medical examination to ensure physical fitness.

The principle of selection in India as in other modern democracies is that the candidate selects his own employer. What this means is that one who secures the highest marks gets the service of his first choice. The most preferred service is the Indian Administrative Service, the second preference being the Indian Police Service or the Indian Foreign Service. The Indian Revenue Service and the Indian Customs and Excise Service which were rated not very high at one time are of late figuring fourth or fifth in the list of preferences. The least preferred could be the Indian Postal Service, the Defence Estates Service, the Central Secretariat Service, etc. Some candidates, particularly those possessing medical and engineering degrees, set their eyes on the more prestigious services like the IAS or IPS; if they fail to get these services they opt to seek their fortune elsewhere in the expanding private sector. Also, many who fail to get selected, try their luck again. A candidate is entitled to four chances, subject, of course, to his being within the permitted age-group of 21–30 years. Generally, most candidates succeed in the second or even third attempt and are in the age-group of 23–5 years. One must join the service as early as possible. Though the age allowed is up to 30 years, those who join in the higher age-group may not reach the highest posts in administration as they may be caught by the age of retirement before they can move to the level of Secretary in the government or they may be left with a very short term at that level.

Over one lakh candidates appear at the preliminary test, out of which nearly 5000 qualify for the main examination. Of this number, over 800 candidates are called for interview. Finally, nearly 400 candidates turn out lucky and are selected. The number of higher level vacancies is as a policy declining since the nineties, when the process of liberalization began in India. Of the 411 candidates selected in the year 2000, 63 were from Scheduled Castes, 30 Scheduled Tribes, 127 from Other Backward Castes the remaining 181 being from the general category. Although candidates may answer in English or in Indian languages, most opt for English. This is because those writing in English possess distinct socialization advantages. The English language exercises a great pull as it is, in India, the employer's language. Candidates have ready access to reading material.

One may be interested to know about the sociological profile of the higher civil service in India. The socio-economic description of the higher civil service becomes relevant to find out whether India's higher civil service is representative in composition of the larger society or not. The higher civil service anywhere in the world is dominated by the middle class in society. Members of the higher civil service in India are generally drawn from an urban middle class background, and have a marked supra-regional all-India leaning. In fact, the regional roots of the direct recruits to the all-India and central services are weak and unsteady. Many of them speak a language at home different from the language of the state they were born in. The language spoken in the office is usually different from the language spoken at home. Many were born in one state, and domiciled and educated in another, and virtually every one of the successful recruits took the competitive examination away from the state where he was born. Their parents are mostly engaged in the modern professions and thus possess strong socialization advantages. They come from a handful of India's 200-plus universities. Delhi, Allahabad, and Rajasthan universities account for nearly 30 per cent of the successful candidates to the higher public services, followed by Jawaharlal Nehru, Panjab, Lucknow, Patna, and Utkal universities. Recently, Andhra University has also joined the club. In short, hardly 10 universities have emerged as the principal contractors of the Union Public Service Commission for supply of the country's mandarins. The social and spatial base of the superior civil service is thus narrow and highly skewed. The social base of the civil service is narrow because the middle class in India is itself tiny in size, although the base of the civil service is steadily expanding as a result of growing educational facilities in society as well as the introduction of reservation of jobs or quota system in the government. In the 1940s, the colonial rulers introduced a policy of reservation in the civil services based on religion. Independent India rejected this criterion but has added a new category of beneficiaries, namely the Scheduled Castes and Scheduled Tribes, and since the 1990s, the 'Other Backward Castes'.

Indian society is an unequal one, a powerful cause of this inequality being the caste system among Hindus. Certain castes have traditionally remained backward, socially, economically, educationally, culturally and otherwise; and they do need a set of concessions vis-à-vis the other more advantageously placed castes so that they may get a fair share in the country's civil service as in other walks of life. The Constitution, while guaranteeing 'equality of opportunity' to all the matters of public employment, allows the state to reserve appointments or posts in favour of any 'backward class of citizens'. The Constitution does not itself define the term 'backward', but B.R. Ambedkar, the chairman of the Constitution Drafting Committee, interpreted it to mean 'Scheduled Castes and 'Scheduled Tribes'. Article 335 of the Constitution enjoins on both the central and state governments to give special consideration to these castes and tribes in the civil services, consistent with the maintenance of efficiency in the administration. The government has accordingly reserved 15 per cent of the posts for Scheduled Castes and 7.5 per cent for Scheduled Tribes. They have an additional age concession in that the upper age limit in their case has been raised by five years: this is purported to neutralize the disadvantages of a late start in life. The result of these concessions may be seen in the increasing numbers of candidates belonging to these castes and tribes entering the civil service. The quota system in jobs has a populist appeal in democratic India and is likely to stay permanently and even expand further.

WOMEN IN THE CIVIL SERVICE

A discussion in the present age of post-modernity is apt to be viewed as incomplete without a mention, however brief, of women in the civil service. Women's entry into a country's civil service is a more recent phenomenon in most countries. The Indian Civil Service was a male service: women as a rule were not allowed admission in it. They entered the educational, medical, and postal and telegraph services and were mostly concentrated in the lower levels of the official hierarchy. Independence of the country changed the situation. The constitution of India granted equality of opportunities to all citizens, thus paving the way for the fairer sex to enter government service. As a result, women have begun entering the civil service in all sectors of administration, although they are concentrated mostly in the lower echelons of administration. According to the Fifth Pay Commission, women employees constitute 7.51 per cent (2.83 lakh) of the total government employees, but 98 per cent of the women employees occupy posts in groups C and D (that is, lower levels) of the official hierarchy. A large concentration of them exists in the ministries of Communication, Railways, and Defence.

As regards the higher civil service, women employees have started entering it in a perceptible number although it is still very small in comparison to their proportion in the population. Women constitute nearly 6 per cent of the total membership of the all-India services and 5 per cent of the higher grades in the governmental service. The lower rate of their employment is due to low literacy among women and high preference for domesticity. Women who succeed in entering the portals of the higher civil service seem to possess certain traits distinctive to themselves. They have received public school education and are the offspring of second generation educated parents. They belong to reasonably good middle class, mostly professional, families possessing a 'big town' background. They thus possess distinct sociological advantages as compared to their male counterparts and are very articulate, commanding a high level of communication skills.

The civil service in India meets its manpower requirement by catching people young. This has its advantage; when young college graduates are recruited, they can be easily moulded to the employer's requirements, which adds to the efficiency of administration. At the same time, these recruits possess no work experience outside the government, thus having little training for handling modern society's complex problems. Those who fail to enter when in the age-group 21–30 miss the bus forever, thus denying the state access to specialized knowledge and experience of different walks of life. The situation is much better than in the past, when the upper age of entry in the government was fixed at 26. Today, many new recruits to the civil service do bring with them some measure of work experience. Also, at present, many persons enter the lower levels of administration, and lack opportunities of moving into higher administration for want of an age-restrictive policy. To provide an incentive to those already within the government but at its lower level, a suggestion is sometimes made to provide for a limited competitive examination: those already in government should be allowed to appear for the higher level competitive examination conducted by the UPSC. The Second Pay Commission's recommendation in this context needs to be considered seriously. The recommendation to open an avenue for recruitment to the higher civil service in India proved to be a non-event. No subsequent Pay Commission picked up the thread and supported the proposal. Nor did any committee on civil service reform pursue the idea. The civil service in India is a closed system with little provision for lateral entry. Recruitment (or appointment) in government takes place at the lowest level of each of the four classes. But these classes are not exclusive of each other. A certain proportion of the posts at the first entry level in class I is reserved for promotion from class II. Similarly, some proportion—larger than in class I—is reserved for persons coming in promotion from class II. In many cases the rules provide for 100 per cent reservation of posts from class III to class II. As said earlier, entry to a class is allowed at its lower level—the higher levels in each class are not open to entry from outside. Exceptions to this general practice are posts requiring a very refined kind of expertise. Limited lateral entry is provided in engineering and technical cadres at higher levels. Hardly any movement from class III to class II in government in presently permitted.

As the recommendation for a special competitive examination to provide young officers in the lower services with an additional opportunity to enter the higher service is a sensible one, it is but appropriate to let the Second Pay Commission speak. 'It should be an essential part of the scheme that only those who are nominated by their Departments should be permitted to take the examination; and the criteria for departmental nominations should be not only good work and good conduct, but also exceptional promise.' A university degree need not, however, be essential. Whatever safeguards are considered necessary to ensure fair nomination —such as selection by a committee—may be adopted. The examination may be open not only to central government employees, but also to those working under the state governments, public corporations, and other undertakings in the public sector. We are presuming that if a scheme of this sort is introduced it would include the Indian Administrative Service/ Indian Police Service as well as the class I central services. The examination papers should not be of the academic type but such as would test intelligence, power of observation, analysis and judgment, and knowledge and understanding of public affairs, etc.—in short, the kind of abilities that are required in the higher services. About three times as many candidates as there are vacancies, might be called for interview in the order of the marks obtained by them at the written examination. The maximum marks for the interview might not be more than half the total marks for the written papers; and the interview marks should be added to those obtained at the written examination to determine the final rank. The interview should be much longer than for the present all-India and central services examination, and the questioning as searching as possible. These are very broad ideas, which would require closer examination if the general principle is found acceptable.[1]

This recommendation would permit lateral mobility, which would weaken the barriers presently dividing the organized services. 'We have felt called upon to suggest this scheme partly because we believe that its incentive value would be far greater than the number of promotions permissible under it might suggest.'[2]

The upper age recruitment presently is 30, but it is too much on the higher side and is imprudent. A majority of the successful recruits are generally seen to enter the civil service between the ages of 23 and 25. Those who enter at the age of 30 are generally repeaters and evince a dogged determination to seek a government job. Those who enter around the age of 30 are left with so many less years in service and may not reach the top. Also, such recruits (who are generally married) do not take training very seriously, being distracted by growing family responsibilities. Most of them bring a measure of work experience, which is not always wholesome. This reduces their propensity to derive benefit from training. The ideal is to enter in the second attempt and before the age of 26.

Lateral entry refers to the provision of entry into different levels of organizational hierarchy, in contrast to the closed system of administration as in India, in which public personnel are recruited only at its lower level within a narrowly prescribed age band, its higher level positions being filled by promotion on the basis of merit or seniority or a mix of the two methods. New Zealand may be an apt example of the closed administration whereas the United States of America represents the other extreme, in which recruitment is made as and when needed at different levels of its hierarchy from wherever possible.

Public administration in India recruits its personnel at the lower age group and restricts entry to the lower level of the service. This prevents fresh blood from entering into public administration. Nor is the practice in complete harmony with democracy, denying all those above the prescribed age group access to public service. A sound personnel system must provide for multiple entry system. This is a particularly pressing need in the sector of science and technology.

Reservation for Scheduled Castes has been in operation since 1943, which means that today second or even third generation members of these disadvantaged groups are availing of these concessions. Most of these beneficiaries of the system of reservation today come from groups with no weak socialization. Also, because 'Scheduled Castes' is an artificial clubbing together of castes which have been socially, economically and educationally neglected, they contain more backward castes as well as less backward castes. Most of the beneficiaries are the offspring of persons from the less backward castes in the Scheduled Castes. One also notices gender imbalance: more male members from the Scheduled Castes join the higher civil service than females. There is a skewed representation of different tribes in the civil service. Tribes like the Meenas from Rajasthan, Negis from Himachal Pradesh capture a disproportionately large number of the reserved seats. A time has perhaps come to debar those whose parents have already reaped the advantages.

The Supreme Court of India has set an outer limit of 50 per cent on reservations in government jobs. It cannot however be said strongly that the political parties have unreservedly accepted the outer limit in support of equity and welfare. Some political sections of society are very vocal in promoting the concept of quotas to meet parochial causes, which plays havoc with the wider question of justice for all in a republican set-up. There is even an attempt to amend the Constitution to break the ceiling on quotas prescribed by the apex court. Such a move, if it ever succeeds, will hardly provide relief to the truly needy, even among the dalits and tribals. The real solution does not lie in reservation of jobs in government. After all, how many jobs are there in the government's kitty? Even if all the jobs in government get reserved for the SCs and STs, the problem of unemployment cannot be solved. Civil society would only be arousing expectations, which it cannot fulfill. The real remedy lies in building a dynamic and equitable economy with fast-expanding economic opportunities.

The syllabus of the competitive examination has registered changes over time in an endeavour to accommodate new areas of knowledge and induct talent wherever available. The trend was triggered by the Kothari Report of the early eighties. The changed pattern of examination is bringing about a slight shift in the background of new entrants to the higher civil service, particularly the IAS. The earlier syllabus in the competitive examination was structured in such away that 'arts' or 'social science' candidates, particularly those opting for history or law, had an edge over others and they also succeeded in fairly large numbers. The premium on history or law has weakened, and now candidates with science, technology, and even medical backgrounds are entering in larger numbers. Indeed, the IAS has of late begun to attract to its fold IIT-trained engineers and even medical doctors. Engineering subjects are included in the list of examination, but not those which medical doctors are required to study. Doctors generally choose zoology and botany. In two successive years—1983 and 1984—they topped the merit list in the IAS.

Whether engineers and doctors should be encouraged to join the administrative career is a subject of debate, but, without taking any firm stand it must nevertheless be pointed out that terms and conditions of service of the specialists must be improved: and no engineer or doctor should be made to think that it would be disadvantageous for him to remain in his own profession. To continue the story of change even though it is internal, confined_as it is within the elitist group of the country, candidates with some work experience have begun to enter the IAS, the upper age of entry being 28 years of age till 1998 and 30 since 1999. A large majority of the successful candidates fall in the age-group of 22 to 25, which moves close to the ceiling in the case of members of Scheduled Castes and Tribes. The argument against 30 years of age being the upper age is that persons of that age-group do not evince seriousness in their institutional training and thus it is difficult to influence their personality formation.

NOTES

1. *Report of the Second Central Pay Commission*, pp. 507–8.
2. Ibid., p. 506.

CHAPTER 7

Chief Recruitment Agency in India
The Union Public Service Commission

India's chief personnel agency is not singular but plural. It has hived off recruitment from other processes of personnel administration, entrusting the former function to a specially designed multi-membership body, namely the Public Service Commission. This body is the theme of the present chapter. It is through the process of recruitment that an individual establishes a relationship with an organization. Of all the processes of personnel administration, recruitment is easily the most critical one. Historically, the method of recruitment was patronage or spoils, but merit began to be adopted in the nineteenth century. Merit as proven in an open competitive examination was adopted in France in 1850. India adopted merit in 1854. The higher civil servants in India are recruited by an independent agency known as the Union Public Service Commission. Clerical personnel are appointed by the Subordinate Staff Selection Commission, while the lower level functionaries are departmentally recruited.

UNION PUBLIC SERVICE COMMISSION

Public recruitment is the cornerstone of personnel administration in all political systems. No amount of in-service training can, for example, make up for the deficiencies in the original 'timber'. Recruitment, at the same time, is a most delicate task. No person, left entirely to himself, can be completely trusted to be thorough, objective, and impartial when choosing someone to fill a post. Even with the best of intentions, one cannot help getting swayed by factors which may be more personal than functional.

Even then, one should not only be fair but should also be seen to be fair. Therefore, proper standards of recruitment for public administration need to be explicitly laid down and strictly observed throughout administrative behaviour. This need is all the more compelling in modern societies where large-scale recruitment for civil service is involved. The Government of India, for instance, employs nearly four million personnel. Enormity is a feature of all contemporary bureaucracies. Large number of people need to be recruited annually, which is best done by a professional body with the exclusive function of recruitment.

Also, today the traditional conception of administration has changed though with varying intensities in different societies. Politically awakened citizenry have made a deliberate decision to create certain institutions, give them a free hand, and make them accountable only to society and its representatives. This is one way in which society imposes suitable curbs and controls over government. In most countries, recruitment of personnel has been taken out of the hands of the executive and entrusted to a separate organization, generally known as Civil Service Commission or Public Service Commission.

NORTHCOTE-TREVELYAN REPORT

The Northcote-Trevelyan Report submitted to the British Parliament in 1854, was the first in the world's administrative history to have visualized the establishment of such a body. Having established a case for a written examination as the basis for public recruitment, the report went on to observe:

The preliminary examination of candidates for civil employment, however, cannot be conducted in an effective and consistent manner throughout the service while it is left to each department to determine the nature of the examination and to examine the candidates. Some on whom the duty of examining devolves feel no interest in the subject. Others, although disposed to do their best, are likely to entertain erroneous or imperfect conceptions of the standard of examination which ought to be fixed, and to be unable to apply it properly after it has been settled. The time and attention of the superior officers are fully occupied in disposing of the current business of their respective departments. To do this in a creditable manner will always be their primary object and as the bearing of the subject under consideration upon the efficiency of their departments, although very important, is not of a direct or immediate end, and is not likely to have much effect during their own tenure of office, what has to be done in reference to it will either be done by themselves in a hurried and imperfect manner, or will be left by them to their subordinate officers to be dealt with at their discretion. In a large department, in which numerous candidates have to be examined, want of time will prevent the superior officers from giving the subject the attention it deserves, and

other matters, although of infinitely less real consequence, will have the prece-
dence, because they press, and must be disposed of at the moment. Moreover, a
large proportion of the persons appointed to a public department usually consists
of young men in whose success the heads of the office or the principal clerks take
a lively personal interest, owing to relationship or some other motive connected
with their public or private position, and an independent opinion is hardly to be
expected from an examiner who is acting under the orders of the one, and is in
habit of daily intercourse with the other. A public officer ought not be to placed in
a situation in which duty might require him to make an unfavourable report under
such circumstances. Lastly, even supposing every other circumstance to be
favourable, it is impossible that each department, acting for itself, can come to
such just conclusions in regard to the nature of the preliminary examination, or
can conduct it in such a fair, and effective, and consistent manner, as would
persons having the advantage of a general view of the subject as it affects every
public department, and who should have been selected for the duty on account of
their experience in matters of this description.

We accordingly recommend that a Central Board, read the Civil Service Commission, should be constituted for conducting the examination of all candidates for
the public service whom it may be thought right to subject to such a test. Such
Board should be composed of men holding an independent position, and capable
of commanding general confidence; it should have at its head an officer of the rank
of Privy Councillor; and should either include, or have the means of obtaining the
assistance of persons experienced in the education of the youth of the upper and
middle classes and persons who are familiar with the conduct of official business.
It should be made imperative upon candidates for admission to any appointment
(except in certain special cases which will presently be noticed) to pass a proper
examination before the Board, and obtain from them a certificate of having
done so.[1]

The Northcote-Trevelyan Report identified for the first time some of the
principles which underlie the development of the modern public service.
Its main recommendations fell into four categories:

(i)   recruitment by competitive examination rather than patronage;
(ii) a division between intellectual and mechanical work;
(iii) promotion by merit;
(iv) measures to unify the civil service, including a common basis of
      recruiting across departments.

It took nearly 20 years to implement fully the concept of open competition
in the British public service. The other principles of the Report were not
fully developed and applied until the 1920s. Commissions after the
Northcote-Trevelyan Report up to 1931 and the reconstruction period
immediately following the First World War established the basis of public
service in Great Britain. These developments included uniform systems of
recruitment; the class division of officials; Whitley machinery; and the
central power of the Treasury over the civil service.

In implementing the recommendations of the Northcote-Trevelyan Report, Great Britain became the first country to set up a Civil Service Commission. The year was 1855, and Great Britain was followed by Canada in 1868. The United States of America was the happy home of the 'spoils system', but after President Garfield was assassinated by a job-seeker the Congress was shocked and quickly passed a law in 1883, known as the Pendleton Act constituting the Civil Service Commission. South Africa set up such a body in 1912, Australia[2] and Northern Ireland in 1923, India in 1926, Sri Lanka in 1931, and New Zealand[3] in 1948. Bangladesh, Burma (Myanmar), Iran, Israel, Pakistan, Philippines, Thailand, Kenya, etc. are other countries having a civil service commission.[4] Whether called civil service commission or public service commission[5] the function of this body is to recruit personnel for public service.

Everywhere, the public service commission is the custodian and inter-preter of the merit principle in the matter of public recruitment. It has always been viewed as the custodian of the public services. Its functions, however, may vary from country to country. The functions of the Public Service Commission in Great Britain are restrictively defined: it is the recruiting arm of the government, being an examining and a certifying body for the purpose of public recruitment. The ambit of its American counterpart was much wider: it recruited personnel for public employ-ment, and administered many laws relating to government employees regarding veterans' preference, classification, security checks, political activity, retirement, insurance programmes, etc. In 1978, the Civil Service Commission of USA was abolished and two independent agencies were created in its place, namely, the Office of Personnel Management and the Merit System Protection Board. The Office of Personnel Management is a personnel policy-making body while the Merit System Protection Board is entrusted with appellate and investigatory responsibilities and is thus the appeals and review board that protects the integrity of the federal merit system and the rights of the employees. The precise functions entrusted to the public service commission of a country are generally determined by the historical experiences and civil culture of that country.

The Public Service Commission may be enshrined in the constitution of the country itself as in India, or it may be set up under a special statute, as was the case in the United States: or by an executive resolution of the government—the Civil Service Commission in Great Britain owes its existence to an 'Order in Council'. The institution of the public service commission has generally been regarded as a product of British influence: the countries which have it as part of their administrative feature were either part of the British empire or came under British influence. Paul P.

Van Reper rightly remarks: The Pendleton Act of USA provided, basically for the adoption of the British civil service system in the United States. A commission was to administer competitive examinations; entrance into the public service would be possible only at the bottom; a full-scale career service was implied; and the offices were not to be used for political purposes.[6] Enacted in 1883, the Pendleton Act continues to be the 'basis of Federal Personnel management to this day'.[7] The merger, in 1968, of the British Civil Service Commission with the Civil Service Department, thereby depriving this body of its separate, independent existence which it enjoyed since 1855, was viewed by many as a retrograde step. The fact, however, is that the independence of the British Civil Service Commission has not suffered any erosion even though it is now an integral part of the executive. The British civil service can rightly feel proud of its traditions of integrity and objectivity, which is a sure enough protection of the commission's independence from ministerial control in matters of recruitment. What is sauce for the gander is not necessarily sauce for the goose. Where unemployment is widespread, political interference pervasive, public opinion weak, conventions and traditions not well crystallized, a public service commission endowed with the highest degree of independence appears to be an inescapable necessity.

THE GOVERNMENT OF INDIA ACT, 1919

The Public Service Commission in India owes its origin to the winds of democracy which began blowing since the Great War (1914–18) and hastened its formation. The need for such a body was not felt so long as the imperial order in India was absolute. It was only after democracy, however truncated, was introduced at the provincial level of government, that a body like the Public Service Commission was first visualized. The British government in India realized that under dyarchy, the hallmark of the Government of India Act, 1919, the civil service was bound to come under the direct influence, and even control, of the politician-minister, which made it essential to take out a decidedly sensitive personnel matter like recruitment from the control of the executive and entrust it to an independent body. Speaking of the need for a public service commission in India, the Government of India's first Despatch on the Indian Constitutional Reforms, dated 5 March 1919, said:

In most of the dominions where responsible government has been established, the need has been felt of protecting the public service from political influences by the establishment of some permanent office particularly charged with the regulation of service matters. We are not prepared at present to develop the case fully for the establishment in India of a Public Service Commission: but we feel that the prospect that the services may come more and more under ministerial control does afford strong grounds for instituting such body. Accordingly, we think that provisions should be made for its institution in the new Bill.[8]

Then followed the Montagu-Chelmsford Report (1919), which recommended that 'for all public services, for which there is recruitment in England open to Europeans and Indians alike, there must be a system of appointment in India.[9] The authors of the report held the view that the traditional system of recruiting for the higher Indian civil service only in Britain needed to be supplemented and we propose to supplement it by fixing a definite percentage of recruitment to be made in India.'[10]

The Government of India Act, 1919, which made a beginning towards responsible government in India, provided:

There should be established in India a Public Service Commission, consisting of not more than five members, of whom one shall be chairman, appointed by the Secretary of State in Council. Each member shall hold office for five years, and may be reappointed. No member shall be removed before the expiry of the term of office, except by order of the Secretary of State in Council. The qualifications for appointment, and the pay and pension (if any) attaching to the office of chairman and member, shall be prescribed by rules made by the Secretary of State in Council. The Public Service Commission shall discharge, in regard to recruitment and control of the public services in India, such functions as may be assigned thereto by rules made by the Secretary of State in Council.[11]

Accordingly, the competitive examination to the ICS was for the first time held in India in 1922. The papers set for this examination, however, were different from its British counterpart. The examination, held at Allahabad, was conducted directly by the British Civil Service Commission. The secretary of that body came to Allahabad to supervise the arrangements. But a public service commission was yet to be established. Writing in 1924, the Royal Commission on the Superior Services to India, popularly known as the Lee Commission (after the name of its chairman) urged action on the setting up of a public service commission 'without delay', regarding it as 'one of the cardinal features of our report and as forming an integral part of the whole structure of our proposals for the future of the (civil) services.'[12] The functions of the commission were to recruit members of the all-India services and the central services, to establish and maintain proper standards of qualification for admission to them, and to hear appeals relating to disciplinary control and protection of the services. It was to consist of five members, two of whom were to possess judicial or other legal qualifications. All of them were to be 'men of the highest public standing who will appreciate the vital and intimate relationship which should exist between the State and its servants',[13] and were to be 'detached so far as practicable from all political associations'.[14]

The Government of India Act, 1919, had already provided for setting up a civil service commission in India itself. The administrative problems involved in supervising the examination from London were many, a consideration that accelerated the setting up of a civil service commission in India. The Central Public Service Commission was inaugurated on 1 October 1926. Sir Ross Barker, a senior member of the Home Civil Service, was invited to be its chairman, this choice being dictated by a determination to fashion the Commission after the traditions of the British Civil Service Commission. Its other members were: A.H. Ley, J.C. Weir, Syed Raza Ali, and A.N. Chatterjee. A.G. Dix, who was a member of the Indian Educational Service, was its secretary .The Central Public Service Commission was made a part of the Home Department in the Government of India.

The Central Public Service Commission advised the Government of India on matters relating to public recruitment. It conducted competitive examinations held in India for the all-India services and the central services and arranged the candidates in order of merit. Where recruitment was made by selection it considered the applications, interviewed the candidates and submitted to the government a list of them in order of preference. Where candidates were to be promoted from a provincial to an all-India service it considered the claims of the candidates nominated by the provincial governments, advised the Governor General of India whether their qualifications suited the service, and finally it arranged them in order of preference. The Commission also lent its services to the provincial governments on their request. The members of the Commission were appointed by the Secretary of State for a term of five years and could not be removed before the expiry of their term except by his order. The chairman was not eligible, on vacating his office, to hold any other post under the Crown in India. Two of the five members were required to have been in the service of the Crown in India for at least 10 years. These provisions were intended to give an exalted status to the recruiting body, make it independent in its functioning, and emphasize continuity in administration.

THE SIMON COMMISSION REPORT

The next stage in the evolution of the Public Service Commission in the country was reached when further proposals for constitutional reform were being framed. The provinces were still without such an outfit. From now on, the general stress was on the need for setting up public service commissions in the provinces and, what is more, the provinces agreeing among themselves to constitute joint commissions to serve two or more of them. The Indian Statutory Commission, known as the Simon Commission (after the name of its chairman), recommending the setting up of public service commissions in the provinces, observed: 'We have no doubt of the necessity for the establishment of provincial public service commissions if an efficient and loyal public service is to be maintained … . The protection of the services from political influences is an essential condition of the constitutional advances we recommend.'[15] The Simon Commission went to the extent of arguing that recruitment of public personnel for the provinces should devolve to the Central Public Service Commission if the provincial governments did not act on this recommendation.

The proposals for Indian constitutional reforms, popularly known as the White Paper (1931), recommended[16] federal public service commission, and for the provinces, provincial public service commissions to serve individual provinces or, for the sake of economy, joint public service commissions to serve two or more provinces. The Joint Committee on Indian Constitutional Reform generally endorsed[17] these proposals, but emphasized the benefits of joint provincial public service commissions. Alternatively, a province could make use of the federal Public Service Commission's services.

THE GOVERNMENT OF INDIA ACT, 1935

The Government of India Act, 1935, devoted chapter II, running from section 264 to 268, to public service commissions. It provided for setting up a federal public service commission for the federation and a public service commission for each province or a joint public service commission serving two or more provinces. As regards the federal public service commission, its chairman and other members were appointed by the Governor-General. At least one half of the members were to be persons who had worked for a minimum of 10 years under the government. The independence and objectivity of the commission were to be ensured by charging the budget of the commission to the revenues of the federation, thus not subject to vote by the legislature. Also, the chairman of the commission was made ineligible, on ceasing to hold office, for further employment under government. Other members, on ceasing to hold office, could not hold any other post under the government without the approval of the Governor-General. Under certain provisions, the government could exempt itself from consultations. Conversely, the Governor-General could refer to the commission any matter for its advice.

The Provincial Public Service Commission was closely patterned after the federal Public Service Commission.

The function of the federal Public Service Commission was to conduct examinations for appointments to the federal services. Besides, it was to be consulted:

(a) on all matters relating to methods of recruitment of civil services and for civil posts;

(b) on the principles to be followed in making appointments to civil services and posts and in making promotions and transfers from one service to another and on the suitability of candidates for such appointments, promotions or transfers;

(c) on all disciplinary matters affecting a government servant;

(d) about paying out of the revenues of the federation the costs incurred by a government servant, serving or retired, if legal proceedings were instituted against him for acts done in the execution of his duty and he had to defend himself;

(e) on awarding pension to a government servant if he was injured in the course of duty.

With the coming into force on 1 April 1937 of the Government of India Act, 1935, the Central Public Service Commission became the Federal Public Service Commission. The provinces too set up public service commissions in 1937. Provinces which set up joint public service commissions were: Bihar, Central Provinces and Orissa; Punjab and North-West Frontier Province; and Bombay and Sindh.

CONSTITUTION OF INDIA

The Federal Public Service Commission caused to operate when the present Constitution come into operation in 1950. Since then, India has had a multi-member Union Public Service Commission (UPSC), and each state has its own public service commission. The provisions relating to the Union Public Service Commission and the state public service commissions have literally been lifted from the Government of India Act, 1935 and little purpose would be served to repeat them. The Union Public Service Commission is India's recruiting agency and is consulted also in disciplinary and promotional matters. There is no obligation to consult the Commission in matters pertaining to the provisions of Article 16 (reservation of posts for backward classes for appointments in the public services) or Article 335 (reservation for Scheduled Castes and Scheduled Tribes for appointments in the public services). The 1958 regulations also truncated the Commission's purview in disciplinary matters. While the Constitution obliges the central government to consult the UPSC in 'all disciplinary matters affecting a person serving under the government in a civil capacity including memorials or petitions relating to such matters', the 1958 regulations restrict consultation to the following types of disciplinary cases only:

(a) where the President proposes to pass an original order imposing any of the penalties specified in the Central Civil Services (Classification, Control and Appeal) Rules;

(b) where the President proposes to make an order on appeal against an order imposing penalty made by a subordinate authority;

(c) where the President proposes to overrule or modify an order made by subordinate authority imposing a penalty; and

(d) where the President proposes to impose any of the prescribed penalties in exercise of his powers of review in cases where no penalty has been imposed.

The UPSC is a recommendatory body but it is required to point out the non-acceptance of its recommendations by the government. The ministry concerned, in turn, has to submit a memorandum to explain why it did not follow the Commission's recommendations. The President causes the report of the UPSC together with the memorandum of the ministry to be laid before each House of Parliament. As a further safeguard, a convention has evolved since 1947 that a ministry which wishes to reject the Commission's advice in regard to any appointment, must refer the matter to the Cabinet Appointments Committee. Other cases in which the ministry proposes not to accept the advice of the Commission have to be referred, without exception, to the Ministry of Personnel and Administrative Reforms. Members of the Commission are given a fixed tenure of six years or till the age of 67 years and are debarred from further employment.

FUTURE PROSPECTS

Though recommendatory in nature, the UPSC commanded the full esteem of the executive in the earlier years of the Republic. Both Jawaharlal Nehru and Indira Gandhi respected it and generally went by its advice, even when not very palatable. The Commission ceased to command that reverence since the mid-1980s, in the sense that non-acceptance of the Commission's recommendations, kept minimal until then, became a serious problem during Rajiv Gandhi's prime ministership. The trend persists, though to a diminished extent.

Today, the UPSC is influenced by two power centres: the technological and the political. More and more scientific and technological posts are being hived off from the Commission's jurisdictional competence. The Atomic Energy Commission and the Council of Scientific and Industrial Research were already excluded from consultation. So are the Departments of Electronics and of Space. The argument advanced is that the UPSC, with its conventional style of staffing and functioning, is ill-equipped to recruit scientific and technological personnel of the level required by an industrializing society. And what remains with the recruiting agency is not gaining routine acceptance by the political executive. The arguments advanced are somewhat unconvincing. The plural membership of the Commission makes readily available to it at the leadership level a wide range of knowledge even in areas of science and technology. Secondly, the Commission functions with the aid of subject of experts and thus its reach is all-encompassing. Above all, people in India repose faith in the Commission's fair play and objectivity, which ad hoc formations can never enjoy. Its members are selected from a pool of distinguished persons drawn from civil service, army, and civil society, including the academic field. Therefore, the employees in these scientific departments themselves protested in the past when their department was sought to be made independent of the UPSC's jurisdiction. Recruitment is a technical job, and the UPSC has developed the necessary expertise in the area. An attempt to rob the UPSC of its jurisdiction and create parallel bodies is ill advised.

In the past, Parliament was seen evincing a keen interest in the Commission's functioning. The print media, too, took a lively interest in matters of public recruitment. This meant that the executive, already seized of the moral parameters of its UPSC's functioning, was kept on its toes by a vigilant environment. Of late, however, a general apathy seems to have descended on opinion-makers of the land, including the mass media and the executive with its shrinking moral values, is becoming increasingly self-aggrandizing and aggressive. As a result, the Union Public Service Commission finds itself a somewhat lonely, isolated body. Of the four pillars of the democratic constitution of India, the Union Public Service Commission is one, the other three being the Supreme Court, the Election Commission, and the Comptroller and Auditor-General. It is viewed as a vital component of healthy democracy in India, and the framers of the Constitution took pains to make the institution as foolproof as humanly possible. This explains why the Constitution makes detailed provisions regarding this institution. Mention also needs to be made of the leadership which the Union Public Service Commission provides by its practice of holding conferences of the chairmen of the state public service commissions, where mutual problems are discussed and future course of action planned.

An organization is no better than the human beings who make it up. It goes without saying that persons of proven competence, integrity, and vision alone should be appointed in the recruiting agency, though this needs to be underscored. The persons appointed as chairman and members of the body must be distinguished in the various fields of knowledge, known also for their integrity, maturity, and impartiality. Critically important in this respect is the appointment of the chairman; he must be very carefully chosen, for he sets the tone and level of the body. The UPSC membership must not be viewed as a sinecure. The Constitution obliges the Union Public Service Commission to prepare an annual report which is placed on the table of Parliament, which is an instrument of shaping public opinions. Parliament must properly discuss it and the mass media should also give adequate publicity to the report and thus help shape public opinion. The Union Public Service Commission is too important a pillar of democracy and a custodian of the merit system in the civil service to be allowed to fall by the wayside on account of continued public apathy.

NOTES

1. *The Northcote-Trevelyan Report on the Organisation of the Permanent Civil Service* is reproduced in the *Report of the Committee on the Civil Service (Lord Fulton)*; Cmnd 3638, London: HMSO, 1968, pp 108–19.

2. Australia had a Public Service Commissioner since 1902.

3. New Zealand had a Civil Service Commissioner since 1912.

4. The Public Service Commission is however, not a universal institution. The countries in Europe do not have it. In France, for instance, recruitment of public personnel is made by the *Ecole Nationale d' Administration*. Nor did Communist countries like Soviet Union have this institution.

5. Strictly speaking, the two terms 'public service' and 'civil service' are not interchangeable. Members of the judiciary and the army are public servants but not civil servants. The terms 'public servant' is wider than 'civil servant'. The present writer uses these two terms as if they are inter-changeable.

6. Van Reper, Paul P., *History of United States Civil Service:* Evanston, Illinois: Row, Person and Company 1958, p. 98.

7. Ibid., p. 113.

8. Paragraph 55 of Government of India's first Despatch on Indian Constitution Reform, see Mukherji, Panchanandass, *The Indian Constitution*, Calcutta: Thacker, Spink, 1920, pp. 71–2.

9. *Report on Indian Constitutional Reform*, Calcutta: Superintendent, Government Printing, 1918, p. 201.

10. Ibid.

11. Section 38 of Government of India Act, 1919.

12. *Report of the Royal Commission on the Superior Civil Services in India*, London: HMSO. 1925, p. 16.

13. Ibid., p. 14.

14. Ibid.

15. *Report of the India Statutory Commission*, vol. II, London: HMSO, 1930, pp. 296–7.

16. *Proposals for Indian Constitutional Reform*, Delhi: Manager of Publications, 1933, proposal 195, p. 71.

17. *Report of Joint Committee on Indian Constitutional Reform*, vol. I, (part I) London: HMSO, 1934, p. 189.

CHAPTER 8

Top Management Staffing

It has been pointed out earlier that filling of individual posts in public administration is not an easy or quick job, for the posts involved are very large, are of very specialized nature and involve both the levels of governance, demanding careful selection of officers. The present chapter discusses the staffing arrangement for the higher level posts in administration. In India, the elite corps of civil servants—group A—has a total strength of about 68,000. Of these, only about 30,000 occupy managerial posts. The rest either spend their career in executive (that is, field) positions, their services being substantially executive in nature, or are still in junior positions. These posts mostly fall in the headquarters organization of the Government of India, known as the Central Secretariat. A few also belong to offices not attached to the Secretariat. The present chapter discusses how managerial positions in Indian administration are filled.

Personnel in the Government of India with supervisory and policy-making responsibilities belong either to the three all-India services or the central services. The central government recruits members of the all-India services and determines conditions of service, including disciplinary action. All members of these services are, however, allotted to one of the 28 state governments by the UPSC soon after their selection, and they work directly under the control of the state government. The state of encadrement exercises day-to-day control over the officer and is his cadre authority. The IAS, however, is an exception in that it has a specific central reserve quota and its members come to the central government periodically on deputation.

For the central services, which also are recruited by the UPSC, the controlling authority is the corresponding functional ministry of the central government. The Indian Revenue Service, for instance, is controlled by the

Ministry of Finance, the Indian Audit and Accounts Service by the Comptroller and Auditor General of India, and so on. Three services, which cut across departmental lines and thus do not belong exclusively to any particular ministry—the Central Secretariat Service, the Indian Economic Service and the Indian Statistical Service—come under the Ministry of Personnel and Training.[1] The headquarters organization of the Government of India thus does not have a service of its own.[2] All the services—whether all-India or central ones—belong either to the state governments or to the functional organizations or ministries even though under the central government. For the purpose of headquarters level appointments, a technical distinction needs to be drawn between the departments and the Government of India.

A PERMANENT SERVICE

Until the Government of India Act, 1919 came into force, the central government and the provincial governments worked at different levels, with the central government primarily and substantially being a referral agency with not much original work of its own: it was a government of the governments in India, rather than a Government of India. This kind of organic inter-relatedness made it extremely expedient that officers with experience of working in the provincial governments and having practical knowledge of subjects should be deputed to the Centre for a limited period to handle these subjects, and at the end of their deputation revert to the provinces with a better appreciation of the purposes which their duties were intended to fulfil. This was the logic behind the central government not having a separate officer cadre of its own.

The Government of India Act, 1919, introduced a kind of 'federalism' in the governmental structure of the country. The line of demarcation between the Centre and the provinces thus became a vertical one, the latter having become autonomous in the 'nation building' sphere of administration. But this constitutional change did not modify the mode of staffing of the central government's headquarters organization, and the old arrangement continued with minor adjustments. A new level of assistant secretaries was, for instance, created, which was a move in the direction of securing an element of permanence in the officer grades.

The question whether the Government of India should have a service or permanent cadre of its own at its headquarters was reopened with the passage of the Government of India Act, 1935, which conferred autonomy on the provinces and visualized, in a formal sense, a federation for the country. The Maxwell Committee on Organisation and Procedure (1937) considered the issue in great detail and its recommendation was to continue the tenure staffing of the Central Secretariat. A permanent civil service of the central government, the committee said, would be one without any direct touch with the life of India, which would be abysmally inadequate preparation for the kind of work performed at the Centre. The background of many of the subjects with which the central government remained concerned could not be understood unless officers dealing with them possessed direct experience of working in the provinces, for it was at this level that the effects of the policies made in the government were felt. A rotating civil service thus provided a valuable link between the central and provincial governments. No less meaningful to the provincial level personnel was the insight into the outlook, method and even difficulties of the central government, which a system of periodic interchange provided.[3]

The traditional method of staffing the headquarters of the central government thus continued. But the workload was increasing. The need arose also for people with specialization in finance in the wake of the Ottawa Agreement on Imperial Preference and the setting up of the Reserve Bank of India (1935). Accordingly in 1937, a Finance-Commerce Pool was constituted which, though recruited mainly from the Indian Civil Service (ICS), had a sprinkling of officers from other eligible central services such as the Indian Audit and Accounts Service, Customs Service, Income-Tax Service, and Military Accounts Service. The pool had a strength of forty-seven.

The outbreak of the World War II in 1939, in which India not only participated but also became an important Allies' centre for military operations in the East, led to a sudden and considerable expansion of the range and scale of governmental activities. The result was that the Centre found itself indenting for a much larger number of officers from the provinces and was disinclined to revert them on the completion of their tenure. Originally, the pool was designed for the Finance and Commerce Departments only, but during the war (1939–45) its members began to be appointed to other departments as well. The 'pool' device eased the staffing problem in the Secretariat, but the independence of the country in 1947 seriously upset the balance as a result of the resignation of a very large number of British and Muslim officers. Recruitment to the ICS had been suspended after 1943. The resulting shortage of officers was examined by the Secretariat Reorganisation Committee (1948), which suggested that while the central government should not pressurize the provinces for additional manpower, it should, as the same time, retain those officers already working under it.

INDEPENDENCE AND AFTER

The first few years after independence became a trying time, with the demand for experienced manpower in the central government growing continually, but not the source of supply. The provinces were themselves under tremendous strain and in no position to supply officers to the Centre under the tenure discipline. An indication of the enhanced need for staff may be had from Table 8.1.

Table 8.1
Staffing Strength of the Secretariat

Positions	1939	1945	1948
Secretaries	9	19	19
Additional Secretaries	–	6	5
Joint Secretaries	8	26	35
Deputy Secretaries	12	51	84
Under Secretaries	16	103	191

These new realities forced the Government of India to prepare, in December 1950, the Indian Administrative Service (Central Cadre) Scheme. Earlier in January 1949, 121 candidates had been recruited to the IAS from the open market. The IAS scheme reiterated the operation of the tenure system and broadened the sources of supply. The door to the Central Secretariat was opened to other services as well, in addition to the ICS/IAS. Under this scheme, selected personnel from these services were to serve at the Centre for the rest of their career. This was purported to ensure specialization in particular departments, and besides, would have the effect of reducing the number of officers to be rotated. Though the plan was not pursued at the time, the underlying idea remained alive, and in 1957, the Central Administrative Pool was announced with the ostensible aim of building up a reserve of officers with special training and experience for the purpose of economic administration and for maintaining continuity of knowledge and experience in the field of general administrate',[4] with little disturbance inherent in the tenure system of staffing. Having introduced planning in 1951, the government considered that the management of the nation's economic affairs needed 'an understanding of economic affairs as well as a capacity for and experience of administration, that is, of handling men and affairs with the tools and techniques of the Governmental machinery'.[5]

The scheme, however, had to be jettisoned in the face of stiff opposition from the higher civil service. Even though the pool scheme was to be applicable only to a segment of administration dealing with economic affairs, it was seen as an attempt to create a new hierarchy of the privileged, and undermine equality of opportunity, which the tenure system stipulates. A few senior civil servants had in fact become quite powerful in view of their continued stay in the Secretariat, especially in the prestigious economic ministries. If the principle of rotation had been allowed to operate uninterruptedly this would not have happened. But the incumbents had sought institutionalization and legitimization of their stay through the 'pool'. Equally strident was the criticism made by the various non-IAS services, which viewed the scheme as a device to restrict the non-IAS officers' opportunity of coming to the Secretariat and contributing to the policy-making processes in the government. Because the proposed scheme entailed change in inter-level rotation of officers, it required consultation with the state governments, many of which also expressed their opposition to it. To divert this opposition, the scheme was abandoned in its original form but revived as the 'Central Economic Pool'—and even this was finally dropped.

SOURCES OF SUPPLY OF MANAGERIAL PERSONNEL

While junior posts in any service are exclusive to the cadre, the senior positions—under-secretary and above, and numbering over 3000—are not reserved for any particular cadre. These may be filled up from the Indian Administrative Service, other all-India services, the central services, and the Secretariat Service. A part of the IAS is recruited through promotion from among ranks of the state level civil service. Among them, those on the verge of promotion may be given Secretariat postings. Those not so placed may also be appointed, but in consultation with the UPSC. Members of the state level civil service do not generally evince any interest in central postings nor are they encouraged by the central government to do so.

Though higher civil servants are recruited through a common competitive examination and the cut-off point for each service is determined by an interplay of market forces rather than by any recognized principle of rationality, the upward mobility of the central civil services is very much reduced. A large majority of the members of the IAS are clustered in the higher income band, and promotion up to the level of joint secretary to the Government of India is virtually automatic. In sharp contrast to this, other services discover themselves most emphatically in an inferior position, concentrated as they are in middle or lower middle income ranges.

Consider, for example, the prospects of the Central Secretariat Services (CSS), first set up in July 1950 and built up as a feeder service to occupy the junior and middle levels of positions in the Secretariat. Its officers, as the nomenclature suggests, remain permanently in the Secretariat, subject only to interdepartmental transfers. Its members hold all posts of section officers and most of those of under-secretaries but their occupancy rate falls steeply higher up the ladder. There is no reservation of posts in the Secretariat for individual services, which means that the posts are open to all services. Yet the largest number of secretaries to the government belong to the IAS, followed by the IPS and IFS (Indian Foreign Service). The IAS is indeed the leadership service in India. Once the near monopoly of the ICS and its successor, the IAS, the higher level positions in the Central Secretariat are today manned by many other services. But here, too, there is a caveat. The lion's share of higher jobs still goes to the IAS. The service unquestionably occupies the commanding heights in the country's public administration, accounting for fifty out of one hundred secretaries. The performance of the IAS becomes prominent in the higher rungs of the ladder, while other services tend to thin out towards the top of the hierarchy. There is also a certain clustering of officers of other services—such as the officers of the various railway services in the Railway Board, of the Postal Service in its own board. Different services, one may thus note, move towards the top, at different speeds—and the rules of the game being what they are, many reach the age of retirement much before sighting the top.

INSTITUTIONAL FRAMEWORK FOR HIGHER LEVEL SELECTION

The competition for the middle and senior management positions at the apex being open to all services, both all-India and central, the procedure for these appointments needs to be streamlined so that clashes of interests, whether inter-service or inter-personal do not get out of hand. Involved in this process are the cadre controlling authority, the Civil Service Board, the Establishment Officer and the Appointments Committee of the Cabinet. The cadre controlling authority is a cell in the department or ministry concerned. It is responsible for personnel matters like postings, transfers, etc., of members of the service. The cell maintains the service records of the members of its service and signifies the availability of an officer for deputation to the Secretariat. No special qualification is regarded as essential for posting in the cell. As a result, its functioning is rather amateurish and ad hoc, with little attention to long-term planning. At the state level, it is the General Administration Department (GAD)—or the Department of Administrative Reforms as it is now called—which controls its all-India service cadres, and it is even worse equipped. The cadre authority necessarily keeps in touch with the Establishment Officer to the Government of India.

Civil Service Board

The Civil Service Board, presided over by the Cabinet Secretary, includes the Secretary in the Ministry of Personnel and a couple of other secretaries. The Establishment Officer to the Government of India is its member secretary. The board recommends names of eligible civil servants for appointment to the posts at levels of deputy secretary, director and joint secretary. For each of these posts the government has prescribed certain qualifications based on length and record of service, work experience, previous Secretariat appointment, sometimes even salary currently drawn by officers, etc. For the IAS officers, the only qualification laid down is length of service, thus making their empanelment for levels up to that of joint secretary nearly automatic. It is the responsibility of the board to prepare panels for various levels of officers who fulfil these criteria.

The collegiate-type board is a result of deliberate policy: it is sound commonsense to invest more than one individual with staffing responsibility so that subjectivity is kept to the minimum. The Civil Service Board had as its precursor the Establishment Board, which was first constituted by the British government in India in 1939. The Establishment Board used to meet regularly. It became the convention that its recommendations were invariably accepted. The present Civil Service Board cannot claim such sanctity of authority. Like any other body in a democracy, it has necessarily to function within a political milieu and is subject to numerous pressures and influences, their intensity increasing as one moves up the Secretariat hierarchy.

Compounding the difficulty of the board in being objective is the lack of objective criteria for assessing merit, especially in annual confidential reports. Individual seniors may be found in a wide range of temperaments, from the crusty to the bonhomous, and this is bound to be reflected in their assessment of their juniors. This apart, the states—which form the cadre authority for the all-India services—have their own personality in assessing merit. Some states—like West Bengal, Tamil Nadu, Karnataka, and Kerala—are known for strictness in writing the annual confidential reports of their officers. In the so-called Hindi belt, on the other hand, the governments are more likely to be effusive with generous use of expressions like 'outstanding', ' excellent' and the like.

The Establishment Officer

The Establishment Officer to the Government of India—the EO as he is commonly called—is member-secretary of the Civil Service Board (CSB) and secretary of the Appointments Committee of the Cabinet. He is thus closely associated with appointments under the government. The EO is invariably drawn from the Indian Administrative Service and generally holds the rank of a joint secretary, though this is not mandatory.

The EO prepares a panel of three, four or more names for each vacancy of the middle management levels. The panel along with the service records of the officers is sent to the ministry or department concerned. The selection may be done out of this panel or, sometimes, a fresh panel of names may be called for. Informal consultation and exchange of views between the parties concerned almost always sorts out the problem of staffing. In this exercise, an effort is always made to secure an adequate spread of officers in terms of services and regions. The EO maintains the confidential files (along with Executive Records Sheets) of all the members of the IAS (except his own, which remains with the Cabinet Secretary). He may also send for the confidential files of any civil servant.

The EO's role is not separate from the work of the CSB he is required to service, but he does wield a varying measure of informal influence, particularly for middle level appointments in the Secretariat. This flows from his working directly and somewhat closely under the Personnel Secretary and the Cabinet Secretary. But the power and position of the EO seem to have suffered an erosion with the increasing weight accorded to political determinants of personnel processes like postings, transfers, etc.

THE APPOINTMENTS COMMITTEE OF THE CABINET

The highest body to approve all appointments of the level of deputy secretary and equivalent and above in the Government, both within the Secretariat or outside it, is the Appointments Committee of the Cabinet (ACC), first set up in 1950 in pursuance of N. Gopalaswami Ayyangar's *Report on Reorganisation of the Machinery of Government* (1949). The ACC consists of the Prime Minister, who is its chairman, the Home Minister, and the minister of the department in which the vacancy has occurred, the EO being its secretary. The committee does not ever meet formally; instead, it disposes of its business by circulation of papers. A case coming to the ACC has already been processed by the appropriate administrative body—the Civil Service Board or the Cabinet Secretary. Over 1500 cases of staffing are annually finalized by this apex level body, the daily average being 6 or 7. The work load on the ACC is steadily increasing: it handles 1500 cases annually.

What has been sketched above is the formally designed framework for senior level staffing in India. As far as presenting the formal setup goes, it is fine. But as regards how appointments are actually made, the sketch would need a lot of filling up of the details of political reality. More and more, the civil service in India is showing decreasing disposition to let personnel practices be governed by abstract rules and regulations. The pressure on Secretariat jobs has been steadily increasing, particularly so for jobs in ministries dealing with economic affairs. Lobbying has become the norm rather than the exception; and with the posts being limited and the pyramid becoming narrower towards the top, many factors such as caste, kinship, region, personal affiliations, etc.—in addition to merit—become critical inputs in the final outcome. The higher one moves up the administrative hierarchy, the more significant becomes the equation with the influential political leaders of the ruling party, and in this chessboard the minister concerned with the appointment generally holds the final key. Like Alice in Wonderland, civil servants have to run hard to stay at the same place, and harder still to move to positions of their choice.

Winners and losers apart, India's mode of headquarters level staffing is so designed as to avoid many of the pitfalls inherent in classical federalism. It seeks to ensure continuous flows of field views and experiences into processes of policy-making and counterflow of corporate level policy perspectives into implementation. Such an arrangement also seeks to foster a measure of emotional cohesion among the members of the higher public services, even though they are posted at different places and work under different political masters.

NOTES

1. The full name is: Ministry of Personnel and Training, Administrative Reforms and Public Grievances, Pensions and Pensioners' Welfare.
2. The only exception is the Central Secretariat Service.
3. *Report of the Committee on Organisation and Procedure, 1937*, pp. 19–20.
4. Quoted in *Ninety-Third Report of Estimates Committee (1956–66)* (Third Lok Sabha), New Delhi: Lok Sabha Secretariat, 1966, p. 71.
5. Scheme for staffing senior administrative posts of and above the rank of Deputy Secretary under the Government of India, 17 October 1957, para 9.

CHAPTER 9

The Establishment Officer
in the Government of India

India is a federation, but its administrative system is unified and integrated. The points of interaction between the two levels of government are numerous. India's higher civil service is commonly shared across two levels. One must note as pointed out earlier, the Government of India does not possess a permanent civil service of its own, strictly speaking but is a perennial indenter, borrowing its complement of officers from the all-India services and the central services. The all-India services are all allotted to the states and are thus state services, even though they are recruited by the centre, the Government of India borrowing its officers from the states, numbering 27 at present. The central services belong to the concerned ministries in the government, not to the Government of India strictly speaking. The Government of India is a large employer. Its requirement is met by drawing officers from all the states in India. This is not an easy or simple task. A special officer is appointed to carry out this responsibility, and he is the Establishment Officer to the Government of India.

The Establishment Officer to the Government of India—or the EO as he is commonly called—is a functionary unique to the Indian subcontinent and is one of the administrative creations of British colonial rule in India. The EO is, indeed, a vital institutional link in the field of selection of managerial level personnel in the Indian government. He has been given a set of functions which are intended to promote, besides administrative efficiency, harmony between the two levels of government in the federal system.

THE SETTING

The special significance of this office lies in a set of ideological formulations underpinning the central personnel system. India was a unitary state from the time of the Regulating Act of 1773 till the enactment of the Government of India Act, 1935, and it was only under the latter statute that a federal system was first outlined for the colony. Though the constitutional change visualized was of a qualitative nature, yet it was not allowed to affect the core values concerning administration, one of which is that the Government of India does not—and must not—possess a civil service of its own. To be sure, there are all-India services, and the central services, but these belong, respectively, to the state governments and the functional departments. The technical position is and has always been, that the Government of India does not own a civil service of its own. Secondly, the staffing of the headquarters organization, namely, the Secretariat, should draw on as many services, both all-India and central ones, as possible, the objective being to attract the most competent personnel from all over the administrative space. Thirdly, appointments in the Secretariat are made for fixed terms, or tenures, thus making the search for personnel a regular and not a once-for-all, exercise.

Until the passage of the Government of India Act, 1935, the practice in regard to staffing in the Government of India was that each department corresponded directly with the lower level provincial governments as and when necessary. This, apparently, did not pose any serious problem, primarily in view of the prevalent unitary system of government in the country. It is true that the government then was small, thus making staffing in the Secretariat quite manageable and even when the government began to expand and posts in the headquarters increased, the practice of departments individually approaching provincial governments independently engendered confusion no less than competition but no change was contemplated. It was the Government of India Act, 1935 with the explicit stipulation of federation for the country which introduced a new measure of permanent uncertainty in regard to supply of officers from the 'autonomous' provinces and thus highlighted the need for a central coordinating point. This made the setting up of a centralized personnel procurement agency imperative, and the initiative in this direction was first taken by the Finance Department. This needs an explanation.

On the analogy of the Treasury in Great Britain, questions relating to the civil service were, in the beginning, dealt with by the Finance Department in the Indian government. The Treasury in Britain, one must note, is much more than a Finance Department, really being in the nature of a residuary legatee in the government, and as such to search for its counter-part in India's Finance Department was not very correct. In India, civil service was, thus, never made an exclusive concern of this department, the other department having a definite share of responsibility being Home. Yet, the fact is that the Finance Department in the past enjoyed a much larger role in regard to the civil service than since Independence. Even the genesis of the office of the EO to the Government of India lies in this Department's Despatch of 15 October 1936 for the proposal for the setting up of an EO was made for the first time in this document. The cue was picked up by the Committee on Organisation and Procedure (1937) presided over by Reginald Maitland Maxwell; indeed a thumb-nail sketch of this office was presented by the Maxwell Committee on Organisation and Procedure.

THE MAXWELL COMMITTEE'S FORMULATIONS

According to the Maxwell Committee, the EO, recommended for the Finance Department would not remain fully occupied, and yet the function contemplated for him was of obvious meaning to all the departments in the government. The Committee, therefore, recommended setting up an EO to the Government of India—that is, with government-wide responsi-bility. 'It should be his duty', the Committee emphasized, 'to keep himself fully informed of possible recruits, both Indian Civil Service and others to the grade of under secretary.' For this purpose, the EO should have a right to obtain any information he may require about any officer in the provinces or other departments with a view to considering whether he is fit for such an appointment. He should, moreover, take an active interest in broaden-ing the channels of his communication with the provinces as well as the cadre authorities of various central services, even visiting their headquar-ters and 'interviewing' possible candidates to assess their suitability for induction in the Secretariat. Besides, he was to be the exclusive pipeline for flow of correspondence in regard to staffing and reversion of personnel. The Committee observed, 'It would probably be a convenience to the provinces if all correspondence regarding the selection and reversion of Indian Civil Service officers in connection with Secretariat or other appointments were conducted by the EO'. Being in touch with all depart-ments in the central government, he would naturally be in a position to keep his eye on probable future requirements and to ensure that provin-cial governments and other cadre authorities received as long notice as possible of impending vacancies. Besides, it was among the important responsibilities of the proposed functionary to maintain 'full' records of the performance of under-secretaries 'both for the periods spent in the secretariat and for the periods spent outside'. For the Secretariat-based officers, he should get the annual confidential reports from the respective secretaries and for those located outside it but 'earmarked' for deputation he should secure them from the provinces and cadre authorities. 'The Establishment Officer would thus be able, on each occasion that a selection had to be made, to put forward the names of all who were qualified for the appointment and to submit detailed records of their previous career.' All said and done, the Maxwell Committee did not want the EO to emerge to a position with the power to recommend individual names for appointment. This responsibility was entrusted to a collegiate body so as to reduce possible subjectivity in judgement. It clearly observed, 'The material (annual reports about officers) so secured should be dealt with by a selection board whose duty it would be to recommend individual officers for appointment. The selection board should consist of three secretaries to Government to be appointed by His Excellency (Governor-General) in his discretion, together with the secretary in the department concerned, if he is not already a member of the board.'

THE ESTABLISHMENT OFFICER TO
THE GOVERNMENT OF INDIA

The office of the Establishment Officer to the Government of India was set up in 1938, its first incumbent being Noel James Roughton, a member of the Indian Civil Service (ICS). Roughton did not stay for long: Indeed, most early EOs had a tenure of less than 18 months, and the term was particularly short during British rule. Perhaps, the job was discovered to be not very challenging. H.M. Patel, a member of the ICS and a 'Commerce-Industry Pool' Officer, was the first Indian to be appointed as EO in 1946. But it was S.B. Bapat of the ICS, who had the longest stay of nearly nine years and who also emerged as a very strong EO.

The EO was originally located in the Finance Department following the practice in Britain, and its justification lay in the interface between its work and the pay and conditions of work of the civil service. Even more importantly, the functionary's location in the Finance Department also equipped him with 'teeth', in the sense that the provinces and other public agencies, always dependent on large financial devolutions from New Delhi, did not dare turn indifferent to his solicitations, much less become non-cooperative. On 1 March 1946, however, the EO was placed under what was officially known as the Secretariat of the Executive Council, named in 1947 as Cabinet Secretariat. This arrangement lasted till the advent of Independence, and since then this office has operated under the administrative control of the Ministry of Home Affairs, and later of the Ministry of Personnel. Also, it was not uncommon in the past to entrust some other responsibilities to the EO in view of a feeling that the office did not have enough work. For instance, he remained as principal of the IAS Training School at Metcalfe House, Delhi for quite some time though this arrangement was temporary. The Economy Committee (1948–9), set up by the Government of India under the chairmanship of Kasturbhai Lalbhai, recommended continuance of the arrangement of the EO also working as the principal of the civil service training school, asserting 'in our opinion, the EO has not got a full day's work'. This functionary was responsible for filling up of middle and senior level management vacancies in the Central Secretariat which then was a sleek organization.

At the time of Independence, the EO to the Government of India was of the rank of a joint secretary and came from the ICS. He was assisted by an office consisting of one superintendent, one assistant superintendent, 6 assistants of whom 3 were designated 'Clerk, Grade A', 7 clerks, and one stenographer. Many of the personnel were temporary, having been recruited during World War II. There was even a proposal early in 1947 that the office personnel under the EO should get an exemption from the general government orders governing recruitment of ministerial staff in the Central Secretariat, the argument adduced being that the EO's work was becoming increasingly complex and continuity of personnel was 'most important'. The request, however, was quickly turned down by the Home Department on the grounds that the provisions of the Ministerial Establishment (Recruitment, Promotion and Seniority) Rules applied all over the Secretariat without any exception, and as such the office of the EO could not be exempted from them. This continues to be the arrangement even now. Personnel in the EO's office, in short, continues to be subject to the well-known system of staffing.

THE EO IN INDEPENDENT INDIA

Drawn from the Indian Administrative Service (IAS) and holding, generally, a rank of joint secretary, the EO to the Government of India is an important functionary in the field of higher level staffing in the headquarters organization of the Government of India. Located in the Ministry of Personnel and Training, he works directly under the Cabinet Secretary and the Secretary in the Ministry of Personnel, his performance being appraised by the latter and 'reviewed' by the Cabinet Secretary. He is secretary to the Appointments Committee of the Cabinet (ACC) and as such receives all communications intended for the latter. He is secretary of the Senior Selection Board (SSB), member-secretary of the Central Establishment Board (CEB) and communicates their decisions to the ministries concerned.

The Maxwell Committee's outline still broadly governs staffing so far as the fundamentals of institutional arrangements are concerned but the modifications introduced are also many. The Committee, one may recall, wanted an Establishment Board to recommend individual names for appointments; and this practice continues but in a modified form, and the new arrangement is discussed in what follows: The Establishment Board was renamed as the Central Establishment Board (CEB) after Independence, and the EO was made its secretary. In 1970, a new Board called the Senior Selection Board (SSB) was created and made responsible for appointments to the posts of Joint Secretary and equivalent and above. The SSB is headed by the Cabinet Secretary and includes the Secretary of the Department of Personnel and some other secretaries nominated by the Prime Minister for a one year term, the EO being its Secretary. The other Board, the CSB, consists of the Personnel Secretary, who is the ex-officio chairman and two other secretaries nominated by the prime minister, and the EO, who is its member-secretary. Every year, the Board prepares panels for under secretaries, deputy secretaries, and directors. It is from this approved panel that individual appointments are made. The indenting department notifies its vacancies to the EO giving a job-profile, and the EO sends a list of three or four or even more names from the panel, out of which the department picks one. The EO is associated with both the Boards and does all the preliminary work necessary for the purpose. He processes appointments to posts of under secretaries, deputy secretaries and directors, and plays a sort of active role so far as selections to these posts are concerned. The posts in the central government being for fixed tenures, the departments keep on indicating the vacancies under them and the job description of each post; and it is among the primary tasks of the EO to find eligible 'bachelors' for purposes of matching the man with the job.

Appointments in the Secretariat are governed by what is called the Central Staffing Scheme, under which all higher vacancies are filled by fixed-term deputation of all services, both all-India and central. For appointment to each level, certain eligibility criteria have been prescribed by the government, and those who fulfill them are put on the panel, which is regularly revised. The exercise of empanelment as well as of recommending individual names is done by the appropriate board, but all the necessary processing is done by the EO. Empanelment ordinarily does not create problems, as the rules of eligibility are comprehensively laid down but the respective board will have to decide some difficult cases. A particular civil servant about to complete his tenure in the Secretariat may seek extension of his term. Or, a civil servant, who reverted to his parent cadre only recently, might want a fresh deputation even though he has not completed his 'cooling off' period. Or, an officer, when moved out of the Central Secretariat, may join some Delhi-based organization in the expectation of his early return. Such difficult cases apart, the jobs in the Secretariat are limited and pressure on them, particularly on economic ministries, is heavy, which adds considerably to the difficulties of both the recommending and appointing authorities including, of course, the EO. The central services have also been making claims on posts in the Secretariat. So does the Indian Police Service. Even high level political and bureaucratic pressures may also be brought to bear on them in a bid to influence placements, especially for higher, more prestigious jobs in the government. The cumulative result is a very heavy load of pressure on headquarters postings and transfers.

Technically speaking, both the SSB and the CEB as well as the EO, enjoy but a recommendatory status. For each vacancy, a panel of three or four or even more names is generally sent to the department concerned, and the secretary of the indenting department may pick up anyone from the list, or may even ask for a fresh panel which, it is true, is not very common. Informal exchange of views between the Personnel Secretary , EO and the departmental secretaries, however, nearly always produces an agreed list of names. This informal pedalling may wield more influence in matters of middle management appointments, especially at its lower rungs in the government. 'It is like a chessboard', one high-ranking civil servant confided to this author, 'and not many can beat the EO in the game. This is because his channels of communication are too many'. But the more specialized the qualifications for a job, the narrower is the discretion left with the EO. Also, his role is limited and of nominal significance when he works for the senior SSB. The proposals for appointments to the posts of the level of Joint Secretary and equivalent and above are initiated by the Cabinet Secretary, and the EO has a reduced measure of initiative or influence.

The EO maintains the confidential service files of all the 5000 and odd members of the IAS, the only exception is his own confidential file which, as a rule, remains with the Cabinet Secretary. A recent innovation is the preparation of 'executive record sheets' or index cards containing qualifications, experience and age of each member of the IAS so that he is able to furnish at short notice names of all eligible officers fulfilling the prescribed qualifications for a particular job. Besides, he has unhindered access to the character rolls of all higher civil servants belonging to other services and may send for them as and when called for. The EO remains in regular contact with the secretaries, including cadre authorities, in various departments and chief secretaries in the states, in his supreme effort to match the demand and supply of officers. From the cadre authorities of various services, he regularly obtains names of officers qualified and available for postings in the Secretariat and the attached offices. Similarly, he is continually fed with information on the likely vacancies, the filling of which is his responsibility. A large number of telephone calls come in his office, and besides, civil servants of various ranks and services call on him at all times of working hours, their daily number being somewhere around 50. It is not necessary that they bring only their individual problems, although many of them do. The chief secretary of a state may, for instance, be discussing with him the deputation or reversion matters of officers of his state. A telephone call may perhaps ask him to expedite a particular case in view of the manpower shortage in the department. It is also not untrue that personal favours too are sought and conferred. Indeed, the higher the job, especially in the economic ministries, the more aggressive is the lobbying for it, and thus caught, the EO too, has his own share of the high level pressure, although the brunt is usually borne by the secretary of the department having a vacancy and the Personnel Secretary/Cabinet Secretary, depending upon the level of the post and the clout which the aspiring candidate may have.

The EO has been designed as an institutional link to ensure flow of officers from the supplier to the indentor, and back. Over the years, the pressure on the headquarters posts has been mounting as an increasing number of officers from the all-India services as well as Central services have begun to demand Secretariat postings, and what is more, those already posted are generally reluctant to move back to their parent cadre at the end of their tenure. The cases of over stay of officers are fairly large. And a very large number of officers otherwise eligible for Secretariat postings have not been tapped at all. Speaking only about the IAS and the Indian Police Service (IPS), the Estimates Committee of Parliament reported in 1984 that as many as 1591 IAS officers and 768 IPS officers (other than those belonging to the cadre of the state of UP) with more than five years service to their credit have never been on deputation to the Government of India. The Committee concluded: 'This shows that the opportunities for deputation to the Centre have not been distributed equitably'. The present tale is one of sub-optimization and points to the need for extended search for manpower in the secretariat.

The EO's responsibilities, one may note, transcend the world of

Secretariat appointments. As the ACC is the final approving authority for all appointments of the level of deputy secretary and above under the Government of India he, naturally, comes to deal with the selection of senior level personnel in the headquarters as well as in public undertakings, nationalized banks, government-owned companies, statutory authorities, etc. Besides, matters like deputation to international agencies and foreign government, selection of officers for overseas fellowships, etc., also claim his time and attention. With growing attraction for international assignments and foreign fellowships, the competition within the civil service itself becomes keen, which, too, makes the role of the EO look important and powerful. In addition, the EO is a member of, or associated with, many committees which, too, keep him occupied.

For proper performance of all these tasks, the EO is assisted by a large-sized office of subordinate officers. The Government of India, today, conducts a large number of training programmes in subjects, including personnel management, but the personnel who look after staffing matters need possess apparently little professional qualifications. Like the EO, they pick up knowledge of the job while actually doing it.

In sum, the EO system seeks to link the states with the Centre, and the field with the headquarters, by a process of appointment of personnel possessing first-hand experience of the other side of the ring, and their rhythmic rotation. This constitutes India's model of institutional response to certain important facets of administrative federalism. But the system necessarily functions within the context of democracy and development, and thus finds it hard not to remain unaffected by pressures and forces released by both. Though both feed on each other, the craze for postings in economic ministries or foreign deputations, for instance, is a consequence of development, and lobbying for placements, of democracy. The same urges dictate that manipulation be permitted by not restricting the discretionary judgement on the part of the members of the system. At present, empanelment of a civil servant does not necessarily imply his eventual appointment, for the simple reason that some departments must also show a readiness to accept him. As the empanelment is done every year and as it has not been prescribed that the present panel must first be exhausted before the new one is opened, some unescorted civil servants may really get bypassed. The present arrangement of letting the departments pick up civil servants from the panel and non-insistence on complete utilization of the year's panel before fresh booking starts, strengthens the manipulative capacity of the system.

Standardization of merit ratings of officers opting for headquarters postings is no less a serious problem. Different officers have different standards of appraising the performance of subordinates. This apart, there being as many as 28 cadre authorities in the case of IAS and IPS, their members, though belonging to the same service and all competing for an increasingly limited number of senior jobs, are appraised differently, creating problems of standardization and comparison.

This notwithstanding, the EO and the boards, of which he is secretary, appear to be a functional necessity in an administrative system under a federal polity under which the central level of government does not possess a civil service of its own for its headquarters. Such a denial, to be sure, is neither constitutionally imposed nor enjoined under any statute, but flows from its own determination to ensure free flow of experience from the constituent states and other field agencies to its headquarters where overall policies affecting society are made. The reverse flow is again motivated by the same resolve to create vacancies so as to enable induction of personnel possessing fresh experience; in the process, the states and field agencies are also enabled to get officers directly acquainted with the objectives of the policies which they are now implementing. It is the responsibility of the EO and the Boards to see that this recycling process keeps going, thus continually integrating the field experience with policy-making, and the states with the government at the Centre.

CHAPTER 10

All-India Services

A remarkable feature of the administrative system in India is the deliberate retention of the all-India services, recruited and controlled by the Government of India and the personnel of which are interchangeable between the central and the state governments.[1] The all-India services constitute an administrative device peculiar to India and to Pakistan, which was a part of the sub-continent prior to Partition. Independent India had two all-India services in 1947—the Indian Administrative Service and the Indian Police Service.[2] In 1963, three more were to be set up: the Indian Service of Engineers, the Indian Forest Service and the Indian Medical and Health Service. The Indian Service of Engineers and the Indian Medical and Health Service, however, proved to be stillborn, owing to the states' sustained refusal to participate in them. Only the Indian Forest Service could see the light of day.

Historically the all-India services, then known as the Secretary of State's services, were formed when India had a unitary, centralized system of government. They were ideally suited to the requirements of that time as their members acquired experience in both the central government and with provincial levels. Recruitment by the Secretary of State for India and his control over conditions of service of the personnel who could be deployed in any part of the country were the defining attributes of the all-India services. Such a power was thought to hold the key to the exercise of British domination over the country, because it guaranteed control over the whole administration. As the British government wanted only British officers in key positions in India, and as these officers were not willing, nor was it expedient to compel them, to serve under Indian control, recruitment to, and control over the top services by the Secretary of State was considered to be critical. The all-India services as an institution exercise strategic control over the country's framework of law and order, which imperial rule considered necessary for its survival in India. The dependence of the imperial government on them became steadily more obvious as the popular desire for fully responsible government became more vocal and assertive.

The phrase 'all-India services' was not used until after the Secretary of State for India's historic announcement of 1917 of a gradually evolving responsible government for India and culminating in the Government of India Act, 1919. The term was first coined by the Committee on Division of Functions set up under M.E. Gauntlett in 1918. The concerned part is worth quoting: 'For the purpose of dealing with the subject, we accept the classification ... viz., Indian (which we shall call All India Services), provincial and subordinate.'[3] The all-India services were not all created at the same time. The oldest was the famous Indian Civil Services (ICS), which owes its origin to the Macaulay Report on the Indian Civil Service submitted in 1854. The last to be added to the list was the Indian Agricultural Service, constituted in 1906. On the eve of the Government of India Act, 1919, there were the following nine all-India services.[4]

(1) The Indian Civil Service (1853)
(2) The Indian Police Service (1905)
(3) The Indian Forest Service (1867)
(4) The Indian Educational Service (1906)
(5) The Indian Agricultural Service (1907)
(6) The Indian Civil Veterinary Service (1892)
(7) The Indian Engineering Service
(8) The Indian Medical Service (Civil) (1897)
(9) The Indian Service of Engineers (1892)

VIEWS OF VARIOUS COMMITTEES

When the Government of India Act 1919 introduced for the first time in 1921 responsible government in a limited sphere at the provincial level through the device of 'transferred' subjects under popular control, described in political parlance as 'dyarchy', the Government of India ceased to be the sole government of the country, although not departing, constitutionally speaking, from the existing unitary set up. From then onwards, the division of responsibility between the Centre and the provinces became vertical, the latter acquiring, free from central control, a sphere of functions defined by the Act itself. The propriety of the all-India services under such an arrangement was questioned for the first time. The Royal Commission on the Superior Services in India, set up in 1923 under the chairmanship of Viscount Lee of Fareham, recommended[5] that no further recruitment be made to four of the nine all-India services then in existence: the Indian Educational Service, the Indian Agricultural Service, the Indian Veterinary Service and the Indian Forest Service[6] (only in Bombay and Burma). 'The personnel required for these branches of administration should in future be recruited and appointed by local governments'.[7] The principle that generally guided the Lee Commission was that responsibility had to be matched with authority, and this meant control over the recruitment and conditions of service of the personnel charged with responsibility. The Lee Commission itself did not carry this reasoning to its logical conclusion. The Indian Medical Service and the Indian Service of Engineers which were recommended for continuance were clearly in violation of the principle. A section of Indian public opinion was, however, averse to the retention of the institution of all-India services. R.K. Shanmukham Chetty, a member of the Central Legislative Assembly, observed:

The Honourable Leader of the House very rightly remarked that the (civil) services must be responsible to the authority whose policy it (sic.) is meant to carry out. The position is no doubt realized by the [Lee] Commission. But in what way have they tried to give effect to it? No doubt, in so far as they recommended that all the services under the departments that have been transferred to the provinces must be provincialized, they recognize this principle. But in so far as they are perpetuating, with regard to the other administrative branches in the provinces, the same system that is continuing at the present day. ... I contend that it is perpetuating the present system which, when the other subjects are transferred in the course of time, will present serious obstacles in the way of administration by Ministers. As was observed in the able memorandum presented by the Madras Officers' Association to the Royal Commission, the all-India hallmark exists only for the purpose of enabling these officers to claim to be appointed, confirmed and dismissed by an extra-provincial authority and to escape effective control either by provincial executive or by the provincial legislature. An all-India service with these extraordinary privileges is an anachronism in any system of provincial responsible government and, we would add, is a violation of the spirit of the Government of India Act of 1919.

Therefore, Sir, in so far as no serious and deliberate attempt is made by the Commission to do away with this invidious distinction, I must say that this House cannot find its way to accept its recommendations.[8]

Such opinions proved of little avail and His Majesty's Government to whom the Report was submitted accepted the recommendations made by the Lee Commission, including its recommendations regarding the all-India services.

The same year the Reforms Enquiry Committee, set up by the Government of India, found itself sharply divided on the question of all-India services. The nationalist members of the committee 'ventured' to think that 'under the present system, the entire Constitution, the methods of recruitment and control of the services are incompatible with the situation created by the Reforms (of 1919) and the possibility of their further developments.'[9]

In 1928, the All-Parties Conference set up a committee under the chairmanship of Motilal Nehru to determine the principles of the future constitution for India. It is significant that this committee did not recommend the continuance of the all-India services in independent India. It recommended, instead, separate civil services for the 'commonwealth' and the provinces.

In 1929, the nationalist members of the Indian Central Committee (1928–9) constituted by the central government to liaise with the Indian Statutory Commission pressed for provincialization of the services. They observed in their dissenting note: '... no self government is possible unless the services are provincialized and all officers are placed under the ministers. If any European officers are required, there is little doubt that the new governments will be able to obtain their services from the Government of India; or would, even after full provincial responsibility is conferred on them, continue to recruit them.'[10] Similarly, the Committee appointed in 1929 by the United Provinces Legislative Council to cooperate with the Indian Statutory Commission showed awareness of the implications of provincial autonomy and of the anomalous position of the all -India services in the emergent political set-up. It remarked: '... we hold that the retention of these (that is, all-India) services in a system of full provincial autonomy would unnecessarily complicate matters'.[11] It also called for an immediate provincialization of the all-India services.

This institution again became the subject of investigation at the hands of a sub-committee which the first Indian Round Table Conference (12 November 1930–19 January 1931) had constituted. The 34 member Sub-Committee on Services, set up under the chairmanship of Sir William Jowitt, lacked, as was not unusual with the committees of this era, unanimity in its recommendation on the future of the all-India services. There was an undercurrent of opposition to the continuance of the all-India services under the new political set-up contemplated for the country.[12] Two out of the 26 Indian members who sat on the subcommittee, B. Shiva Rao and Sreepad Balwant Tambe, demanded immediate and total discontinuance of the all-India service while three others—Bhim Rao Ambedkar, Zafrullah Khan, and Saropuran Singh—were averse to further recruitment on the all-India basis for the Indian Civil Service and the Indian Police Service. The majority of the members, however, recommended the retention of the Indian Civil Service and the Indian Police Service as all-India services except that recruitment for judiciary offices from the Indian Civil Service, as was the prevalent practice, was to be discontinued.

A few years later, the British Indian Delegation in its memorandum[13] to the Joint Committee on Indian Constitutional Reform (1933–4), constituted as its name implies to frame the Government of India Act, 1935, under the British rule urged that the officers serving under the provinces should be recruited on a provincial basis, and that the all-India services were incompatible with provincial autonomy. The joint committee, while appreciating 'the force of this line of argument', did not accept it. It regarded the need for a regular supply of officers: both Indian and British, of the highest quality as vital to the stability of the proposed constitution itself, and the all-India services, recruited and controlled by the Secretary of State for India assured this. Secondly, it wanted to play safe by not introducing any change in the civil service, 'simultaneously with the introduction of fundamental changes in the system of government'. 'It is of the first importance that in the early days of the new order, and indeed until the course of events in the future can be more clearly foreseen, the new Constitution should not be exposed to risk and hazard by radical change in the system which has for so many generations produced men of the right calibre.'[14] In addition to the Indian Civil Service and the Indian Police Service, the two 'security' services, the Joint Committee recommended the continuance of the Indian Medical Service (Civil) in deference to the British officers in that service, though it had been recommended for abolition by the services sub-committee of the First Round Table Conference. The Joint Committee remarked: 'We are ... convinced on the information supplied to us that the continuance of the civil branch of the Indian Medical Service will provide the only satisfactory method of meeting the requirements of the war reserve and of European members of the civil services, and that it will be necessary for the Secretary of State to retain the power which he at present possesses (although medical matters have since 1920 been under the control of ministers) to require the provinces to employ a specified number of Indian Medical Service officers. In making these recommendations we have not been unmindful of the natural desire of the provinces to develop medical services entirely under their own control. *But the requirements of the army and of the civil service have an overriding claim.*'[15] (italics supplied). These recommendations found expression in section 244 of the Government of India Act 1935, which listed three services, the Indian Civil Service, the Indian Police Service, and the Medical Service (Civil) as all-India services.[16]

Political India had thus set its face resolutely against the institution of all-India services. The same, however, may not be said so firmly about the attitude of the Indian Muslim League, although Sir Shafaat Ahmed Khan, a prominent member of the All-India Muslim League, argued for provincialization of all-India services in his book *The Indian Federation*, published in 1937.[17] The Muslims appeared to be equivocal in their views on the all-India services. They were a major community in some provinces and a minority in others, which put them in a dilemma. To the Muslims of the provinces where they were in a minority, all-India services with a British element in them offered protection against domination by the Hindus. So they wanted the retention of all-India services with a suitable provision for the employment of British officers. Sir Shafaat, who has been quoted above in favour of provincialization, had taken in 1929 the opposite view and pleaded for the continuance, 'for some time to come', of the Indian Civil Service and the Indian Police Service.'[18] However, Muslims could, at the same time, see dangers in all-India services. As the central government would be controlled by Hindus, these services might be a useful instrument for the Centre to contain and even thwart the autonomy of the Muslim majority provinces. It was this apprehension which in 1946 impelled the Muslim majority provinces of Sind, Bengal, and Punjab to opt out of the scheme of all-India services prepared by the Interim Central Government in 1946.

INDIAN REACTION AT THE TIME OF INDEPENDENCE

History has the uncanny habit of often thrusting on people and institutions roles of which they were at one time outspoken critics. When in 1946 the independence of India appeared to be in sight, the nationalist stance on the all-India services underwent a sudden and fundamental change. The all-India services were, verily a mote in the nationalist eye, and yet when political power was passing into the hands of the nationalist leaders they unhesitatingly changed their stand and supported their retention. It is not easy to discover the true motivation. Did the earlier opposition flow from their commitment to the concept of federalism? This is not proved by their later orientation. One may even argue that the nationalist leaders never hoped that they could gain political power at the Centre at least during their lifetime; what they might have expected was their obtaining power in the provinces, which conditioned their disposition towards the all-India services. The national leadership, in short, took a leaf out of the Secretary of State's book and assumed a role which the latter had consistently played in regard to the all-India services. This is reflected in the interim central government's quick initiative in convening a provincial premiers' conference in October 1946 to consider the question of replacement of the Indian Civil Service and the Indian Police.

ALL INDIA SERVICES IN THE NEW ORDER

The Secretary of State for India had stopped recruitment to the ICS and the Indian Police during wartime, and even when peace returned it could not be resumed on account of the constitutional changes taking place in India. The interim government under the prime ministership of Jawaharlal Nehru was installed in 1946, with independence well in sight now. When a new India was in the offing, the institution of all-India services, at one time the proverbial thorn in the Indian leadership's flesh, began to be wooed; and in this saga Sardar Vallabhbhai Patel played a pioneering role.

Provincial Premier's Conference

With the plan of resurrection of the All India Administrative Service in his mind, Sardar Patel convened a Conference of Provincial Premiers[19] on 20 and 21 October 1946. Those invited to the Conference were the provincial premiers but the provinces ruled by the non-Congress parties were represented either by a politician of a minister's rank or civil servants. Punjab, where the Unionist Party was in power, was represented by its revenue minister. Sind deputed its chief secretary, whereas Bengal, where the Muslim League was in power, sent a civil servant of the rank of an additional secretary. Dr Khan Sahib, the premier of NWFP, attended the conference in the afternoon of the second day only. Of course, Sardar Vallabhbhai Patel, the guiding spirit, was present on both days, and he was accompanied by the secretary in the Home Department and three deputy secretaries. The premiers who attended the conference were Pandit Govind Ballabh Pant from UP, T. Prakasam from Madras, B.G. Kher from Bombay, Sri Krishna Sinha from Bihar, Hare Krushna Mahtab from Orissa, Pandit Ravi Shankar Shukla from the Central Provinces, Gopinath Bordoloi from Assam, and Dr Khan Sahib from the NWFP.

Sardar Patel's Advocacy

Sardar Patel, in his introductory remarks, raised the question whether a central or a provincial service should replace the Indian Civil Service and the Indian Police, recruitment to which had been stopped by the Secretary of State for India in view of the impending constitutional changes. He expressed the central government's support for the setting up of an 'All India Administrative Service', and the advantages he cited were many and were to both the Centre and provinces. Such an All-India Administrative Service would facilitate liaison between the Centre and the provinces, ensure a certain uniformity in standards of administration, and keep the central administration in touch with realities. He went on to emphasize that the provincial administration would on its part acquire a wider outlook and obtain the best material for the higher posts. The Home Minister emphasized that there was need for ensuring contentment and security in the services and for ensuring that the civil service was free from communal or party bias.

Provinces' Views

Of the nine persons who spoke on the first day, the premiers of UP, Bombay, Bihar, Assam, Orissa, Central Provinces, and Madras, supported, with varying levels of reservations, the creation of such a service, and wanted the control of the Secretary of State for India to be terminated altogether. Gopinath Bordoloi, the premier of Assam, lent support to the service but wanted the provincial control over it to be adequate and sons of the soil to be given more opportunities. Pandit Govind Ballabh Pant, the Premier of UP, however, took a different line, arguing that the central government be responsible only for recruitment and training; he was not in favour of the substitution of the central government for the Secretary of State for India, and wanted full control of the provinces over the service. Dr Khan Sahib of NWFP, a Congress-ruled province, was present only in the afternoon of the concluding day, and the proceedings of the Conference do not indicate his participation or intervention in discussions at any stage.

The premiers who belonged to the Congress party, one may note, fell into three catagories in respect of their stand towards the all-India service: (1) B.G. Kher, Ravi Shankar Shukla, and Hare Krushna Mahtab supported the All India Administrative Service, apparently without any reservations; (2) Bordoloi (Assam) wanted 'adequate' control of the provinces over these services, (3) Pant (UP) favoured an all-India service but would give only two functions to the Centre—those of recruitment and training—other responsibilities including those of discipline and control vesting in the provinces. The provinces where the Congress party was not in power such as Bengal, Punjab, and Sind expressed their firm unwillingness to participate in the all-India service. But the non-participation was not declared to be absolute and total. Punjab's revenue minister, Nawab Sir Muzaffar Ali Qazilbash (who represented his province), wanted the ICS and the IP to be wound up at the earliest but expressed the view of his government that the services should be provincialized. 'The provinces must have full control over the services and, to have full control, they must also select their own services. This would ensure proper representation of communities and greater attention to local problems and on the whole be conducive to efficient administration.'[20] As regards the mode of linking the two levels of government, Qazilbash said the provinces should place the services of their officers on deputation with the Centre. Though arguing for provincialization of the services, he expressed the view that his government was in favour of centralized prescription of standards and centralized training arrangements. The chief secretary to the Government of Sind who was representating that province in the Conference emphasized the determination of Sind to form its own service. He, however, added that Sind was disposed to join in a scheme of central training of the officers. Bengal was represented by its additional secretary, who conveyed the decision of his government against the all-India service adding, however, that Bengal was 'willing to agree to central prescription of standards for selection and to join a central scheme for training.'[21]

What emerged very clearly from the discussion was a stand against the Secretary of State for India's role in regard to the ICS and the IP; the conference insisted on his control to go at the earliest. But on the successor service, the views expressed were not unanimous. While provinces such as Bombay, Orissa, and the Central Provinces supported the proposal in favour of an All India Administrative Service, Assam wanted 'adequate control' of the province and large intake of the local people in the service and UP stood for full provincial control, the Centre to restrict itself to only recruitment and training. Bengal, Punjab, and Sind—the Muslim majority provinces—stood for the provincial civil service and gave to central government a definite role in only two subjects—that of laying down of standards of recruitment and imparting of training to the newly recruited personnel.

Proposal Accepted

Sardar Patel, the 'Iron Man of India' would not give in and stood by his original proposal most tenaciously. He summed up the discussion by emphasizing a general feeling in favour of the formation of an All India Administrative Service', and expressed the hope that 'after the general scheme was framed, those who were at present not in favour, would be convinced that adequate allowance had been made for provincial susceptibilities regarding control and would agree to join in'.[22] The conference then proceeded to discuss other related matters. On the mode and method of recruitment, it favoured the adoption of rules and regulations prevalent in the case of the Indian Civil Service. Accepting the suggestion of Govind Ballabh Pant, it recommended a combined competitive examination for the proposed Administrative Service and the Indian Foreign Service. Decisions taken on many other matters were demonstrably respectful of the provincial susceptibilities and left substantial autonomy with the provinces. With regard to the fixation of cadre strength, the provinces were to work out the number of posts for which officers of the All India Administrative Service were required. The central government would determine its own requirements, and after receiving the provincial proposals, would work out the details of the cadre. The quota for promotion of the provincial civil service officers in the proposed service was recommended to be 25 per cent of the superior posts. The provinces were left free to select and to devise rules of selection for the provincial service quota, but the persons finally selected were to be subject to a certificate of fitness by the Federal Public Service Commission. It was also suggested that benefits of leave, pensions and other conditions of service should be designed on the basis of the rules applicable to the provincial services. Above all, allotment of officers was to be made in consultation with the provinces and, as the conference recommended, 'in making allotments, selected candidates should, as far as possible, be allotted to their provinces of origin'.[23]

The conference made recommendations on many other matters. On the question of rates of remuneration for the proposed All India Administrative Service, it regarded the existing pay scales of the ICS on the high side, and recommended a five years' scale at Rs 300–50–400–450–500, leaving the final decision in this respect to the (First) Central Pay Commission, which had already been appointed by the government. The representatives of the provinces also agreed that uniformity of pay-scales even in the other provinces which would not come in the central scheme would be desirable so that if they later decided to join, the absorption of the officers of the provincial cadre into the all-India service would not be difficult. Besides, inter-provincial competition would be avoided.

By removing the point of control from the provinces, where its members would mostly be working, to the central government, an all-India service is viewed as marking diminution of the provincial autonomy, and not very appealing, even suspicious to the provinces. Equally compelling is the need for security of tenure of the higher civil service without which the civil servants, exposed, as they would be to political and partisan pressures, may not be expected to work efficiently, independently, and impartially. Indeed, reconciliation between the need for conferring a sense of security on the civil service with the provincial demand for full control over its officers is, and has always remained, a thorny problem. In the interests of efficient administration, it was desirable that an officer should not be subject to removal or dismissal from service before his case is examined by an independent and impartial authority not under the thumb of the provincial government. Sardar Patel suggested that the power of major punishments like removal and dismissal should vest with the appointing authority, namely the central government. But in the same breath he assured that 'a convention should be established under which the Centre would accept the provincial government's recommendation whenever the provincial government and the Federal Public Service commission were in agreement'.[24] In the case of disagreement between a province and the Federal Public Service Commission the central government would decide the case on merit after considering the recommendations of the provincial government and of the Federal Public Service Commission (FPSC). The government under which an officer was serving for the time being would have full authority to award other punishments subject to a reference to the Federal Public Service Commission. In so far as the central government is concerned, it will accept the advice tendered by the FPSC; but provinces, if they so wished, might disregard such advice for adequate reasons.

B.G. Kher, Hare Krushna Mahtab, and Pandit Ravi Shankar Shukla accepted the proposal. Sri Krishna Sinha also expressed his agreement though with some misgivings. Gopinath Bordoloi suggested that even in respect of removal or dismissal, the provincial government should be the final authority but there could be a right of appeal to the Government of India. Pandit G.B. Pant and T. Prakasam expressed the view that it was undesirable that an officer serving under the provincial government should be in a position to look to an authority other than the provincial government for protection. They felt that if the administration were to run smoothly and without friction, provincial governments should have full control over their officers. There was no objection to consultation with the Federal Public Service Commission and any recommendation made by the Commission would be given due weight but the final authority to decide must be the provincial government. Nawab Sir Muzaffar Ali Qazilbash, revenue minister of Punjab, said that it would be desirable to entrust the government of the day with full disciplinary powers over its officers. Under such a system it was likely that the services would become subject to political intrigue and influence. The Punjab government accordingly proposed to establish a civil service committee to whom all such cases could be referred and whose recommendation would be accepted by the government as binding by convention. The Punjab government's view that the civil services should be provincialized was largely influenced by the consideration that it was undesirable that control over its officers be shared by any outside authority. He realized that the central government would require officers trained in the provinces but for this purpose the Centre should be given full liberty to pick the best officers out of the provincial services. Recruitment to the provincial services could also conform to prescribed uniform standards and there should be arrangements for centralized training of recruits.

Sardar Vallabhbhai Patel concluded the discussion by emphasizing the provincial premiers' general support to the proposal for the creation of the Indian Administrative Service and the Indian Police Service. That the conclusion did not logically flow from the discussion held did not apparently bother the Sardar much. He wanted these services; and he got them. All this was a magnificent victory for the Centre and, more truly, a personal triumph for Vallabhbhai Patel. Indeed, Patel may rightly be acknowledged as the true architect of the all-India services. His task was probably rendered less arduous by the Muslim League's initial abstention from the Interim Central Government. The Muslim League joined the central government after the provincial premiers' conference had finished its deliberations.

A week after the conference, there was an interpellation in the Central Legislative Assembly. Patel's terse reply was: 'A conference of provincial premiers was convened on the 21st October 1946 by me to discuss arrangements to replace these (the Secretary of State's) services. The consensus at the conference was in favour of the formation of new all India services for this purpose. Details are being worked out in consultation with the provinces and when arrangements are finalised a public announcements will be made.'[25] When a member (Sri Prakasa) further asked: 'Have the government assured themselves that such services are at all necessary in future? Patel merely said: 'That is the consensus of opinion of the provinces.'[26] The partition of the country in 1947 cleared the way for the acceptance by all of the all-India services.

Nevertheless it must be stated that the provinces evinced little enthusiasm for the all-India services: the latter were pushed down their reluctant throats by Vallabhbhai Patel. A view was expressed that matters like initial recruitment and training could be centralized but control over the service, including placement, should remain with the provinces. The Unionist party under the leadership of Sir Khizar Hayat Khan, premier of Punjab, lost no time in publicly repudiating such an administrative arrangement, declaring 'Punjab is one of the provinces which would prefer to have a superior service of their own instead of the all India administrative service under contemplation for this purpose.'[27] Punjab was soon joined by Sind and Bengal in its opposition to an all-India administrative service.

All-India Services and the Indian Constitution

The drafting committee of the Indian Constituent Assembly did not originally provide a constitutional base to the all-India services. Explaining its views, the committee observed: 'The committee has refrained from inserting in the Constitution any detailed provisions relating to the services; the committee considers that they should be regulated by the acts of the appropriate legislature rather than by constitutional provisions as the committee feels that the future legislatures in the country, as in other countries, may be trusted to deal fairly with the services.'[28]

The draft Constitution accordingly makes no mention of the all-India services. Yet the Constitution which finally emerged from the Constituent Assembly not only embodies reference to it, but also includes a provision for the creation of new all-India services. The Constituent Assembly accepted these without demur.

Such sudden solicitude for the all-India services was due to the Home Ministry's special insistence on its inclusion in the supreme constitutional document of the land. A constitutional base was deliberately preferred to make it more lasting and less vulnerable. Vallabhbhai Patel, who was then the Home Minister, was the principal advocate of this institution. The 'steel-frame of the whole structure', a sobriquet for the all-India service, endeared itself to the 'Iron Man of India'. The then prevalent single party dominance system in India rendered its acceptance easy. Besides, the times were such that there was firm support for whatever appeared as an agent and symbol of centralism and national unity. As the nation was at this time passing through a critical period in its history in the wake of Partition, communal riots and other disturbances, the Constituent Assembly plumped for an extraordinarily powerful central government. The constitutional provision for the all-India services, a manifestation of the prevalent national mood, is reproduced below:

312. All-India Services
  (1) Notwithstanding anything in[29] [Chapter VI of Part VI or Part XI], if the Council of States has declared by resolution supported by not less than two-thirds of the members, present and voting that it is necessary or expedient in the national interest so to do, Parliament may by law provide for the creation of one or more all-India services [(including an all-India judicial service)] common to the Union and the States, and, subject to the other provisions of this chapter, regulate the recruitment, and the conditions of service of persons appointed, to any such service.
  (2) The services known at the commencement of this Constitution as the Indian Administrative Service and the Indian Police Service shall be deemed to be services created by Parliament under this article.[30]

(3) The all-India judicial service referred to in clause (1) shall not include any post inferior to that of a district judge as defined in article 236.

(4) The law providing for the creation of the all-India judicial service aforesaid may contain such provisions for the amendment of Chapter VI of Part VI as may be necessary for giving effect to the provisions of that law and no such law shall be deemed to be an amendment of this Constitution for the purposes of article 368.]

Legal Framework

Though the Constitution recognizes the Indian Administrative Service and the Indian Police Service as two all-India services and even provides for a procedure for the creation of more such services, parliamentary legislation was essential to regulate the recruitment and conditions of service. Article 312 creates a constitutional lacuna and to fill that gap, a law by Parliament was necessary. This is done by the All-India Services Act passed by Parliament in 1951.

The Constitution came into force on 26 January 1950, and until a law was enacted the IAS and the IPS were being governed by what are called 'non-statutory executive orders'. This exactly was the situation from January 1950 till October 1951. The All-India Services Bill was introduced in the Lok Sabha on 15 October 1951 and was passed the same day. In addition to the Home Minister and the Minister of State in the Home Ministry, only three MPs—H.V. Kamath, Ruthnaswamy, and P.S. Deshmukh—participated in the discussion, which covers barely 20 columns of the printed proceedings. The members talked about the need to strengthen administration, and welcomed the all-India services. P.S. Deshmukh observed: 'The All-India Services is a matter of supreme importance for the country; it is a question of supreme importance in any country, but it is more especially so in a country of the size of India with various sections and factors which compose the Indian community ... . The British Government ruled this country so well and for so long because of the All-India Services they had organised. ... We used to abuse the 'steel frame' and we used often to say that our own people were enslaving us for the benefit of the British people. Nonetheless, when we have achieved independence we can not only not do without the all-India services, but I for one would suggest that it should be made as strong a steel frame as it was in the past.'[31] He continued to emphasize that the necessity for this was greater because India chose the parliamentary form of government under which ministries may come and go but 'we will have to rely essentially on the composition of the services'.[32]

More than what was thought of by the constitution of India, the introduction of planning brought into being a significantly enlarged area of central control. It connotes that certain things have to be done all over the country even though India has a federal system. Acceptance of planning, in other words, makes a commonness of approach imperative, and this is provided, at least facilitated, by the all-India services.

The All-India Services Act, 1951, amended from time to time, is a simple one, seeking to regulate the recruitment and the conditions of service of persons in the all-India services. The Act empowers the central government to make rules, in consultation with the state governments, to this end. The rules and regulations made are required to be laid before each House of Parliament for a period of 30 days, and it is only at the end of this period that they can come into force. Parliament is free to make changes in them.

The All-India Services Act, 1951, delegates rule-making power to the executive but at the same time requires that the government would lay on the table of each House of Parliament the rules it proposes to promulgate. These rules are framed in consultation with the state governments concerned and the Union Public Service Commission where necessary. The state governments are required to be consulted when the Centre proposes a new rule or a modification of an existing one, but the term 'consultation' has been given a purely technical meaning. The Centre gives an opportunity to the state governments to react to its proposals but it is not necessary for it to be bound by them. Theoretically the central government can frame a rule even though it has been opposed by all the states in India. In practice, what sometimes happens is that many states do not care or bother to reply to the Centre's proposals for new rules. This is interpreted in New Delhi as equivalent to the conveying of consent!

These rules may be said to fall into four categories. There are rules which apply to the all-India services as a whole. Besides, rules have also been framed for the Indian Administrative Service, the Indian Police Service, and the Indian Forest Service.

The central government has so far promulgated the following rules:

1. The All-India Services (Leave) Rules, 1955.
2. The All-India Services (Special Disability Leave) Regulations, 1957.
3. The All-India Services (Sunday Leave) Regulations, 1960.
4. The All-India Services (Medical Attendance) Rules, 1954.
5. The All-India Services (Provident Fund) Rules, 1955.
6. The All-India Services (Compensatory Allowance) Rules, 1954.
7. The All-India Services (Travelling Allowances) Rules, 1954.
8. The All-India Services (Conduct) Rules, 1968.
9. The All-India Services (Discipline and Appeal) Rules, 1969.
10. The All-India Services (Death-cum-Retirement Benefits) Rules, 1968.

11. The All-India Services (Commutation of Pension) Regulations, 1960.
12. The All-India Services (Conditions of Service-Residuary Matters) Rules, 1960.
13. The All-India Services (Remittances into and payments from Provident and Family Pension Funds) Rules, 1958.
14. The All-India Services (Confidential Rolls) Rules, 1970.
15. The All-India Services (Joint Cadre) Rules, 1972.
16. The All-India Services (Dearness Allowance) Rules, 1972.
17. The All-India Services (Leave Travel Concession) Rules, 1975.
18. The All-India Services (House Rent Allowance) Rules, 1977.
19. The All-India Services (House Building Allowance) Rules, 1978.
20. The All-India Services (Group Insurance) Rules, 1981.

Though there are as many as 20 sets of separate rules regulating different aspects of service, the most important perhaps is the All India Services (Discipline and Appeal) Rules.

CONTROL OVER ALL-INDIA SERVICES

It is on the question of control over the all-India services that a controversy has been raging right since their inception and more particularly since the mid-sixties. Generally, the state governments have criticized the all-India services on the grounds of the latter's weak commitment to them and this attribute is viewed as a direct consequence of the paucity of control they have over these services.

HISTORICAL EVOLUTION OF CONTROL MECHANISM

The question of control over the all-India services and its mode and mechanisms were discussed at the time of the formation of these services, and the consensus then was to leave maximum autonomy for the states.[33] The Provincial Premiers' Conference of 1946 tilted itself in favour of the provinces as most provisions relating to the all-India services formulated by it respected the latter's sensitivities. Sardar Vallabhbhai Patel assured the provinces amply that while the power of removal and dismissal of members of the all-India services was to vest with the appointing authority, namely, the central government, a convention needed to be established under which the central government was to accept the provincial government's recommendation whenever the provincial government and the Federal Public Service Commission were in agreement. Where there was disagreement between these two, the central government would decide the case on merit after taking into consideration the recommendations of the provincial government and of the Federal Public Service Commission. The government under which an officer was serving for the time being would have full authority to award other punishments (that is, except removal and dismissal) subject to a reference to the Federal Public Service Commission. In so far as the central government was concerned, it was to accept the advice tendered by the Federal Public Service Commission; but provinces, if they so wished, could disregard such advice for adequate reasons.[34] This approach was applauded by the provincial premiers who asserted that it was undesirable that an officer serving under the provincial government was to be in a position to look to an authority other than the provincial government for protection. Indeed, the all-India services which emerged from this conference were put on par with the provincial civil service (PCS). Nor was the Premiers' Conference inclined to look at the latter as a kind of service inferior to any other service in the new political order. Other matters concerning the all-India services were also decided in a way supportive of the provinces' position. The cadre strength of the all-India services was to be determined by the provinces and the Centre was not to intervene in the exercise.[35] Similarly, appointment to vacancies in any province was also to remain, 'as far as possible', restricted to persons within it.

The principal provisions of the 'Scheme for Formation of an All India Administrative Service' are summarized as follows.

Candidates selected for appointment to the Indian Administrative Service were to be allotted to the participating provincial governments by the central government which would consult the latter and comply with their requirements. Candidates were to be allotted 'as far as possible' to their province of origin or domicile.[36] The original scheme left many powers in the hands of the provincial governments—an act which did not arouse the latter's misgivings vis-à-vis the all-India services—and thus facilitated their acceptability. A province could, for instance, suspend a member of the all-India service but the original scheme did not refer to any right of the affected officer to appeal to the central government against such a decision and the Centre had no right to reinstate him. All that the scheme said was: 'An officer may be suspended by the government under which he is serving. An officer under suspension shall be paid by the government suspending him a subsistence allowance equal to one-third of the average monthly pay earned by him during the preceding twelve months. In addition, that government may direct payment of any compensatory allowance of which the officer was in receipt on the date of suspension to such extent and subject to such conditions as it may direct.' Besides, penalties other than dismissal or removal from service could be imposed by the government under which an officer was serving. The scheme, however, visualized that before imposing any punishment, the government 'shall consult the Federal Public Service Commission and a convention will be established that the Federal Public Service Commission's advice shall be departed from only for exceptional reasons'.[37] The scheme visualized a formal enquiry where the officer had a fair opportunity of explaining himself before any punishment could be awarded to him. Above all, the scheme made it clear: 'The officer will have no right of appeal whatever.[38]

It would thus be clear from the foregoing that the scheme originally formulated for the Indian Administrative Service conferred effective power in many matters on provincial governments. The fixation of the cadre strength remained with the provinces. The scheme fixed the percentage of promotion to IAS from the state administrative service (PCS) at 25 but the operational responsibility remained with the provinces subject to approval of the Federal Public Service Commission. The decision taken was that 'the provinces should be left free to select and to devise rules of selection for the provincial service quota, but the persons selected would be subject to a certificate of fitness by the Federal Public Service Commission'.[39] It also decided to allocate to a province those officers who, 'as far as possible', belonged to it, indicating thereby that it was to be generally an insiders' service. Similarly, minor punishments were left with the provincial governments and no appeal could lie with the Centre. The Federal Public Service Commission was to be consulted in many matters, but the provincial autonomy in the management of the all-India service was no less marked.

Over the years, the Centre's control over the all-India services has steadily expanded and consolidated, and that too at the expense of the state governments whose control over these services has been continually attenuated, so much so that this has caused a somewhat marginalization of their position. The overriding challenge of nation-building has induced the central government to strengthen its control over the all-India services—as on many other institutions of the land—in a bid to keep the new nation-state intact though the presence of an element of partisan motivation on the Centre's part might not be completely ruled out. Also at work has been the subservient political culture at the state level fostered by the single-party dominance system, so characteristic of India under Jawaharlal Nehru's active leadership.

CONSTITUTIONAL POSITION

The civil service in India including the all-India services enjoy protection under article 311 of the constitution of India. As this article points out, a civil servant including a member of the all-India services cannot be dismissed or removed from employment by an 'authority subordinate to that by which he was appointed', and, further, no such person can be dismissed or removed or reduced in rank except after an enquiry in which he has been informed of the charges against him and given a reasonable opportunity of being heard in respect of those charges. This provision has been viewed as offering rather excessive security of job to erring public servants but the recent judgements[40] of the Supreme Court are interpreted as having made punishment easy and thus taken away the safeguard against arbitrary action. The members of all-India services are appointed by the President of India, and as such dismissal from service, discharge or reduction in rank cannot be imposed by any authority lower than the appointing one. This is the constitutional position, and needs to be made clear even though this area has rarely caused any difficulty either to the Centre or to the states in managing the civil service.

DISCIPLINE AND CONTROL

The system of control over these services is codified in what are known as the All-India Services (Discipline and Appeal) Rules, 1969. There are, besides, other codified rules which regulate the conduct and behaviour of members of these services, This chapter deals with the punitive powers of the employer, which are as follows:

1. Suspension;
2. Censure;
3. Withholding of promotions;
4. Recovery from pay of any pecuniary loss caused to government or government controlled organization;
5. Withholding of increments of pay;
6. Reduction in rank;
7. Compulsory retirement.

Suspension of a civil servant is listed above as a punishment but it is generally not so viewed by the judiciary in India and is not recognized as a punishment under the All-India Service (Discipline and Appeal) Rules though instances are not lacking where the judiciary has interfered with executive discretion in this regard, Yet, it is listed here as a punitive mechanism deliberately. Suspension is loud in its very nature: the officer comes to be identified as soon as put under suspension and as such necessarily carries a definite social as well as official stigma. Its psychological effect is crippling, and its very prospect is demoralizing, even chilling. Major punishments to members of the all-India services can be awarded only by the central government, and the state government enjoys no power in this area. For instance, no one from these services can be dismissed, removed or compulsorily retired except under the order of the Centre. Informal consultation with the state concerned is held but the Centre alone can inflict this category of punishment.

Though suspension of a civil servant is not officially treated as punishment, it is this which, in practice, is widely resorted to by state governments with the express intent to penalize an officer. The legal position is that a state government has the power to suspend a member of all-India services and, what is more, for this no prior central approval is necessary. The existing rules, however, envisage a definite reporting mechanism. The central government is required to be reported when a suspension takes place; a detailed report of the case is required under the rules to be sent to the Centre within fifteen days of the suspension order. One may note here that a state government may suspend an officer; but the suspension order can remain valid for a maximum period of three months unless disciplinary proceedings are initiated against him or such an order is confirmed by the central government. The officer concerned has, besides, a right to appeal against his suspension to the Centre, which has the object of preventing any deliberate victimization of the officer. It is because of the right of appeal with the Centre that the state government feels aggrieved, and wants this to be removed. What happens is that the affected civil servant is first inclined to seek remedy in the state government itself; it is only after he has failed in these informal efforts that he seeks the Centre's intervention through appeal or goes to the judiciary to seek redressal of his grievance.

As said earlier, the members of the all-India services remain under the control of their state government so long as they are posted under it, and it is only when a major punishment is to be awarded that the Centre's concern becomes activated, for it alone is competent to award it. The award of a major punishment is the prerogative of the central government. Besides, the members enjoy the right of appeal to the Centre against the action of the state government leading to suspension or inflicting of minor punishments. This is a safeguard against political proximity adversely affecting the independence and morale of the services. The provision for appeal assumes that the Centre, being a remote authority, is likely to be more objective and impartial in its decision-making concerning civil service matters.

NATURE AND EXTENT OF STATE GOVERNMENT CONTROL

The state government has many ways of exercising control over the all-India services, and these include local victimization for political reasons also. Postings and transfers of officers are under its command, and this right is unabridged. What has now become a rather common practice, at least in some places, is the state governments exercise not a small measure of control by a high degree of selectivism that it brings to bear on the postings of officers, particularly in the case of strategic jobs. The state government may supersede an officer; recourse to this, as already mentioned, is also on the increase, particularly since the mid-sixties. And, of course, it can punish an officer by censure, stoppage of increment, and recovery of the quantum of loss caused by him. There are informal methods also which are pressed into service. Chief Ministers are seen to take up with the Centre deputation cases of politically inconvenient officers. To protect the officers from unjust treatment, a provision for

How Control over All-India Services is Shared

State governments	Central goverment
1. It enjoys power of posting and transfer of an officer.	The central government cannot interfere.
2. It can suspend an officer.	A detailed report of the case is required to be sent to the Centre within 15 days of the date of suspension. The officer may make as appeal to the central government, and the latter may allow or disallow the appeal.
3. It can award minor punishments (censure, withholding of promotion, and recovery of pecuniary loss caused to the government).	The officer make an appeal to central government and the latter may confirm or withhold the punishment.
4. Apparently no control, the views of the state government concerned invited.	The central government may award major punishment (reduction in rank or pay, and compulsory retirement.
5. In case of a difference of opinion between the state government and the central government the former's opinion does not prevail.	In case of a difference of opinion between the state government and the central government the latter's opinion prevails.

appeal to the Centre has been made, and an aggrieved civil servant can knock at the Centre's door to seek redressal. The Centre, thus, has the last word in the matter of minor punishments as in the case of suspension. The table on p. 127 describes how control over all-India services is exercised.

The participatory process of decision-making, a mark of the all-India services, seems to be becoming dispensable of late and the view presently taken by the Centre is that while consultation with the state governments is obligatory under the rules, their concurrence is not mandatory. This may mean that even if all the states are unanimous in their opposition to a proposed rule the Centre may still legally go forward and enact it. If this view is taken, which is presently the case, the state governments remain completely out of the picture and the Centre can regulate the all-India services on its own terms. A member of the IAS serving under a state government could until recently be brought on deputation to the Centre only with the former's consent but in 1984 this rule was superseded; and the amended rule provides in regard to the deputation of cadre officers that 'in case of any disagreements, the matter shall be decided by the central government and the state government or state governments concerned shall give effect to the decision of the central government'.[41] What this means is that New Delhi has now the power to pull out an officer from the state government and post him under it even if the state government does not want it. Such powers through technical interpretations of rules are not strictly speaking, in conformity with the participative culture, which is the nourishing force behind the all-India service, but have perhaps become necessary become of the low behaviour of state governments. Some members of the all-India services, it is true, do not hesitate to act like commissars while their true role is that of a yogi; and the civil service ethos must discipline such deviants.

ADEQUACY CONTROL

Does the state government enjoy adequate control over the members of the all-India services working under it? Does it need increased power of control over them? Or, what should be the role of the central government in regard to the members of the all-India services? These are important questions even though an easy, universally acceptable answer may not be in sight.

'There is no control over the all-India services which the state government does not have,' argued a former chief secretary of a state when the present author was interviewing him. Another person who had also held the office of chief secretary told the present author: 'During my term as chief secretary, there were seven changes of ministries ... . Unless a civil servant is protected he cannot function independently.' He advised: 'The power of suspension should be taken away from the state government.' But he added in the same breath, 'The state government would not agree to withdrawal of such a power, I admit. The states, today, want complete control over the all-India services, for the want a subservient civil service.' It is perhaps good to familiarize ourselves with his views on the interface between the emerging political leadership and the all-India services:

There was a time when as an IAS officer I only expected a transfer. Over the years, the government is not that just. There is undue interference with the delegated powers of the officers with the consequence that there is, today, complete disappearance of confidence among the members of the All India Services. It is only while in opposition that the political parties clamour for administrative reform and demand that the civil service should be independent and impartial. Once in power, the ministers want all the civil servants to be under their thumb. ... Coalitions are notoriously weak governments. The Muslim League, a coalition in Kerala, wants— and has—Muslim officers in key positions in departments headed by its leaders ... . In 1957 I, on many occasions, said 'No' to E.M.S. (who was the Chief Minister) and he never interfered. I can't do so in the 1980s. Today, there is constant interference with the power and authority of the civil service leading to erosion of the morale of the All India Service officers. Every officer is subject to the ministers' whims. The All India Service officers are getting rapidly politicized. But the answer to the problem does not lie in destroying the edifice of All India Services; instead, the policy-makers should better analyse the process responsible for the present state of affairs and take appropriate action in the right direction.

This is the tale which the civil servants have told, and one finds a deeply pessimistic note in it. What the ministers and others think about the all-India services should be equally insightful.

A politician holding a key portfolio in a coalition-led state observed:

I admit that the all-India services provide a uniform standard of quality in administration all over the country, and the credit for this goes to the fact that they are recruited by the Central government. The members of these services however show, unmistakably, their leanings towards the Centre. I, therefore, plead that after a member of all-India services is recruited he should remain under the control of the state government and the Centre should be completely divested of control over him. All India services are acceptable to us only when control over them gets vested in the state government. The responsibility of the Central government should be restricted to recruitment and post-entry training at the National Academy of Administration.

Another politician, a prominent leader of the Communist Party of India (Marxist) and a former chief minister, emphatically asserted:

The manner in which the all-India services have functioned in at least some states have given rise to serious apprehensions because on many occasions they have functioned as agents of the Centre within the administration. It is of paramount importance that the basic loyalty of these services should be to the state government to which the members have been allotted and they are guided and disciplined by the state government. It follows, the Central government must respect the decisions of the state government with regard to the service and disciplinary matters. Unless these services are put under the discipline of the state they are apt to create administrative problems for it. Dual loyalty is improper, vitiating as it does the relations between the Centre and the state.

When asked to elaborate the 'agent of the Centre' image of the all-India service, he observed: 'During 1957–59 when we first came into power there was an important event when the state government made a serious complaint to the Centre about a senior officer belonging to these services. This officer was not fair and loyal to the state government and was instrumental in creating problems at the behest of his masters in Delhi. On our protest, the Centre adopted an attitude of complacency, and eventually it took no action in the matter.'

He concluded:

The state government finds that it does not have adequate disciplinary control over members of the all-India services. The members of these services are inclined to look to the Centre over the head of the state government. When there is a conflict between the Centre and the state the former (i.e., Centre) has given an unmistakable impression that it is *the* government which matters, and the states are inconsequential. When a state government takes action against a delinquent officer it should stand and not be set aside by New Delhi, which often happens at present. My contention is that an officer should be under the undivided discipline of the state government during his tenure in the state, and, to this extent, the present arrangements need modification.

Another state-level chief executive complained against the central government's control over the members of the all-India services posted in his state. This, according to him, has resulted in the officers looking to New Delhi for protection, and in the process the authority of the state government gets systematically eroded. He pointed out that his government had suspended a few delinquent officers and even initiated action against some but the central government intervened and negated the action. He lamented: 'We have come into power because people of the state have reposed their confidence in us. We are people's representatives but we do not have control over members of the all-India services working under us. How can we deliver the goods?' His view was that all officers working in the state government must remain under its control and appeal against its decisions, if any, were to lie with the administrative tribunal which must be set up. It would be fit to sum up the foregoing analysis in the words of R.P. Noronha, a member of the ICS and who retired as chief secretary of Madhya Pradesh in 1974. In his *A Tale Told by an Idiot*, he observes:

Today the politician distrusts the IAS man. ... He distrusts him because he belongs to an All India Service, whose loyalty must be more to the Centre than to the state. This is utter nonsense, but the politician believes it, and it is what he believes that is the important thing, not the truth. Any politician will tell you that he prefers a State Civil Service officer to one from the IAS, as a Collector, and one of the headaches of a Chief Secretary is to persuade his government to accept the annual quota of IAS probationers. At state level, therefore, the IAS is a foundling. So far as the Centre is concerned, he has been put out for adoption and they wash their hands of him. The state can kick him around as much as they (sic) please and the Centre will not interfere, even unofficially. It is only when the state proposes dismissal that the Centre is consulted, and then they (sic) content themselves (sic) by passing the buck to the Union Public Service Commission. Washing their hands with the blood of innocent men was a popular pastime in the Home Ministry. All this leaves the IAS in the unenviable position of being disliked by the states and disowned by the Centre.[42]

Noronha sums up: 'It was a source of never-ending astonishment to me that they (All-India Service members) could function at all.[43]

SOME OTHER MANAGERIAL ISSUES

The Indian Administrative Service (IAS) is the successor service to the 'heaven-born' ICS and is the first choice of nearly all the candidates. Every year the competitive examination includes some who have already got selected in some other service; yet they appear in it to qualify for the IAS. The respect in which this service is held may be measured from the fact that 'repeaters', as they are called, are always for the IAS. Many successful candidates are the offspring of bureaucrats themselves. Commanding many socialization advantages, the sons and daughters of higher civil servants are good in social interactions and possess, besides, a total picture of India because of the relatively high mobility of their life, which equip them admirably with qualities valued by the selectors.

Before appointment, two more formalities have got to be completed. A candidate must be certified to be physically fit and, secondly, there is his police verification. The government wants to find out the antecedents of the candidate including, at one time, information on whether he is or was actively associated with the Communist party or a student association affiliated with that party. The policy of the government was not to appoint any candidate having association with the Communist party. This procedure of verification was criticized by the Communists in Kerala in 1967 when they came in power, and they refused to have this carried out. The police verification continues but political dispositions of the candidates are now not probed. Nor is such an enquiry advisable in view of the growing federalizing process under way.

STATE-WISE ORIGIN OF THE IAS MEMBERS

Statistical information about the Indian Administrative Service alone is not available as the UPSC holds a common examination for the two all-India services as well as the central services and the data it publishes in its annual report relates to all the services.[44] It will, however, be certainly of interest to probe into the state-wise origin of the IAS successfuls. This effort, too, is handicapped as the UPSC publishes only the university-wise breakdown of such candidates. In the absence of state-wise figures, one is left with no alternative but to depend upon the university-wise distribution of the successful candidates, assuming that a university draws its students only from the state in which it is located, which may be questionable and indeed is in the case of many including the Delhi, Jawaharlal Nehru, and Aligarh Muslim universities, as well as IITs. This, however, may be a crude measure of state-wise origin of the IAS successfuls, and it is in this belief that the following observation is made.

The leading supplier states to the IAS are Delhi, Punjab, Uttar Pradesh, Haryana, and Bihar, closely followed by West Bengal and a few others. Last in the row are states like Jammu & Kashmir, Gujarat, Maharashtra, north-eastern states, etc., which have not sent any sizeable number of candidates to the IAS. Jammu & Kashmir is educationally backward and besides, lacks as yet the notion of civil service as a career. Gujarat, on the other hand, is a 'forward' state in India with abundant career opportunities for its people besides having what may be called a business culture, which makes academic/administrative employment unattractive. In short, both backwardness and forwardness may act as a drag, and graduates from such states tend to view 'service' as something not within the range of their habitual thinking. A society, it seems, has to reach a certain level of consciousness in order to gain awareness of various options of earning a livelihood. Some communities have yet to graduate to this point. At the same time, others have diversified their options; and government career does not hold much attraction for them.

The scale of regional representation has not remained static. In the fifties, the universities of Allahabad and Madras were the principal suppliers of successful candidates to the higher civil service, but they have since slided back, yielding place to the Delhi and Jawaharlal Nehru universities. Much depends upon factors like quality of education, level of economic development, cultural, orientation of the student community, etc. One senior bureaucrat told the present author: 'The regional representation in the all-India services does not remain unchanged but varies from time to time. When I was a boy, all my brothers insisted on writing the IAS examination. Today, I find a change; no one in the family is interested in IAS. What I am trying to say is that new communities which never thought of such services in the past are now aspiring for the all-India services. Many write the IAS examination because the only alternative open to them is a clerical career. The Kerala culture is government job-oriented, and yet not many Kerala boys and girls succeed in the higher civil services competitive examinations. This is because the quality of education is somewhat unimpressive even though there has been extensive expenditure on it in the state.'

Many states, one may further note, practise discriminatory policies today in respect of recruitment of personnel, and as a result candidates belonging to certain castes or regions remain kept out of public employment or are made to work under several disabilities. Brahmins in Tamil Nadu, for instance, grow up under cumulative disadvantages, starting with the stage of admission to educational institutions. Caste is a rather powerful factor in many other states such as Bihar, Haryana, Uttar Pradesh, etc. In Punjab and Jammu & Kashmir, there is discrimination on the basis of religion. As a result of such ascription-based discrimination informally practised, the principle of 'equal opportunity' comes to lose its validity, and candidates otherwise qualified are discouraged from serving the state as its servants. Brahmins, for instance, were entering government service in large numbers in Tamil Nadu—as in many other states. As a result of discrimination practised by the party in power since Independence, they find public avenues shut, and discover themselves under a steady compulsion to become self-employed or to compete at the UPSC-held examinations or to join the private sector. Many of them appear at the IAS examination but do not want home postings, the states preferred being Gujarat, Maharashtra, Madhya Pradesh, etc., where working conditions are much more congenial—at any rate, until recently. It is not without a message that no Brahmin in the IAS has been able to become a chief secretary in Tamil Nadu for quite some time. The point sought to be driven home is that the all-India services are being prevented from acquiring a representative character by a variety of factors, including the partisan orientations of some of the state governments.

The steady expansion of university education has brought a very large number of students within the field of eligibility for the all-India services. As against 10,000 graduates annually coming out of the universities in the early thirties, it is around 2 lakh spread all over the country in the eighties. This should enlarge and strengthen the field of choice, which however has not happened. In 1982, as many as 26 universities have not claimed a single position out of nearly 140 vacancies in the IAS. The standard of education, especially university education, therefore, can safely be assumed to have fallen, and besides, they vary from university to university.

PROMOTION FROM 'PCS'

As already mentioned, the IAS is partly recruited from amongst the members of the state civil service, the originally fixed percentage of 25 having been increased to $33^1/_3$.[45] Making the provincial civil service a feeder to the IAS serves two purposes: a much needed incentive to the state service, and presence, in adequate numbers, of the 'sons of the soil' in administration. Whether the promotion quota of the state service should be increased or not is a subject of debate and discussion. The members of the state civil service have acquired mastery over details of administration by working in the field for long periods. By the same virtue, they are down-to-earth and have a deep grasp of field realities. When they get promoted into the IAS they bring a wealth of experience—an undoubted asset—to the new service. At the same time, the critics point out, being local persons, they are weak in the quality of independence which is upheld as one of the marks of the all-India services. Having worked in the same state all their life, they have become politically vulnerable and even accommodating. When the present author was discussing this aspect with a high-ranking politician, he remarked: 'It is not true that they are necessarily politically vulnerable: they are politically sensitive and understand the local climate much more intimately.' As regards their promotion quota, most believed that the present arrangement was all right and its further raising may dilute the character of the all-India service.

Though one-third of the vacancies in the IAS are filled by promotion of PCS officers, the time they take to get into the IAS is not the same in all the states. In some states a PCS officer may take only 10 years to get into the IAS while in states like UP and Bihar one may hope to get into this service only after 28 years.[46]

This is a rather shocking situation proving that the management of the PCS has been wholly unsystematic, even haphazard. When promotion comes too late in life it ceases to be an incentive and this is precisely what is happening in the case of some PCS officers.

MANAGEMENT OF THE SERVICE

Historically, matters relating to the all-India services were dealt with by the Ministry of Home Affairs in the central government. As these services are organized and maintained on behalf of the central and state governments, the Ministry of Home Affairs was responsible not only for matters of a general nature but also for their detailed application to individual cases. This institutional arrangement was not conducive to efficiency.[47] The Administrative Reforms Commission (1966–70) recommended the setting up of a separate Department of personnel to serve as a nodal agency for the personnel functions of the government. It observed: 'It is necessary to set up a central personnel agency ... . A Central agency with overall responsibility in all important matters and manned largely by specialists will obviously be able to devote concerted attention to formulation of new policies, set new standards and raise the quality of administration.'[48] The central government accepted this recommendation and, in August 1970, constituted the Department of Personnel. In February 1973, the Department of Personnel and the Department of Administrative Reforms, in existence since 1964, were merged to form the Department of Personnel and Administrative Reforms. Again, in 1985, the Department was elevated to the level of a ministry, and it is now known as the Ministry of Personnel and Training, Administrative Reforms and Public Grievances and Pension[49]—a tortuously longish name for a ministry. The Ministry carries wide-ranging responsibilities in the field of personnel management but a particular reference to the IAS must be made here. Matters relating to this service have since become the direct concern of this ministry .The cadre control in respect of the Indian Police Service and the Indian Forest Service was transferred to the Ministry of Home Affairs and the Ministry of Agriculture respectively.

The cadre control over the all India services is decentralized, the governing criteria being that 'the specialist should be the concern of the ministry which deals with that specialized subject' and that in case (of the service where) the user ministries were more than one and if it (the service) cannot be controlled by one ministry, the control of that service should vest in a central agency.[50] Such a decentralized arrangement is with regard to the day-to-day operation in cadre control but the overall policy control is still exercised by the Ministry of Personnel, to call it by a shorter name.

At present, the Indian Administrative Service is being managed by the Ministry of Personnel, which has in it a services division headed by a joint secretary under the overall control of the secretary. Besides a joint secretary, this division has deputy secretaries, under secretaries and desk officers besides other staff. The services division·is the cadre-controlling authority for the IAS and exercises the powers of the Government of India under various rules and regulations. Besides, it formulates policies for the all-India services in general and maintains liaison with the state governments in regard to matters relating to the Indian Administrative Service.

At the state level, matters relating to the Indian Administrative Service are dealt with by the General Administration Department (GAD) or the Department of Personnel. Though Kerala has a Department of Personnel, the Indian Administrative Service is dealt with by the General Administration Department, which functions directly under the chief secretary and the chief minister. Matters relating to the all-India services, it may be emphasized, are directly under the chief secretary although there may be a secretary to assist him in his multifarious responsibilities.

Mention must also be made of the Union Public Service Commission which participates in the management of the all-India services even though not as directly, pervasively and intensively as the other two agencies do. As is well known, it is the UPSC which sets the ball rolling by making recruitment of the members of the all-India services. Every year, each state notifies to this body the number of vacancies it has, and the UPSC then computes the total number of selections to be made.

There is also an examination at the end of the probationers' training at the Lal Bahadur Shastri National Academy of Administration, and the marks secured at the terminal test are added to the marks secured in the earlier examinations, and the total marks determine the officers' ranking in their service.

This is one function of the UPSC. Besides, the Commission gets itself involved in two other types of situations. The Commission is constitutionally required to be consulted in respect of disciplinary cases contemplated against central civil servants including, of course, the members of the all-India services and this consultation is in regard to the findings of the departmental inquiry set up to examine an officer's transgressions as well as to the quantum of punishment proposed. This role of the Commission flows from its broader function of being the protector of the civil service: the Commission has been visualized by the Constitution to ensure that civil servants are not subjected to arbitrary punishment. Disciplinary cases coming before the Commission are nearly 1200 a year, out of which not more than 12 are from the members of the all-India services.

The second situation in which the UPSC is involved is in relation to the promotion of state civil service officers into the IAS, the IPS and the Indian Forest Service as well as in the promotion of what may be called 'non-PCS' officers into the IAS. As is already mentioned, the promotion quota to the IAS at present is $33^1/_3$ per cent and to recommend promotion into IAS, promotion committees are set up. They are presided over by the chairman or a member of the Union Public Service Commission to ensure complete objectivity, and the recommendations made by such committees are always accepted. A criticism often heard against the UPSC is that it has hardly provided the level of leadership expected of it in this area, and, as a result, such confabulations are held just to fulfil the constitutional requirements and have become more or less routine affairs.

CONCEPTUAL FRAMEWORK OF MANAGEMENT

Technically speaking, the Government of India does not possess a permanent civil service of its own, except the Central Secretariat Service. It has always been the policy to fill the middle and higher management level positions at the headquarters by deputation of the all-India services (mainly IAS) officers from the state governments and to a lesser degree from the various central services, controlled as they are by their respective departments. The exceptions are the External Affairs, Railways and Posts and Telegraphs ministries. Such an arrangement was always defended, and even when the federation-creating Government of India Act, 1935, was enacted, no departure from this principle was permitted.

The principal argument advanced in favour of it is that higher civil servants engaged in policy-making and advising ministers must possess first-hand as well as fresh experience of working in the field to keep the actions and decisions of the union government as close to reality and as meaningful to the people as possible. This is precisely what the tenure principle seeks to do. At any rate, the background of most problems dealt with in the Secretariat cannot be understood or appreciated in a vast and diversified country like India unless the public servants concerned have direct experience of working in the states and field agencies. Having worked in the Secretariat, the civil servants get directly acquainted with the objectives underlying the policies and programmes which they have to execute. In the process, implementation does not lose sight of the objectives of a given programme, thereby contributing to its success. Also each level of government comes to gain direct insight into each other's constraints and concerns, and this itself facilitates reaching a healthy equilibrium in a federal system.

This principle of staffing has remained firmly established in India, and though modifications were attempted in the recent past in the shape of 'pools', these were always viewed as aberrations. The rigorous discipline of the tenure system postulates appointment of the best, which is not a very simple exercise in view of the occasional clashes of interests, because posts in the Secretariat are limited and there are many aspirants drawn from various all-India as well as central services. Moreover, as the ability of a civil servant is ascertained from his annual character roll, now called performance appraisal, standardization poses a problem. Varying individual dispositions and differing norms of evaluation prevail in the states and the services.

The tenure system must remain rhythmic and the civil servants must revert to their parent organizations on completion of their tenure, so that the vacancies may be filled by new groups of officers. This, again, is not easy, for personal factors may try to defeat the reverse flow of officers as these do the process of inflow. On return from the Secretariat, the civil servants should be welcome to their states and field agencies and must not be greeted with what are known as 'punishment postings'.

At a fixed period every year, the central Ministry of Personnel notifies the government's requirements to the state governments which then send lists of officers whom they can spare. An informal practice on the part of the states is to consult the concerned officers and take their consent. The Ministry of Personnel gets the officers screened and it has for this purpose a board to assist it. Thereupon it constitutes panels for various levels in the government, from the names sent to it by the states and does placement in various ministries and departments. On completion of the tenure, the officer reverts to the state, and the same exercise is repeated in search of new incumbents.

This is the theoretical position, but the practice makes it tiresome and tortuous.

It is an assumption of the all-India services that all officers belonging to them are basically of more or less equivalent ability. But some are more hardworking as is nature's law and thus acquire greater ability than others. This provides the justification for an element of selectivity in promoting officers to what are referred to as selection-grade and supertime scale levels in the government. The supertime scale posts for the IAS are the divisional commissioners, secretaries to the state government and joint secretaries in the Government of India. All these posts are of equivalent responsibility, and yet an officer's appointment as a joint secretary is not possible without his empanelment. This kind of selectivity for postings in the Centre has made one former member of the IAS, M.N. Buch, observe: 'What justification can there be for denying officers at this very senior level the opportunity of deputation under the central government on the grounds of unsuitability? A person unfit to be a joint secretary is unfit to be commissioner of a division or secretary to a state government also.' What this statement implies is that since the reverse logic is untenable, the imposition of a screening test for purposes of posting as joint secretaries in the Centre is weak in logic. While the net for catching officers for central deputation should be cast wide, the state governments should also devise some screening mechanism so that officers do not succumb to complacency and instead continue working hard.

The claim that the central government (that is, the Ministry of Personnel) prepares the panels and determines the postings objectively is not always borne out by facts. Despite the enthronement of the tenure system, it is only a small number of nearly 300 officers[51] who keep hovering around Delhi out of the total membership of nearly 5000 and who act as gate-keepers preventing their other colleagues from getting central postings. It is significant that, 1591 IAS officers and 768 IPS officers (other than those belonging to the UP cadre) with more than five years' service to their credit have not been able to come on deputation to the Union government.[52] The fact is that, today, without political patronage, a civil servant is unlikely to get a senior posting at the Centre, at least in a prestigious ministry. The deputation of officers to the Centre, especially at the top levels, depends on social and political factors also in addition to their merit. A minister, for instance, would be more inclined to induct civil servants of the state he himself comes from. Some IAS officers are very skilful in managing Delhi jobs: when threatened with a transfer; they leave no stone unturned in forestalling it. To this end, they deliberately design linkages with those who know the ropes. When even this strategy fails, many civil servants, who are loath to revert to their parent states, manoeuvre postings in the numerous quasi-governmental or autonomous organizations in Delhi. M.N. Buch observes: 'The fact is that officers make concerted efforts to have their names empanelled, then try and influence their postings to the ministry of their choice and, when faced with the possibility of returning to the state, use the Indian Institute of Public Administration as a means of staying on for a year or two in Delhi, whilst they persuade the Department (Ministry) of Personnel to accommodate them at the centre again.'[53] Buch testifies to the influence exerted by factors like kinship in determining postings in the Central Secretariat, more so in the case of economic ministries, carry as they do enormous perks, power and patronage. He observes: 'When Mr. P. C. Sethi was Chief Minister of Madhya Pradesh I told him that the (Central) Ministry of Commerce was referred to as the ministry of sons and sons-in-law. I counted five officers in this category. Mr Sethi corrected me and said that there were eleven.'[54]

The discipline expected of this mode of staffing has thus become considerably lax. The broad profile of the Secretariat today is that those who had an advantage of an early deputation are generally reluctant to go back to their cadre. A typical civil servant of today is not prepared to take postings quietly and as a routine, and makes, instead, efforts to prolong his stay at the headquarters. Even when an extension is not granted, he incubates in one of the autonomous organizations in Delhi to get 'cooled off' before he becomes formally qualified for another deputation. A few succeed in finding a place in their state bhavans in Delhi as resident commissioners. These exercises deny them valuable field experience, and, what is more, a very large number of officers otherwise eligible for Secretariat postings remain unutilized. Opportunities for deputation to the Centre have not been distributed equitably, but much more disturbing is the manner of allocation of personnel among the various ministries and departments.

Postings in the Secretariat are governed by the Central Staffing Scheme under which the doors are theoretically open to all higher civil services. Practice, however, belies the profession. Indeed, today, the members of the all-India services appear to fall into two broad categories when viewed from this angle. There is a group of officers who have developed an inordinate liking for central postings and who avoid reversion to their 'home' state, while the second group would not like to come to the Centre, happy and contented as they think they are in their states. All the same, like Alice in Wonderland, they have to run hard to stay at the same place, and harder still to move to positions of their choice.

One may probe a bit more deeply into the two emerging profiles. Generally, those who have been raised in Delhi or those who have spent their early years in Delhi, for education or some other purpose, develop a fascination for the city. Delhi commands a strong, continually expanding infrastructure, and many think of settling down in the metropolis to take advantage of its facilities and partly also perhaps to escape from the many disabilities characterizing life in the states today. These attractions are particularly appealing to those members of the IAS who do not hail from the state of their encadrement as well as to those for whom Delhi is culturally and temperamentally compatible. Also, an extended stay at the Centre itself acts as a handicap to an officer's career in the state: such an officer has meanwhile distanced himself from the political and bureaucratic leadership in the state and thus may not get proper postings. This group has a sub-group in it with its own sharp style of functioning. A typical member of this cluster manipulates postings in the economic departments in his earlier years in the state. He may even move to a state-level public corporation, and the expense account at his disposal convinces him of the pay-offs built into the managing of economic and industrial affairs in a developing society. When he comes to the Centre he strives for a posting in the economic ministries and even stakes his claim on merit in view of his past specialization and experience. While occupying this position, he gets many opportunities to make foreign trips to deal, for instance, with international organizations. In the process, he is adding to his experience as an economic administrator and his personal acquaintances also increase. His ultimate target may be to move into an international organization like the World Bank or its subsidiaries, ancillaries or tributaries with its seven/ eight times higher emoluments and equally impressive perks. A civil servant of this kind of a profile is very skilful in making his bio-data look formidable, and he uses it very effectively. He is a pre-emptive personality.

The other group is not enamoured of postings in the central government and indeed resists coming to the Centre. Stay in the state has its own charm and bounties: big houses with numerous creature comforts, more personalized and less hectic lifestyle with a high measure of psychological satisfaction. This apart, officers of this disposition have many opportunities of compensating themselves by buying up property and other real estate such as agricultural farms, which may not be possible at the Centre. Generally, the 'insider' element in the IAS with its already deep roots in the local soil evinces this propensity more to stay in the state, where, because of its proximity to the scene of action, life is also very thrilling. It has also been noticed that officers prefer staying in their state if working conditions are good and the political climate is congenial. The gradual polarization of these two groups is subjecting the all-India services to distortions and is imparting disorientations to their members.

The tenure system at present covers officers up to the level of additional secretary. When a joint secretary at the Centre gets promoted as additional secretary, his previous stay as joint secretary is not counted and he starts his tenure of three years afresh in his new capacity. Secretaries to the government are kept exempt from tenure; the justification apparently advanced is that by the time an officer reaches this level he is left with barely five or six years of service before retirement and as such he need not rotate. It is this interpretation of tenure which complicates the placement practices, for some officers manage to continue indefinitely in the Secretariat till their retirement. Additional secretaryships in the government should preferably go to officers working in the state governments or executive departments so that freshly gained field experience is brought to bear on policy-making. This means that joint secretaries must be enabled to have a field exposure immediately before assuming the responsibilities of the higher position. Also, it may not be prudent to keep out the secretaries to the central government from the application of the rule of tenure. Bureaucratic politics, never absent at any level but aggressively operative as one moves up the administrative hierarchy, does not seemingly accept any such boundaries. In 1985, four full-fledged secretaries to the government were transferred out to the states, and they can never be dubbed as incompetent. This apart, conceptually speaking, senior officers are as much needed at the Centre as in the states, and rotation even at the highest level is bound to be beneficial to both the levels of government. Care should at the same time be taken to ensure comparable terms and conditions of services to such homebound civil servants.

NEGLECT OF FIELD EXPERIENCE

It has been a principle underlying the Indian Administrative Service that field experience in the state is most valuable for a member of this service and he must continually replenish it so that he may participate rationally and competently in policy-making, his rightful role in the government. This is why the Indian Civil Service, of which the IAS is a successor, was regarded as a 'camp service', implying that it was a service of field postings. When it was decided to wind up the ICS and replace it by the Indian Administrative Service, it was felt that the latter should inherit the strength that had made the ICS a legend. It must be remembered that many members of the ICS spent as many as 20 years in the field (that is, province) and it is after accumulating such an asset that they came to the Centre on policy-making positions.

The field component of an average member of the Indian Administrative Service is rather low as compared to his prototype of the Raj, and, what is more, this is declining over the years. It is said that today nearly 50 per cent of the IAS officers have remained without the experience of functioning as district collectors, which is an alarming state of affairs. It is absolutely essential to restore the importance of district experience for administrative careers. Utmost attention must be given to the grooming, refining, and training of these officers, and for this they must be placed under district collectors who are themselves model civil servants and who take a deep and continuing interest in their junior colleagues. The best civil servants know how indebted they are to district collectors under whom they had spent their initial years. It is equally necessary that the IAS officers should be appointed as district collectors in due course of time and have a respectable term of stay in the post. The Administrative Reforms Committee set up by the West Bengal Government in 1982 under the chairmanship of Ashok Mitra recommended that an IAS officer of at least nine years' seniority may be placed in charge of a small district and of 15 years for holding the charge of a major district. 'It is our view', the Committee wrote, 'that, following the completion of probationary training, an officer belonging to the Indian Administrative Service should have at least two tenures, of a minimum period of two years in each case, as either Sub-Divisional Officer or Additional District Magistrate to be followed by a tenure with a government department ... for a further period of two to three years, before he or she should be asked to assume the charge of administration of a relatively small-sized or less sensitive district. The seniority we envisage in such cases is of a minimum period of nine years. After completing a tenure as District Magistrate in such a district for a period of two to three years, the officer should be brought back to the secretariat for a further tour of duty with a department, following which he should be asked to hold charge of a major district ..., a minimum period of service of at least fifteen years should be regarded as essential for an officer belonging to the IAS.'[55] The district collectorship is itself the best training one can get. While functioning as a district collector, one has to take numerous decisions on numerous matters, which builds up his decision-making capabilities. He is continually exposed to all social and political pressures and learns how to steer clear of them. He sees people from the closest range and therefore acquires rich insight into human motivations and behaviour. All these contribute to his building in a way perhaps no other posting can do. Some states practise discrimination and officers belonging to certain castes or categories are generally not given charge of a district. Such discriminatory practices must be firmly discouraged. It is equally necessary to let a functionary remain in his post for a reasonably long time so that he can show results. A district collector in Uttar Pradesh has an average tenure of 60 days and a superintendent of police serves a district for an average of 35 days, according to a recent research study. This may not be exactly true, yet it is not way off the mark. Governments have been changing in a parliamentary democracy but the pattern of civil service transfers remains more or less the same. Over 7000 higher civil servants were transferred in the state of Uttar Pradesh during the period 1992–2002, though the combined strength of IAS and IPS in the state including Uttaranchal is nearly 960, of whom nearly 30–5 per cent remain on central deputation. At the back of most such transfers are extra-administrative factors such as political affiliations, personal obligations, and caste. Officers show too much keenness to get key posts. Frequent transfers are inimical to work, uncomfortable to the individual, and expensive to the state. A district collector's period of stay should not be less than three years. And, why not five years, which is the span of India's Five-Year Plans?

The shrinking of the field dimension in the IAS has happened for a variety of reasons, some of which are impinging on administrative policies themselves. This may be illustrated. The post of a divisional commissioner was earlier higher in rank than that of a secretary to the state government, the only senior position, perhaps, being that of the chief secretary. This implied that an officer had compulsorily to go to the field on reaching a certain level of seniority. After some time, the office of the secretary in the state secretariat was also upgraded and made equal to the post of divisional commissioner. This measure removed the incentive for an officer to go to the field and acquire experience of this level to be fit for the higher post. There are other reasons also. It is common knowledge that it is easier to create a higher-level position in the Secretariat but extremely difficult to add even an ordinary position in the field. The proliferation of positions in the Secretariat is enormous and only a part of this expansion can be accounted for by genuine increase in the work load. Moreover, the fact is that senior level officers are increasingly reluctant to work in the field and prefer positions at the headquarters of the government to escape from the pressures of the district level politicians or to reap the benefits available at the seat of government.

INTER-CADRE TRANSFER

Members of the all-India services are allocated to individual states in which they are required to serve for the whole of their career except for fixed terms of service at the Centre. The allotment of state thus carries enormous personal meaning for an officer. For a variety of reasons, he finds himself under a compulsion to seek a change of state, called inter-cadre transfer. The state, too, arms itself with the power to effect such transfers in what is called 'public interest'. Change of state is provided under the rules. The Indian Administrative Service (Cadre) Rules, 1954, lays down:

The central government may with the concurrence of the state governments concerned transfer a cadre officer from one cadre to another cadre.[56]

Such changes may be allowed by the government subject to the fulfillment of certain conditions. The requests of inter-cadre transfers were considered on the following grounds:

1.   In public interest;
2.   When two all-India service officers borne on different cadres marry;

3.   When the climate of the state of allocation was injurious to the health of the officer or the spouse or the dependent children;
4.   On compassionate grounds on merits of each case.

Since January 1983, inter-cadre transfers are permitted on the following two grounds, taking care at the same time that the officer is not transferred to his or her home state:

1.   In public interest;
2.   When two all-India service officers borne on different cadres marry.

The provision for inter-cadre shifts cannot be altogether eliminated from the rule book, but such changes must not depend, even remotely, on extraneous considerations. This is said here by way of a warning for it has been abused in practice. Zail Singh, the Home Minister in the Centre during 1980–1 imparted an overly liberal interpretation to the rules and got transferred to Punjab a number of officers particularly from far off states. H.M. Patel, the Home Minister in the Janata Government (1977–9) got the rules liberalized and, what is more, interested himself in inter-state transfers. Officers who have succeeded in having their cadres changed have generally been the sons or sons-in-law of very influential persons at the Centre and, what is more, contrary to the official profession, they have been brought back to their home-states. This should not have happened, weakening as it does the very foundation on which the all-India services is based, conceptually speaking.

A crucial question yet remains: will the state governments withdraw the opposition and see the virtues in them exactly the way the various committees later see them? The states are openly vociferous in their opposition to them. Basically, the issue of whether to have new all-India services or not has become one of patronage. Ostensibly, the Centre musters its plea for all-India services on the criteria of administrative efficiency, but control over a service inevitably gives it a silent but very effective tool of manipulation and pressure and it is this capacity which tends to arouse the state government's fear of them. And they are not completely unjustified and mistaken for nursing such fears. The government at the Centre has not always successfully resisted the temptation of using the accredited tools and agencies of Indian federalism for short-term partisan ends.

An abuse of institution of governors of states is widely known. This being the track record of the government of India, the times are not propitious for the creation of new all-India services, even though they may be warmly recommended by a high-powered commission as the Fifth Pay

Commission and the Commission on Centre-State Relations (the Sarkaria Commission). Emphasis should be to run the existing all-India services along purely professional lines so that these services evolve in course of time a distinct personality of their own and become an institution which begins to be sought after in society for its own absolutely professionally motivated behaviour. Equally it would be prudent to nurse the two security services—IAS and IPS—and abandon the pursuit for fresh all-India services.

Today, many even question the existence of these services. The IAS displays belief in its sure ability to deal with all matters under the sun and its distrust of specialists. Self-conceit is barely hidden in the generalist service. The remedy for present maladies and problems does not lie in recruiting more engineers and doctors to the IAS. Nor does the solution lie in creating special streams of agriculture, information technology, conservation and other areas where technological change is very rapid. Nor does the way out out lie in recruiting more and more specialists. All-India services connote dual control, which is plainly not acceptable to the lower state government in India. The constitution of all-India services erodes the autonomy of the states: the latter resist proposals which adversely affect their power of patronage.

DRIVE TOWARDS ESTABLISHMENT OF NEW SERVICES

Anxious to invoke this constitutional provision, the government has been making conspicuous efforts for the creation of new all-India services, and it is but appropriate to turn one's attention to them even if in the process, chronological discipline does not get fully observed. Both the historical past and the constitutional feasibility of creating new all-India services have been tempting the central government to create more of them in newer spheres of activity. The existence of as many as nine such services in the past provided the content of the Centre's dream, and action was initiated to realize the latter. Besides, the Constitution holds out a possibility of creating new all-India services, which itself tempts the Centre to action. The demand has often arisen from other sources also. For instance, these services have been viewed (see the States Reorganization Commission 1953–5) as a check on the separatist trends in the country, posing a threat to national integrity.

In the sixties, social turmoil in many parts of the country was steadily increasing, to curb which the Government convened, in August 1961, the Chief Ministers' Conference to formulate an effective strategy of action.

The chief ministers' deliberations covered many areas but their recommendation for the creation of three new all-India services is significant.

1. The Indian Services of Engineers (Irrigation, Power, Building and Roads)
2. The Indian Forest Service
3. The Indian Medical and Health Service

The Centre was in fact waiting for such an opportunity and thus reinforced, it initiated the necessary constitutional action in the winter session of Parliament. On 6 December 1961, the Rajya Sabha adopted a resolution in favour of these three services.[57] The advantages claimed by the Centre for all-India services are principally three.[58]

1. These services ensure a uniform and high standard of recruitment and training of officers.
2. The rotation of officers between the Centre and the states and the interchange of experience is beneficial to both the Centre and the states.
3. These services develop an all-India outlook.

The necessary legislation for the creation of all-India services in the fields of engineering, forestry, and medicine was passed by Parliament on 6 September 1963. This involved an amendment of the All-India Services Act, 1951. As a result, Section 2A was inserted into the Act of 1951, making provisions for these three new services.

This was a distinct victory for the Centre and a notable event in the history of the all-India services. Even official orders were issued announcing the constituting of the Indian Medical and Health Service; and basic rules regarding recruitment and cadre management were notified in the Gazette of India. All this, however, was being done without taking into account the state government' susceptibilities. Several state governments, not without reason, were opposed to the proposed services, which compelled the Centre to go slow and thus not constitute these services.

However, in the mid-sixties, the Centre again looked buoyant and was poised for further moves. The immediate success gained in the enactment of the legislation itself reinforced its confidence in regard to extended deployment of all-India services. At any rate, this success emboldened the Centre to initiate bolder moves. The Centre, in 1965, initiated the move for the creation of two more all-India services, namely the India Agricultural Service and the Indian Educational Service (General Education, Technical Education).[59] The resolution was eventually passed by the Rajya

Sabha, which was but expected in view of the majority of the Congress party in the House.

In the winter session of 1965 of Parliament, the Government introduced the all-India services (Amendment) Bill, 1965[60] to set up the India Agricultural Services and the India Educational Service (General Education, Technical Education). The bill however lapsed as the Lok Sabha was in the meantime dissolved. Meanwhile, the Indian Forest Service was formally constituted on 1 July 1966, and initially it consisted of officers all selected from the State Forest Service. The first examination for direct recruitment to the Service was conducted by the Union Public Service Commission in September 1967.[61]

The general election held in 1967 radically changed the political complexion of India, for the hitherto ruling party, the Congress, suffered defeat in several states and could form its government at the Centre with a much-reduced majority. The new political equilibrium was not auspicious for the all-India services. The non-Congress parties came into power in as many as nine states, out of the then total of 17. These states did not hide their absolute disapproval of the scheme. Thus, the plan of three new services in the fields of forestry, engineering, and health to be supplemented by two others in education and agriculture appeared to have been shelved, with the disappearance of single party dominance in the country. What is really of interest is that the all-India services were discovered to be not very welcome not only to some non-Congress state governments, but also to some Congress-ruled ones. When the Janata Party came to power at the Centre in 1977, it abandoned the proposal for the setting up of the remaining two services in view of the opposition of several state governments.

The Congress (I) party, came to power at the Centre in 1980, and again revived the move stating 'the proposal' that was earlier dropped was now under the consideration of the government'.[62] Rajiv Gandhi's government, however, preferred no action. Nor are the subsequent governments show any inclination to promote these services in view of their constituent parties' consistent opposition. All India servicing is not a live topic since the commission on Centre-State Relations, commonly known as the Sarkaria Commission (1988), examined the institution of All-India Services in the context of India's Centre-State relations, and recommended a further strengthening of these services with greater emphasis on selection, training, placement etc., and on more regular consultation between the Centre and the states on matters relating to the management of these services. It recommended the creation of all-India services in the fields of engineering, medicine, and education, and even lent its support to constituting such services in other sectors like agriculture, cooperation, industry, etc.[63]

The Sarkaria formula envisages a much larger and fuller role for all-India services. The Central Fifth Pay Commission (1991–6) is the latest body to support the creation of new all-India services.

In contrast to its predecessor the Indian Civil Service, the Indian Administrative Service is much larger in size and is inevitably drawn from a larger number of castes, religions and regions. The profiles of both the political masters and the administrative echelons have also changed. The populist parties which came to power in the coalition government at the Centre and the states since the nineties or even eighties witnessed a kind of caste-based coalition between the politicians and the bureaucrats, both practicing the art of the possible.[64] During 1941–59, Tamil Nadu had 10 chief secretaries, of which only five had served in the central government. All-India service is becoming a rhetoric, according to S. Guhan, himself a member of the IAS.[65] Nirmal Mukerji, the former cabinet secretary and Rebeiro, a former director general of police, have considered the IAS and the IPS dispensable. The Indian Administrative Service particularly claims to be the higher management pool in Indian Administration, thus being the sole supplier of the managerial skills in the government. This claim is not very true. Today, the market has become much more developed and diversified and is even in a position to supply lateral entries to the public sector. Several of the activities presently handled internally may be outsourced to the private sector as well as to non-governmental organizations. Also, such a move is sure to downsize the IAS. The case for the public bureaucracy to cut itself down is urgent, but this is not happening owing to lack of political will and determination, even though the problem of downsizing is itself made a tricky one. The first task is to identify the 'surplus'. These have then to be shifted to the surplus pool. Thereafter they have to be shifted to departments short on staff. Posting would be preceded by re-training. Since the employee can not be placed on a lower pay scale, there is hardly any saving from the exercise. How hollow is the claim of bureaucratic downsizing can be seen from the following.

Cadre Strength of the IAS

Year	Strength
1951	1232
1961	1862
1971	3203
1981	4599
1991	5334
2001	5159

Size of the Civil Service

Year	Staff Strength	No. of Secys, Addl, Jt &Dy, Secretaries
1997	38.95 lakh	1371
1998	38.47 lakh	1459
1999	37.46 lakh	1553
2000	38.26 lakh	1692
2001	38.55 lakh	1692

The all-India services are not notable for maintaining high standards of integrity among their members. The extent of corruption among them is subject to speculation, but the widely shared fear is that it is high and, what is more, is not on the decline. One cannot do better than reproduce an excerpt from a letter received in the mid-eighties from a distinguished former public servant, N.S. Saksena (of Indian Police), in reply to a query made by the present author:

I joined the Indian Police in 1941 and retired in 1977. Being a member of the police service I had occasion to watch the integrity of my own service carefully in Uttar Pradesh, where I served in all ranks—Assistant Superintendent of Police, Superintendent of Police, Deputy Inspector-General and Inspector-General—from 1941 to 1953 and again from 1960 to 1971. I worked in the Ministry of Home Affairs from 1953 to 1960 and again from 1972 to 1977. Here I came in close contact with police officers of practically the whole of India. Later I went up and down the country several times as Member, Union Public Service Commission, from 1977 to 1983 and as Member, National Police Commission, from 1977 to 1981, and was able to learn about the integrity of both Indian Administrative Service and Indian Police Service officers.

I was Superintendent of Police, Anti-Corruption, in U.P. from March 1948 10 June 1952. Later I served as Director of Vigilance, U.P. from April 1965 to August 1968. In both these assignments it was my job to beep an eye on dishonest senior officers.

During the last five years of British rule in India—August 1942 to August 1947—the integrity of the administration had taken a plunge because the administration was dominated by politics. Quite a few dishonest officers escaped notice because they rendered good service in fighting the Congress movement.

For a few years after independence there was an improvement in the general integrity of the administration because the Council of Ministers consisted of honest men, who valued integrity. From about 1955 or so a slow deterioration started. After 1967 the downward trend became quite fast and since then we are continuously going downhill. In 1948, U.P. had eight ministers of whom as many as seven were honest. In 1970s and 1980s the percentage of honest ministers in the U.P. cabinet has hardly exceeded fifteen-twenty. There have been quite a few thoroughly corrupt Chief Ministers.

The fall in the integrity of the Indian Administrative Service/Indian Police Service has been simultaneous with the fall in the integrity of the political executive.

In the years 1948–1952 when I was Superintendent of Police, incharge Anti-Corruption, in U.P., I watched the integrity of both Indian Administrative Service and Indian Police Service officers. My two Home Ministers were Shri Lal Bahadur Shastri and Dr. Sampurnanand—both men of sterling integrity. Quite often they enquired from me about the integrity of the Indian Civil Service—Indian Administrative Service/Indian Police—Indian Police Service. The percentage of dishonest officers did not exceed fifteen or so. When I served as Director of Vigilance in U.P. from 1965 to 1968 the percentage had doubled to about thirty. During my all-India tours from 1972 to 1983, as Inspector-General, Central Reserve Police Force, Director-General, Central Reserve Police Force, and Member, Union Public Service Commission, and Member, National Police Commission, I have seen the percentage of dishonest officers continuously rising and today it has definitely reached fifty.

Of these fifty per cent dishonest officers it will be quite unrealistic to call them equally dishonest. There are milder forms of corruption, which are well known, while there are quite a few who are blatantly corrupt. The situation is not irremediable. Our Finance Minister, Mr. V.P. Singh, has shown the way. In both the Indian Administrative Service and Indian Police Service there are about fifteen per cent officers in senior age-groups who are multi-millionaires. This truth can be revealed by a detailed enquiry into their assets.

Is there any method by which moral qualities can be judged? There is no foolproof method but if the probationary period is long enough—say, three years—it will be possible to weed out at least a few bad specimens. After the probationary period ends it is necessary to scrutinize carefully the total movable and immovable assets of the officer. I need not go into details here but quite a few corrupt officers can be caught if the will is there. Unfortunately the vast majority of Indian Administrative Service/Indian Police Service officers have enough political clout to escape the consequences of their corruption.

These are wise suggestions, but demand firm political and high civil service determination to assimilate them with strong follow-up action.

EVALUATION OF ALL-INDIA SERVICES

India is unique among federations in its having some of the most important civil services in common between the Centre and the states in the form of all-India services, distinct from central and state services. All-India services are a legacy of the past and the result of a federal system evolving through a process of devolution from a unitary government. Their continuance after Independence is due to the belief that these services are needed for maintaining and strengthening the unity of the country; to ensure uniform and high standards of administration in the state, to provide competent administrative personnel for the new development tasks of the state and to make possible better coordination of policy between the Centre and the States and greater cooperation between them. The A.R.C. Study Team on 'Personnel Administration' stated that the need for all-India services was greater than in the past to provide 'a uniform administrative base, an easy communications system' and for the natural development of personnel at the higher level and as 'an organic administrative link between the three tiers of government'. It was further argued that the all-India services would be able to attract the best talent in the country and the constitutional protection afforded to them will enable them to act impartially and offer independent advice to ministers. The rotation of officers between the Centre and the states, which is a part of the system of all-India services, would make the experience gained in the states available to the Centre and be of help to it in dealing with country-wide problems and also enrich the state administration with experience gained in the wider sphere of the nation. A review was undertaken, consequent on the passage of the Act of 1935 with its features of federalism, whether a bifurcation of civil service in India was desirable and even necessary. The Maxwell Committee on Organization and Procedure (1937) discussed the issue but recommended firm continuance of the existing tenure staffing of the Central Secretariat. According to it, a permanent civil service of the central government would verily be one without any direct touch with life in India which would be an inadequate preparation for the kind of work performed at the Centre. The background of many of the subjects with the central government cannot be understood unless officers dealing with them possess direct experience of working in the provinces, for it is at this level that the effects of the policy made at the higher levels of government are felt. A rotating civil service thus provides a valuable link between the central and provincial governments. No less meaningful to the provincial government personnel is the insight into the outlook, method and even difficulties of the central government which a system of periodic inter-change provides.[66] Thus, the traditional method of staffing of the headquarters organizations of the Government of India continued. But with the expanding functions of the central government under the new 1935 Constitution, it discovered itself under mounting stress especially in regard to the recycling of officers. In 1937, a Finance-Commerce Pool, exempt from the traditional tenure system, was constituted. The outbreak of the Second World War in 1939 in which India not only participated but also became an important Allies' Centre for military operation in the East expanded suddenly and considerably the range and scale of government activities, leading to an expansion of the Secretariat and necessitating appointment of a fairly large number of additional personnel. The result was that the Centre found itself indenting for a much larger number of officers from the provinces and at the same time showed a strong disposition not to revert them on the completion of their terms.

A sudden and substantial drop of the British element in the higher civil service in India occurred during this period even though the joint committee, whose report formed the basis of the Government of India Act, 1935, put it on record that 'we are convinced that India for a long time to come will not be able to dispense with a strong British element in the Services.'[67] For the ICS, it was accepted that the British proportion should be one-half. In practice, the arrangement was that part of the Indian half was to be recruited by examination in India and the remaining vacancies by examination in Britain. In 1936, the vacancies for the ICS were 20 and for the Home Service 33. The first 20 places on the joint list went to British, candidates of whom not one accepted the ICS. In fact, none of the 20 candidates who could secure any home appointment elected for the ICS. More than that, of the 12 British candidates who were not high enough for the Home Service, but high enough for the ICS, 10 refused the latter service.[68] The declining fortunes of the all-India services were in evidence since the Constitution of 1919. The Constitution of 1935, though based on provincial autonomy, did not do away completely with the institution of all-India services. The Indian Civil Service, the Indian Police, and the Indian Medical Service (Civil) were retained, the first two being the security services and the last named to cater to the medical requirements of the European civil servants. Competitive examinations had begun to be held in India also.

In 1937, popular ministries were formed in the provinces amidst a widespread national movement for independence. Before the Constitution of 1935 could settle down to its normal level of functioning, the Second World War broke out drawing India into the global conflict on the side of the Allied powers. The Congress ministries resigned on ideological grounds, leaving the task of governing in the hands of the career bureaucracy. Under the pressure of war, public administration in India had to take up new functions to cope with the new requirements. An expansion of the machinery of administration thus took place at various levels of governance. A sudden demand for additional public personnel could be met only by relaxing the usual standards of recruitment. As many war-time activities were viewed as temporary, the persons recruited were kept temporary. Recruitment to all all-India services stopped from July 1942 because of extremely unsettled conditions. Even when the end of the Second World War was in sight, recruitment in London was not resumed as meanwhile the political situation in India had changed drastically. In 1947, India won its independence, but the country was partitioned along communal lines. As part of the partition plan, the public personnel were also given the option of service in either of the newly created countries or retirement with generously planed pensionary benefits.

The all-India services have undoubtedly many advantages in greater or less measure. But they also raise a variety of problems, especially in the field of inter-governmental relations. The question whether the all-India services are incompatible with a federal system of government is perhaps only of theoretical interest. But it will have to be admitted that these services restrict the autonomy of the states in several ways. All-India services must be recruited by the Government of India, which removes a considerable area of patronage from the domain of the states. Besides, recruitment to all-India services must be based on a nation-wide competition. States which are backward in the field of higher education, tend to go unrepresented or under-represented in such a competition. The control over the services is divided between the Centre and states, with the former having the ultimate word in disciplinary matters. The states' control over its services is thus restricted. The loyalty of the all-India services is divided between the Centre and the states and they tend to look up more to the Centre than to the states for the protection of their interests. This makes them suspect in the eyes of the state governments which they serve. Joint control is likely to become increasingly difficult, with different parties in control at the Centre and in the states. The system of rotation of officers between the Centre and the states cannot be worked rhythmically under such circumstances. Difficulties in this respect have already been experienced with one party in control at the Centre and other party governments in some of the states.

The impact of the all-India services on the state services has been a neglected aspect of the question, and needs careful study. Extensive state services are an essential complement and base for the all-India services and much of the work of administration is carried on by them. The role of the all-India services is one of direction, coordination, and control. The layering of the services is horizontal, with little or no movement from the subordinate level to the middle level and superior services. A wide gap separates the different layers of the services. It has been claimed that the top layer—the all-India services—act as a leaven to improve the quality of the middle and bottom layers. This is true only to a limited extent as the numbers of the all-India services are far too few, about 5000 (many of this number serving at junior level) in a civil service numbering 10 million in the three levels of government, to significantly affect the quality of the work of the latter. On the contrary, the presence side by side of the all-India services with their better scales of pay, higher status and of state services with their modest emoluments and inferior status, breeds envy and tends to lower the latter's morale and efficiency. The higher costs of the all-India services are seen as a burden, which the state cannot afford, and which may be regarded as unjustified. The difficulties of the states in recruiting well-qualified persons for their services are greatly enhanced.

The question of all-India services needs to be examined from several angles. It is necessary first to assess their contribution to the maintenance and improvement of a high standard of administration in the states and the Centre, which is the primary reason for their creation, and to national unity. The efficient maintenance of internal order and stability is the ability of the services to carry out development tasks under the plans. Secondly, the question of all-India services has to be considered from the federal angle. Their impact on the character of the administration in the states and on their autonomy must be assessed. It may be noted here that no effort has been made to explore whether alternative means, which are not inconsistent with the federal system, can be devised to serve the purposes for which the creation of the all-India services has been urged. The third angle from which the question should be considered is whether all-India services with their special privileges, powers and emoluments and the horizontal layers of the civil service are compatible with the principles of democracy and socialism to which the country is committed.

No critical appraisal of the work of the all-India services since Independence and of their contribution to the improvement of administrative standards or to national unity has yet been attempted. The closest to such an appraisal is to be found in Paul Appleby's classic report of a survey of public administration in India (1953). The report, while admitting the relatively high position of the Indian administrative system among the administrative systems of the world, is highly critical of the organizational structure, personnel policies, financial and administrative procedures, and of the capabilities of the administrative system for the speedy accomplishment of development tasks. The efficiency of an administrative system must be manifest in the manner of its working and the concrete results achieved. Judged by these tests it can hardly be maintained that the all-India services and the Indian bureaucracy in general have been conspicuously successful in the accomplishment of either their traditional law-and-order functions or their new development planning and administration. The fault may not be entirely that of the all-India services. Political independence and the social policies of the new state have placed on the administrators developmental tasks which were wholly novel to them and which they were not adequately prepared to handle. They had to work under political heads who were themselves ill-equipped to direct them and who frequently misdirected them either through ignorance or other less valid reasons. Notwithstanding these difficulties, the higher echelons of the services, which necessarily direct the administration, must take a large part of the responsibility for the deterioration of standards that has been observed since Independence. The all-India services have not themselves been able to maintain high standards characteristic of them before Independence and have more or less failed to arrest the deterioration of the standards of administration in the states and in the Centre. They have also failed to provide the needed leadership to the other services. They have also not shown any marked independence in their relations with their political bosses in spite of the constitutional guarantees of their position and career. A nexus is developing between the higher bureaucracy, the politician and the mafia (as referred to in the Vohra Committee Report). The top levels of the services with a few exceptions have generally tended to follow their political.bosses and carry out their behests rather than risk their displeasure and jeopardize their own careers by offering them unpalatable advice. They have lost the sense of camaraderie and betray an increasing tendency to be mere puppets under their respective political leadership. The professionally motivated proper relationship between the political and administrative wings of the government is yet to emerge. By and large two services have collectively shown low motivation for improvement in their standards of efficiency. They have also not been very receptive to new ideas and innovations. They have been very largely concerned with their own careers, service prospects, emoluments, and other rights and privileges. The preoccupation of the services with their careers has militated against their achieving the level of efficiency that is needed today and which they are not incapable of achieving, given the proper motivation and incentives. A large majority of members of the services who are individually excellent are yet collectively ineffective in giving the people the purposeful government that they need.

The modern administrative system of India was essentially the work of the all-India services, especially of the Indian Civil Service. It was built on the English model. Its members were made subject to the law and infused a high sense of responsibility for the welfare of the people over whom they ruled. The best products of British universities were recruited to them. The result was a competent and incorruptible administration to which a simple rural society looked up to for justice and help in solving its problems. A service, with a similar background of education, traditions and culture, and identical interests was an apt instrument of control and a 'steel frame' for holding the country together. Because of their European background and education, they were also the agents for modernizing the Indian administrative system.

Could the personnel of the all-India services play a similar modernizing and integrating role? The all-India services since independence differ radically from the predecessors. Their personnel is wholly Indian. This, of course, is necessary and should increase the efficiency and sense of commitment to the nation's interests. They have had their education mostly in Indian universities, which unfortunately is in many ways inferior to that of their British predecessors. The background of the members of the new all-India services is more heterogeneous. They are subject to conflicting linguistic and regional loyalties and lack the cohesiveness and homogeneity of the British personnel of the civil service before independence. Under these circumstances, the new all-India services cannot serve as modernizing agents or an effective integrating force to the same degree as their predecessors. If the aim is that the all-India services should play such a role, the government's policies in regard to recruitment, training, and placement will have to be different from what they have been or are at present.

As in the country at large, the loyalties of the personnel of the civil services tend to be confined to their linguistic group or state. A broad national outlook is becoming less and less evident and the sense of loyalty to the nation is weak. National integration postulates the unreserved acceptance of the equal rights of the citizens of the country irrespective of their domicile, language, or religion or caste. This is not the case at present. The problem of national unity is essentially psychological, though it has economic overtones. Institutions such as a national Parliament, national political parties, a national language, and a national educational system, etc. greatly help in the process of integration. But the solution of the problem has to be sought essentially in the educational and cultural fields. The all-India services can at best play only a minor role in this sphere. They are not among the more important institutional aids to national integration. The ability of the new all-India services to play an integrating role has been greatly affected by some of the recent policies of the Government of India in regard to recruitment to the services. The adoption of the 18 languages of the Eighth Schedule of the Constitution as alternative media in the competitive examination for recruitment to these services can only lead to the breakup of the unity of the service and its ultimate division into separate linguistic groups with their loyalties confined to their own language group and states. Services so fragmented can hardly be expected to play an effective integrating role or raise the standards of administration. A re-orientation of policy in regard to the language of examinations, training, allocation, and rotation would seem to be needed to make the all-India services effective as a unifying force. There are some obvious weaknesses of the all-India services, to which reference is necessary. As the superior services, they are divided from other elements of the civil service by a very wide gap. The wide disparity between them and other civil services breeds a sense of superiority in one and a spirit of envy in the others. The exclusiveness and the casteist spirit of the all-India services are notorious. The treatment of other civil services, even all-India technical services by the generalist IAS has been the subject of bitter complaint. The widespread discontent among the technical services and their plea to be constituted as all-India services at par with the administrative services is largely the result of the attitude of the general administrative services towards them. The existence of rigid caste hierarchies in the civil services is hardly conducive to the teamwork needed in modern public administration. They are inconsistent with democracy and any socialist philosophy.

From the point of view of federalism, services common to the Centre and the state are an anomaly. They cannot be reconciled with the autonomy of the states. More than any other characteristic of the Constitution, the control of the most important civil services of the states by the union through the all-India services tends to invest it with a pronounced unitary bias. Federal control may be only potential rather than actual. But nonetheless it seriously limits the states' control over their own public services and their sense of autonomy. Common all-India services were instituted after independence partly to assure the political neutrality of the civil service and to protect them against political victimization by the governments of the states. In the conditions of India at present, the constitutional protection of the civil service is perhaps necessary to avoid their ill treatment and to give them the independence necessary to function efficiently. It should be possible to afford such protection to the services without creating all-India services working in the state but controlled by the Centre. An independent statutory authority such as the Union Public Service Commission or an administrative tribunal could be entrusted with such duties. The best protection would, of course, be the development of public opinion on the legitimate sphere of political direction and control over the services and of the rights and obligations of the services.

The concentration of attention of the all-India services as the necessary instrument or the improvement of administration in the Centre and the states has tended to obscure the fundamental problem of Indian administration, which is to improve the state administration at the headquarters, district and grassroot levels to make them adequate instruments of government and of social and economic development. Many states have undertaken enquiries of their administrative systems and a plethora of recommendations have flowed from these enquiries. A great deal of advice has been offered to the states by the Planning Commission and central ministries on the method of reorganizing the states' services. The administrations continue to be run on traditional lines and little change has taken place in their machinery or procedures. Two new major developments in state administrations since the fifties may be noted. One is the creation of a hierarchy of rural local self-governing institutions set up to make local development planning democratic and the other is the vast expansion in public employment since independence. This is more a quantitative rather than a qualitative change. Neither seems to have markedly improved the quality of administration in the states, but both have added to their financial burdens. The greatest need in the state seems to be of highly qualified staff in the technical fields of engineering, agriculture, medical and veterinary services, small scale industries, higher education, economics and statistics, and planning. It should be emphasized that even the most competent of general administrators can be no substitute for experts in these specialist areas. The disparities in the emoluments, powers, and status of the specialists in these fields and generalist administrators have militated against the recruitment of the most qualified staff. These would need to be brought on par with those of the generalist all-India services.

Personnel administration in the states no less than in the Centre has been concerned largely with the protection of the rights of existing personnel and the closeness of the service hierarchies. It has not concerned itself with staff development and the training of the civil servant for his job or with the incentives necessary to draw out the best work on the part of the staff. In spite of the existence of public service commissions, recruitment to the services is often determined by considerations other than merit. Incentives to secure the best work, delegation of responsibility and authority, the concept of team work, job description, evaluation and training and other aspects of sound personnel administration are mostly neglected at present and need the attention of the states. Administrative organization and procedures need to be examined from the point of view of their suitability for efficient work. Receptivity to new ideas and the tools and techniques of modern administration are needed. Administration procedures in the states no less than in the Centre are at present control-oriented. They inhibit action and the taking of responsibility and lead to red tape. Changes are necessary to make administrative action purposeful, swift, and responsible. The magnitude of the problems, both traditional and new of the states and in the Government of India requires the most efficient administrative system, fully abreast of modem developments in administrative science and able to deal effectively with the problems of development planning and administration. Equally, the general administration would need to be streamlined, especially on the procedural side. The size and resources of the states, some of which are comparable to the major countries of Europe, makes the creation of such administrative systems in the states both necessary and possible, constituting as they do the delivery system of public administration.

CONCEPT OF ALL-INDIA SERVICES SINCE INDEPENDENCE

The threefold classification of higher civil service in British India, namely, the all-India services, the central services, and the provincial services, rested no less on the level of the appointing authority, the underlying belief being that the higher the level of appointing authority the greater is the security conferred on the particular service. While the all-India services were recruited and controlled by the Secretary of State for India-in-Council, the central services and the provincial services had the Governor-General-in-Council and Governor respectively to carry out the functions of the Secretary of State vis-à-vis their respective services

With the independence of the country in 1947, the Government of India ceased to be under the control of any higher-level authority, and the Secretary of State's services, naturally, came into its hands. Indeed, one of the factors behind the powerful position of the central government under the Indian constitution is its unabridged acquisition of the role and functions, which the Secretary of State for India was performing. The members of the all-India services are, under the Constitution, appointed and controlled by the President of India who, one may recall, is also the appointing authority for class I services. The uniqueness of the all-India services in independent India lies in their functioning in fields directly under the jurisdiction of the states, in the interchangeability of its members between the Centre and the states, and, finally, in the concept of joint management, the day-to-day control being with the government under which a member happens to serve, the ultimate control vesting in the Centre. The members of these services are allotted to different state cadres soon after their recruitment, and they serve in their state unless they come to the central government under deputation. But members of a particular service, wherever located, constitute one service, with common terms and conditions of employment and compensation plan.

From the point of view of a uniform system of administration in the country, in turn leading to sustenance of sentiments of national unity, the retention of all-India services has been one of the significant steps on the part of India's constitution-makers. This is at the political plane. The argument is reinforced by the logic at the administrative level also. More than what was thought of by the constitution of India, the introduction of planning brought into being an enlarged area of central control and implementation of common programmes all over the country. It means that certain things have to be done all over the country even though India has a federal system. Acceptance of national planning makes a commonness of approach necessary; and this is precisely what is expected to be provided by the all-India services. Thus, both politically and administratively, the all-India services have their uses. They have given broadly a common framework of administration to the country. Besides, all-India services provide for exchange of experience between the Centre and the states, as the members of these services rotate between the two levels of government, which has the effect of bringing the Centre nearer to the states. As one state-level chief executive remarked to the present author, 'the Centre, unrealistic as it is even now, would have been much more unrealistic without the all-India services'.

It is a normal feature of a federation to make the two levels of government autonomous and independent of each other. Not only are functions and resources kept clearly demarcated but the machinery of public administration too is kept separate and distinct. This, however, should not be taken to imply that inter-level cooperation and collaboration is forbidden in federalism or, for that matter, kept to the minimum. What is conveyed here is the separateness of public administration with each level equipped with its own administrative machinery and personnel to carry out its tasks. 'all-India services' is an administrative innovation of the Indian subcontinent which has its echo both in Independent India and its partitioned part, namely Pakistan.

NOTES

1. Members of the appropriate all-India services are also seconded to local governments by the state governments.

2. It should be noted that the all-India services of pre-1947 origin were not abolished abruptly or altogether. A decision to abolish a particular service meant discontinuing fresh recruitment to it, thus enabling its painless extinction through the natural process of retirement, resignation and casualties of its members. Independent India deliberately retained in 1947 only two all-India services: the

Indian Civil Administrative Services (which included the old Indian Civil Service) and the Indian Police Service. It inherited, however, the other all-India services as well, which were on their way out. The last member of the Indian Civil Service retired in 1979.

3. *Report of the Committee on Division of Functions*, para 70.

4. *Report of the Reforms Enquiry Committee*, Calcutta: Government of India, Central Publication Branch, 1924, p. 163.

5. Ibid., chapter II.

6. It also recommended provincialization of the roads and buildings branch of the Public Works Department.

7. Ibid., p. 8.

8. *Legislative Assembly Debates*, vol. IV, part V, 3–16 September 1924, p. 3261.

9. *Report of the Reforms Enquiry Committee*, Calcutta, Government of India, Central Publication Branch, 1924, p. 163.

10. *Report of Indian Central Committee*, Calcutta: Government of India Central Publication Branch, 1929, p. 136.

11. Report of the Committee appointed by the United Provinces Legislative Council to cooperate with the Indian Statutory Commission, Allahabad: Superintendent, Government Press, 1929, pp. 104–05. Also see Note 17.

12. Three viewpoints emerged in the committee. One section was in favour of retaining the status quo in this matter, holding that the Secretary of State for India should continue, as in the past, to bear responsibility for the recruitment of members of all-India services and for determination of conditions of their service. Another section recognized the desirability of retraining the Indian Civil Service and the Indian Police Service but wanted the Government of India to recruit and' control the members of these services. Yet another section insisted on the provincialization of all-India services. Hafiz Hidayat Husain argued: 'The great objection, which to my mind seems to be insuperable, is that we are going to have provincial autonomy and if every subject is going to be transferred to the administration of the legislative council, the retention of the Indian Civil Service and the Indian Police Service is, to my mind, fraught with considerable difficulties and inconvenience'. Husain, however, did not press his views. (*Indian Round Table Conference: Proceedings of Sub-Committees*, vol. VIII, Calcutta, Central Publication Branch, 1931, p. 36). B. Shiva Rao said: 'I think it would be satisfactory to work these services on an all-India basis, and at the same time ensure a proper relationship between the services and the Ministry'. (Ibid., p. 54). Bhim Rao Ambedkar, who was also against all-India services, observed: 'We are framing a Constitution in which we propose to give as large a degree of provincial autonomy to the provinces as possible, and it seems to me that no province can be deemed to have provincial autonomy if it has not the right to regulate the civil service that is going to work in its area'. (Ibid., p. 55).

13. Quoted in *Report of Joint Committee on Indian Constitutional Reform*, vol. I, (part I), London: HMSO, 1934, para 296.

14. Ibid., para 297.

15. Ibid., para 299.

16. Section 244 said: '(i) as from the commencement of Part III of this Act appointments to the Indian Civil Service, the Indian Medical Service (Civil), and the Indian Police Service (which last-mentioned service shall thereafter be known as "The Indian Police") shall until (British) Parliament otherwise determines, be made by the Secretary of State '.

17. Sir Shafaat Ahmed Khan observed: 'Provincial self-Government logically necessitates control by the provincial government over the appointment of its servants. A public servant cannot serve two masters. If he is appointed by the Secretary of State, it may be extremely difficult for the provincial Government to exercise sufficient control and supervision. The authority of such government may be undermined, and in some case actually flouted by a public servant who is determined to assert his legal rights'. *The Indian Federation*, London: Macmillan, 1937, p. 216.

18. Vide his 'explanatory' note in the Report of the Committee appointed by the United Provinces Legislative Council to cooperate with the Indian Statutory Commission, *op. cit.*, pp. xxviii–xxxiv.

19. The Chief Ministers were designated as Premiers or Prime Minister at that time, and such practice continued till the inauguration of the present Constitution.

20. Government of India, Home Department, File No. 45/3/46–ESTS(R), para 9.

21. Ibid.

22. Ibid., para 13.

23. Ibid., para 19.

24. Ibid., para 20. .

25. Starred Question 71, *Legislative Assembly Debates*, 30 October 1946, p. 213.

26. Ibid., p.214.

27 *The Hindu*, 25 October 1946, p. 4.

28 The Constituent Assembly of India, *Draft Constitution of India*, New Delhi: Government of India Press 1948, p. xi.

29. Subs By the Constitution (Forty-second Amendment) Act, 1976, sec. 45, for 'Part XI' (w.e.f. 3–1–1977).

30. Ins. By the Constitution (Forty-second Amendment) Act, 1976, sec. 45 (w.e.f. 3–1–1977).

31. *Parliamentary Debates: Parliament of India Official Report*, Part II, XVI, 15 October 1951, col. 4925.

32. Ibid.

33. Government of India, Home Department, File No. 45/3/46–Ests (R), para 20.

34. Ibid., para 20.

35. File No. 45/3/47–Ests (R)–1946, Government of India, Home Department, Ests (R), para 23.

36. File No. 174/47–Ests (R)–1947, Rule 5 of the Scheme.

37. Rule 12(a) of the Scheme for Formation of an All-India Administrative

Service. See File No. 174/47–Ests (R) of 1947, Government of India, Ministry of Home Affairs.

38. Paragraph 13 of the Scheme, ibid.

39. Government of India, Home Department, File No. 45/46 Ests (R), para 16.

40. *Union of India* versus *Tulsiram Patel*, 11 July 1985. For summàry, see *The Statesman*, 25 July 1985. An able interpretation of the Supreme Court judgement is given by S. Sahay: 'Rights of Civil Servants', *The Statesman*, 1 August 1985.

41. Notification 11030/15/83, dated 14 March 1984.

42. R.P. Noronha, *A Tale Told by an Idiot*, New Delhi: Vikas, 1976, p. 74.

43. Ibid., p. 17.

44. It may, however, be safe to remark that the IAS is the aspiration of all the candidates appearing at the examination, and almost without fail their first choice is this service.

45. One may note that the Ashok Mitra Administrative Reforms Committee, set up by West Bengal in 1982, recommended raising the annual induction to the IAS from the State Civil Service from the current level of 33 per cent to 50 per cent. *Report of the Administrative Reforms Committee*, Calcutta: Government of West Bengal, 1983, para 9.11.

46. *Seventy-Seventh Report of the Estimates Committee* (Seventh Lok Sabha), New Delhi: Lok Sabha Secretariat, 1984, pp. 18–19.

47. *Ninety-Third Report of the Estimates Committee* (Third Lok Sabha), New Delhi, Lok Sabha Secretariat, 1966, pp. 18–19.

48. Administrative Reforms Commission: *Report on the Machinery of the Government of India and its Procedures of Work*, 1968, p. vi.

49. The Ministry of Personnel and Training, Administrative Reforms and Public Grievances and Pension, headed by a deputy minister but under the overall charge of the Prime Minister, comprises the following three departments: (i) Department of Personnel and Training, (ii) Department of Administrative Reforms and Public Grievances, and (iii) Department of Pension and Pensioners' Welfare. The administrative head of the Ministry is a secretary to the government and he is also head of the first-named Department: The other two departments are headed by additional secretaries who are under the overall control of the secretary.

50. *Ninety-Third Report of the Estimate Committee*, Third Lok Sabha, 1966.

51. M.N. Buch, 'Dismal Pattern of Postings of Delhi', the *Times of India*, 24 October 1985.

52. *Seventy-Seventh Report of the Estimates Committee*, Seventh Lok Sabha, 1984, p. 58.

53. M.N. Buch, ibid.

54. Ibid.

55. *Report of the Administrative Reforms Committee*, Calcutta: Government of West Bengal, 1983, para 9.0.

56. Rule 5(2).

57. One must note that the resolution by the upper chamber is constitutionality obligatory for the creation of All-India services.

58. Ministry of Home Affairs: *Report* 1961–62, p. 4.

59. *Parliamentary Debates: Rajya Sabha Official Report*, Vol. II, No. 26, March 1985, Col–4782.

60. Ministry of Home Affairs: *Report* 1965–66, p. 1.

61. Ministry of Home Affairs: *Annual Report* 1967–68, p. 1.

62. Department of Personnel and Administrative Reforms: *Annual Report* 1981–82, p.38.

63. *The Report of the Commission of Centre-State Relation*, Part I, pp. 219–31.

64. See *Asian Age*, 25 October 2000, H.Y. Sarda Prasad, 'Heaven born once, earth bound now?'

65. Balveer Arora and Beryl Radin (ed.), *The Changing Role of the All India Services*. Also see author's Working Paper No. 16 entitled 'All-India Services: Retrospects and Prospects', published by Centre for Policy Research, New Delhi, 2004.

66. *Report of the Committee on Organization and Procedure*, 1937, pp. 19–20.

67. *Report of the Joint Committee Indian Constitutional Reforms*, Vol. I (Part I), London: HMSO, 1934, para 2758.

68. Government of India, Home Department (Establishments) f.21/4/36–Ests., 1936.

CHAPTER 11

The Central Civil Services

The higher civil service in India is not monolithic in composition. It comprises all-India services and the central civil services. The latter services by definition are recruited by the Government of India and are under its exclusive control. All-India services, on the other hand are binary, jointly controlled by both the Government of India and the state government, to which a member is allotted though recruited by the former. This chapter deals with the central civil services. They are the established civil services known as the central civil services as well as miscellaneous isolated posts lying outside the established services which are clubbed together to what is known as the general central service. The central civil services, or central services as they are called constitute a separate category and as such have formulated their own rules governing their members. These rules are the Central Classification and Appeal Rules, Conduct Rules, Fundamental Rules and departmental rules. The central services, including the general central service, are classified in descending order of responsibility as well as qualification as class 1, class 2, class 3, and class 4, (now known as groups A, B, C, D, respectively). The central civil services have been established from time to time and their number is increasing in view of increasing work load. Their growth is marked by incrementalism. They were 30 in 1971, and 49 in 1984 and new services are created from time to time. They account for the bulk of the class I posts under the central government: 55,000 out of total of 75,000 class I. The proliferation of the organized services inevitably entails a measure of overlapping of functions. This also creates problems of unequal service conditions and promotional prospects among the members of various services. The central civil services may be classified into technical and non-technical services, an example of the former being the scientific and engineering services while the non-technical services are the Indian Audit and Accounts Service, the Indian Revenue Service, the Indian Postal Service, etc. Similarly, the central civil services contain both categories of isolated posts, the technical as well as non-technical. The central civil services are uni-functional (the Indian Police Service is also uni-functional) and are constituted in the form of a pyramid. It is common to have well-organized time-scales in each service like junior time-scale, senior time scale, junior administrative grade, senior administrative grade, selection grade, etc.

As a rule, a central service is confined to one department or ministry. Members of the Indian Postal Service work in a single department, namely the department of posts. But there are central services such as the Indian Economic Service or the Indian Statistical Service which cut across department boundaries and serve the entire government according to need. But the general fact is that the Central services are unifunctional and specialized.[1]

Some of them are small in size. For example, the Indian Salt Service has a strength of 11 and the Central Legal Service has 70 posts. In fact, there are only 20 services with a cadre strength exceeding 500. The Central Health Service has a cadre strength of about 3500. The Indian Economic Service and the Indian Statistical Service has a total strength of 600 and 500 respectively.

Unlike the all-India services, the central civil services as said earlier are under the exclusive control of the central government and their personnel man positions only in the central government. The civil services of the central government comprise established services known as the Central Civil Services as well as civil posts created outside the established services, which constitute the 'general Central service.' These services are mutually exclusive. As Sundaram his pointed out, 'Different services operate in vertical sides and are jealous about influx from other services'.

There are, today, the following Central Civil Services—Class I,

CENTRAL SERVICES IN 2003

Central Services (Non-technical)

1.   Indian Audit & Accounts Service
2.   Indian Trade Service
3.   Indian P&T Accounts & Finance Service
4.   Indian Postal Service

5. Indian Defence Accounts Service
6. Indian Defence Estates Service
7. Indian Ordnance Factories Service
8. Indian Foreign Service
9. Indian Civil Accounts Service
10. Indian Customs & Central Excise Service
11. Indian Revenue Service
12. Indian Information Service
13. Indian Railway Accounts Service
14. Indian Railway Personnel Service
15. Indian Railway Traffic Service
16. Railway Protection Force
17. Central Secretariat Service
18. Railway Board Secretariat Service
19. Armed Forces Headquarters Civil Service
20. Customers Appraisers Service
21. General Central Service

Central Services (Technical)

1. Indian Inspection Service
2. Indian Supply Service
3. Indian Telecommunication Service
4. P&T Building Works Service (Architectural, Electrical & Civil Wings)
5. Border Roads Engineering Service
6. Indian Naval Armament Service
7. Military Engineering Service
8. Central Power Engineering Service
9. Indian Broadcasting Service (Engineering)
10. Indian Railway Service of Electrical Engineers
11. Indian Railway Service of Engineers
12. Indian Railway Service of Mechanical Engineers
13. Indian Railway Service of Signal & Telecom Engineering
14. Indian Railway Stores Service
15. Central Engineering Service (Roads)
16. Central Architects Service(CPWD)
17. Central Electrical & Mechanical Engineering Service (CPWD)
18. Central Engineering Service (CPWD)
19. Central Water Engineering Service
20. Overseas Communication Service

21. Central Health Service
22. Indian Railway Medical Service
23. Indian Ordnance Factory's Health Service
24. Central Reserve Police Health Service
25. Border Security Force Health Service
26. Indo-Tibetan Border Security Police Health Service
27. Indian Economic Service
28. Indian Statistical Service
29. Indian Legal Service
30. Indian Cost Accounts service
31. Defence Research and Development Service
32. Defence Aeronautical Quality Assurance Service
33. Defence Quality Assurance Service
34 Central Company Law Service
35. Survey of India Service
36. Geological Survey of India Service
37. Indian Meteorological Service
38. Central Labour Service
39. Indian Broadcasting Service (Programme)
40. Indian Broadcasting Service (Engineering)
41. Indian Salt Service

Other Services

1. Central Reserve Police Force
2. Border Security Force
3. Indo-Tibetan Border Police
4. Central Industrial Security Force

One thus notices that India does not have a unified civil service. Each service is separate and distinct and inter-service transfers are not permissible. The size of a service is fixed according to functional requirements. While some services claim a fairly large membership, a large number of them run into two digit figures, making them unviable—in the sense that career prospects of members become narrowly restricted. The size of a service is reviewed periodically to take into account changing functional requirements. The management of a service vests in the functional ministry which is known as the cadre-controlling authority. That of the Indian Administrative Service is the Ministry of Personnel, of the Indian Police Service, the Ministry of Home Affairs, and of the Indian Forest Service, the Ministry of Environment. The following table describes the cadre-controlling authorities of some of the major central services:

Central Service	Controlling Authority
1. Indian Audit and Accounts Service	Office of the Comptroller and Auditor General of India
2. Indian Foreign Service	Ministry of External Affairs
3. Indian Information Service	Ministry of Information and Broadcasting
4. Railways Services	Railway Board
5. Indian Postal Service	Ministry of Communication
6. Indian Revenue Service	Ministry of Finance

The day-to-day administration of these services rests with the individual ministry (called the cadre-controlling activity) under which the posts exist. Also involved in the management of the services are the Ministry of Personnel, which determines the conditions of services (of administrative nature), and the Ministry of Finance, which is concerned with the pay scales and other financial aspects of the conditions of service, such as fixation of provident fund, etc.

The total membership of a central civil service is determined in the light of its own requirements. Period cadre-reviews are undertaken to look into the problem of stagnation. These services therefore command different strength as would be clear from the following table even though the data belong to the year 1972 as given by the Third Pay Commission.

Name of the Central Civil Service	Strength in 1972
1. Indian Audit and Accounts Service	757
2. Indian Defence Accounts Service	215
3. Indian Railway Accounts Service	428
4. Indian Railway Traffic Service	810
5. Indian Income-tax Service	1827
6. Central Customs and Central Excise Service	692
7. Indian Postal Service	302
8. Defence Estates Service	95
9. Indian Ordnance Factories Service (non-technical)	96
10. Indian Information Service	315

These services perform important functions falling within the central sphere of administration like the statutory audit of the accounts of the union and the states, accounting and financial management of expenditure, collection of all-central revenues through direct and indirect taxes and administration of the relevant statutes, division of essential services to the community at large, such as railway transportation and postal administration, management of military estates and ordinance factories, and dissemination of information regarding the policies and programmes of the central government. Along with the Indian Administrative Service, these services have also been conceived as and utilized as reservoirs of talent for manning senior administrative posts in the headquarters organization of the central government. With the progressive growth in the activities of the Government of India in these areas, the role and importance of these services has also grown commensurately.

Members of the technical central civil services are generally employed under the Department of Atomic Energy, the Department of Mines and the ministries of Defence and Food and Agriculture. Their other employees are the ministries of Finance, Railways, Industrial Development, Irrigation and Power, Tourism and Civil Aviation and Supply and the Department of Science and Technology. Isolated posts exist in other departments as well. The scientific face of the Government of India is becoming more and more visible, as reflected in the number of scientific posts in class I, class II, and class III that has increased from 7120 at the time of the Second Pay Commission to over 22,000 in 1971. This expansion is in addition to that which has taken place in the autonomous scientific organizations.

The present chapter discusses the following central civil services briefly:

1. Indian Foreign Service
2. Indian Audit and Accounts Service
3. Indian Broadcasting (Programme) Service
4. Indian Civil Accounts Service
5. Indian Cost Accounts Service
6. Indian Custom and Central Excise Service
7. Indian Defence Accounts Service
8. Indian Defence Estates Service
9. Indian Economic Service
10. Indian Information Service
11. Indian Ordnance Factories Service
12. Indian P & T Finance and Accounts Service
13. Indian Postal Service
14. Indian Railway Accounts Service
15. Indian Railway Personnel Service
16. Indian Railways Traffic Service
17. Indian Revenue Service
18. Indian Statistical Service
19. Indian Trade Service
20. Central Secretariat Service

Recruitment to the above services, excepting the Indian Economic Service, Indian Statistical Service, Indian Cost Accounts Service, and Indian Broadcasting Programme Service, is made through the combined civil services examination conducted by the UPSC. By and large, direct recruitment to the extent of 50 per cent of the posts at the lower level is resorted to, the remaining 50 per cent posts are filled through promotion from the respective feeder services. The posts above the lower level are filled by the method of promotion only or by selection through departmental promotion committees constituted for the purpose.

The Indian Foreign Service (IFS) was established following India's independence for the conduct of the full range of India's foreign relations. The cadre control of this service rests with the Ministry of External Affairs. The Indian Audit and Accounts Service is the principle instrument by which the Comptroller and Auditor General of India discharges his constitutional obligations. This service aids and assists the C&AG in the performance of his duties and in the exercise of his powers in relation to audit of accounts of the union and of the states and of any other authority or body prescribed by or under any law made by Parliament or state legislatures. The Indian Broadcasting (Programme) Service was constituted on 5 November 1990 under the administrative control of the Ministry of Information and Broadcasting to provide a specialized programme cadre to All India Radio and Doordarshan. This service was bifurcated media-wise and further divided into two streams comprising Programme Management and Programme Production. As such IB[P]S provides for four independent cadres, namely (i) Programme Management cadre of All India Radio, (ii) Programme Management cadre of Doordarshan, (iii) Programme production cadre of All India Radio and (iv) Programmme Production Cadre of Doordarshan. The initial constitution of the service was made by appointing officers holding corresponding posts in respective cadres in All India Radio and Doordarshan. Consequent to the departmentalization of accounts, the Indian Civil Accounts Service was constituted on 1 April 1977 to man the group 'A' posts in the departmentalized accounting formations. Initially, officers from the Indian Audit and Accounts Service were derived and the first direct recruitment to this service began from the year 1978. The officers of this service are responsible for formulation of policies and procedures in matter of government payments and accounting; and internal audit functions in the various ministries/departments except railways, defence, posts and telecommunications, space and atomic energy which have their in-house accounting setup. The Controller General of Accounts (CGA) is the head of this service. The Indian Cost Accounts Service is comparatively a young civil service and is manned by qualified cost/chartered Accountants. The officers of this service are required to tender advice to various ministries on a variety of complex cost and pricing related issues. This service is being administered by the Department of Expenditure, Ministry of Finance. The organization of Indian Customs and Central Excise is a part of the Department of Revenue the Ministry of Finance. The Central Board of Excise and Customs (CBEC) is the apex body of Central Excise, Customs and Narcotics Departments which is headed by the Chairman, CBEC and the Board, comprises five other members. The posts of chairman and members are ex-cadre posts for the Central Excise & Customs Service. The officers of this service are entrusted with the task of collection of much needed revenues though indirect taxes, notable among them being customs and excise duties and tax on services.

The Indian Defence Accounts Service caters to the in-house accounting, and financial advice needs of the three defence services, Defence Research and Development Organization (DRDO), Border Roads Organization, ordnance factories and other inter-services organizations. The Controller General of Defence Accounts is the head of the Indian Defence Accounts Service and functions as an internal financial adviser. The Indian Defence Estates Service was originally constituted as the Military Lands and Cantonment Service. This service has been assigned the task of management of civic—administrative and local self-government in cantonments, developmental works in cantonments, administration of defence land, procurement of immovable assets and lands for deference purposes, etc. The Director General, Defence Estates, is the head of the Indian Defence Estates Service. The Indian Economic Service was constituted with the objective of having an organized higher class A service to formulate and implement the economic policies and programmes of the country. The service is inter-departmental in nature and after a training programme, the young recruits are groomed to function as economic administrators and economic advisers and are posted in different ministries

The Indian Information Service, which was originally known as the Central Information Service, was constituted in March, 1960. It was renamed as the Indian Information Service in 1987. The service has been entrusted with the functions of dissemination of information on government policies, programmes and activities through print, audio and visual media and providing feed back on the reactions of the people on government programmes, policies, and advising the government on information polices.

The Indian Ordnance Factories Service (IOFS) was constituted for the overall management of ordnance factories in India which are the sinews of self-reliant indigenous defence production capabilities of the nation. It comprises both technical and non-technical posts. Technical posts constitute about 99 of the total cadre strength and are filled mainly through the Combined Engineering Service Examination. The remaining 10 per cent non-technical posts are filled through the Combined Civil Service Examination conducted by the UPSC. About 84 per cent of the total posts in the IOFS cadre are operational and the remaining 16 per cent posts are for staff assignments.

The Indian Postal Service manages the vast domestic and international postal and mails network, money transfer and certain agency functions, banking transactions, life insurance, postal operations and administration. The Postal Services Board, the apex postal body, comprises a chairman and three members, assisted by the Member (Finance) of the Telecom Commission. The Secretary (Posts) is the chairman of the Board and also the Director General of Postal Operations. The Indian Posts & Telegraph Accounts and Finance Service has been assigned the task of providing financial advice and financial management to the Departments of Posts and Telecommunications.

The Indian Railways Accounts Service plays a pivotal role in the arena of financial management and management accounting network of the Indian Railways. The Indian Railways Personnel Service is a unique service in the sense that it is the only service amongst the higher civil services catering exclusively to personnel management discipline in the government. The Indian Railways Traffic Service (IRTS) is responsible for management of transport services, business development and generation/collection of revenues in the Indian Railways. The Indian Revenue Service manages the administration of direct taxes in the country. It is responsible for administering a wide gamut of fiscal laws like the Income Tax Act, Wealth Tax Act, Gift Tax Act, Interest Tax Act, Expenditure Tax Act, etc. Their immediate objective is to collect direct taxes and to detect and deter evasion.

The Central Board of Direct Taxes is the apex body dealing with matters pertaining to direct taxes. It comprises of a chairman and five other members.

The Indian Statistical Service was constituted by encadring statistical function posts in different ministries/departments of the Government of India. Since 1984, the Department of Statistics, advised by the ISS Board, has been functioning as the cadre controlling authority. Prior to this, cadre control functions rested with the Department of Personnel and Training. There has been no cadre review since the inception of the service in 1961, which is a shocking failure. The Indian Trade Service (formerly Central Trade Service) was created to cater to the requirements of a specialized cadre of officers to man the Import-Export Trade Control Organization. In tune with the economic liberalization of the Indian economy, the Imports and Exports (Control) Act, 1947 was repealed and substituted by the Foreign Trade (Development and Regulation) Act, 1992.

One of the central services, namely the Central Secretariat Services, is discussed below:

THE CENTRAL SECRETARIAT SERVICE

The Imperial Secretariat Service was renamed the Central Secretariat Service when this Service was established in 1948. The cadre of assistant secretary was abolished, and existing personnel in this cadre were included in the grade of under secretary. Originally, the service had the following four grades:

Grade I	Under Secretary	Class I
Grade II	Section Officer	Class I
Grade III	Section Officer	Class II-non-gazetted
Grade IV	Assistant	Class II-non-gazetted

The grade I and the selection grade of the CSS are in class I and the rest of the grades in class II. Officers in these grades of the CSS are employed in the Secretariat as well as in the attached and subordinate offices. But the Railway Ministry has its own Secretariat Service. The Central Secretariat Service is designed as a support service in the government and fulfils its 'memory' function. Grade III was created primarily as a kind of training post for direct recruits. 'The idea originally was that there would be an equal number of posts in the two grades of section officer—those in the lower grade would be in charge of smaller and less important sections. Further, for direct recruits the new grade was to be a training grade.'[2] But the scheme did not operate in the intended manner, and there was free interchange of positions among the section officers of the two grades. 'In the circumstances, and also, in the interest of improved recruitment', wrote the Second Pay Commission, 'we recommend the amalgamation of the two grades.'[3] The government accepted this recommendation, and merged the two grades into a continuous class II grade. There is also the addition of a new grade called the selection grade comprising deputy secretaries and above. Fifty-five posts of deputy secretaries in the Secretariat were reserved for Central Secretariat Service personnel.

More recently, members of the Central Secretariat Service have begun to be appointed as directors and joint secretaries and their number is also increasing. Thirty-two deputy secretaries in the Central Secretariat Service have been included in the select list for the post of joint secretaries. Above the level of joint secretary, personnel of the Central Secretariat Service have not yet made their impact felt in any significant number.

The present organization of the Central Secretariat Service is as follows:

1. Selection Grade (Joint Secretary,

    Director,

    Deputy Secretary)
2. Grade I (Under Secretary or equivalent)
3. Section officer
4. Assistant's Grade

Appointed to the selection grade is made by promotion on the basis of merit of permanent officers of grade I having five years service in the grade. For the purpose of promotion, a select list of officers of grade I is prepared. Similarly, appointment to grade I is made by promotion on the basis of merit of permanent officers of the section officers' grade having at least 10 years' service in that grade. In this case too, a select list of section officers is prepared. Appointment to the section officers' grade is made partly by direct recruitment and partly by promotion. Normally one-third of the vacancies are filed through direct recruitment, the remaining by promoting assistants with eight years' minimum service, and by holding annually a limited departmental competitive examination. Assistants are appointed through direct recruitment and partly through promotion, the ratio being 3:1.

A significant development since 1962 has been the decentralization of the Central Secretariat Service 'in the interest of better personnel management and better utilization of the training received in each ministry.'[4] The Ministry of Personnel is the controlling authority for selection grade and grade I but control over personnel up to and including section officer has passed into the hands of the administrative ministries. The decentralization has, however, raised the following problems:

1. It has led to atomization of the Central Secretariat Service, preventing personnel from acquiring a wider experience of the various activities of the Government. This breeds too narrow- and confining-specialism.

2. After decentralization, no single agency is, as a matter of course, responsible for collecting, keeping and processing vital service statistics in regard to the various decentralized services. 'The (Estimates) Committee feels that without a regular and systematic study of these statistics, it would hardly be possible to keep a centralized watch over the growth of

individual cadres or take effective steps to correct imbalances in promotion prospects of the decentralization categories of staff in different cadres.'[5]

3. Some ministries are more expansion-oriented than others. Promotion prospects in different ministries are thus bound to be uneven.

4. Allocation of staff to the decentralized cadres is being disturbed because of the frequent reorganization of ministries/departments in the Government of India.

NOTES

1. This is not the distinguishing feature of the central services, however. Even all-India services like the Indian Police Service and the Indian Forest Service are unifunctional. The Indian Administrative Service, on the other hand, is the multifunctional service cutting across union and state boundaries serving both central government and the state government. The Indian Administrative Service serves the various ministries and departments of central and state governments and is designed to man positions of a general administrative nature at different levels of government.

2. *Report of the Commission of Enquiry on Emoluments and Conditions of Service of Central Government Employees, 1957–59*, New Delhi: Ministry of Finance, 1959, p. 113.

3. Ibid.

4. *Ninety-third Report of the Estimates Committee*, New Delhi: Lok Sabha Secretariat, April 1966, pp. 68–9.

5. Ibid.

CHAPTER 12

The Specialists in the Higher Civil Service

The civil service in India is a generalist one, a generalist being defined as 'a person with a broad general knowledge and skill in several disciplines, fields or areas'.[1] This character was imparted by the British colonial rulers, as their own civil service in their homeland was a generalist one. The Northcote-Trevelyan Report of 1854 imparted to the home civil service the generalist stamp. The civil service in India was given the generalist character by the famous Macaulay Report on Indian Civil Service, 1853. The report said:

We believe that men who have been engaged, up to one or two and twenty, in studies which have no immediate connections with the business of any profession, and of which the effect is merely to open, to invigorate, and to enrich the mind, will generally be found, in the business of every profession, superior to men who have, at 18 or 19, devoted themselves to special studies of their calling. The most illustrious English jurists have been men who have never opened a law book till after the close of a distinguished academic career; nor is there any reason to believe that they would have been greater lawyers if they had passed in drawing pleas and conveyances the time which they gave to Thucydides, to Cicero, and Newton. The duties of a civil servant of the East India Company are of so high a nature that in his case it is peculiarly desirable that an excellent general education, such as may enlarge and strengthen his understanding, should precede the special education, which must qualify him to dispatch the business of his cutchery.[2]

The generalist is thus said to be an all-rounder, sometimes also dubbed as 'jack of all trades but master of none.' Many generalist administrators claim that they are no less specialist— they have specialized in administration, this person is defined as one engaged in planning, organizing, staffing, directing, coordinating, reporting, and budgeting (Posdcorb). In other words, the administrators are specialists in administration—they engage themselves in carrying out all.these processes, their successful execution resulting in the fulfillment of the governmental goal. The Indian Civil Service was a leadership service in the entire area of public administration. Its members even used to occupy specialist posts like director of agriculture, inspector general of police and post master-general. They even manned the higher judiciary. The early days of the British Raj indeed constituted the golden age of the generalist administrators in India. But the generalist predominance in administration could not remain unchallenged for long. The events following the Government of India Act, 1919 for the first time questioned the supremacy of the generalists in administration. Under the Government of India Act of 1919, nation-building activities were transferred to popularly elected ministers. The budget of this sector of administration increased under popular control as a result of which more and more specialists began to be recruited. As was to be expected, they showed more independence of outlook and did not take kindly to the customary overlordship of the generalist district collector. Also, the popularly elected minister exerted direct control over his district-level functionaries and was unwilling to allow them to work under the undisputed hegemonic control of the district collector. In other words, both departmentalism and specialism undermined the authority of the district collector. The process of ascendancy of the specialist persisted in years to come.

Independent India inherited the legacy of the generalist credo, now symbolized by the Indian Administrative Service, the successor-service to the Indian Civil Service. More and more specialists began to be recruited in public administration under the country's firm developmental commitments. The country's ethos had also changed, the brightest students were getting attracted to science, engineering, technology, medicine and such professional fields and those with less exalted qualifications were joining humanities and social sciences courses. The increased induction of the specialists in administration brought to the fore the problem of the generalist-specialist relationship in the civil service. The vexed question was examined by the Second Central Pay Commission, 1959 (Jagannadha Das) which observed:

Where the work of a department is mainly technical, it is desirable, in our view, that the Secretary should be a person who, while possessing administrative ability and capable of taking abroad government-wide view of matters, has a technical background in the particular field. In a department which has a considerable amount of technical as well as administrative work, the Secretary may be either a technical officer, with proved administrative capacity, or a generalist administrator; technical officers should not be excluded from the field of choice on *a priori* considerations, but should be considered on merits. Further, the top technical advisers or heads of departments should have full opportunity to have their views considered by the Minister, along with any views which the Secretary of the department may have; for which a suitable arrangement may be a joint discussion with the Minister, whenever there is an unresolved difference of opinion between the technical head and the Secretary .The basic idea governing the relationship between the two must be the recognition that the former should have an affective share in the framing of policies and programmes at the highest official level. We are, however, clearly of the view that the function of head of department and Secretary should not normally be combined—whether the Secretary is a general administrator or a technical or a professional officer.[3]

It was however, left to the Administrative Reforms Commission (1966–70) to examine this problem in a much more comprehensive way and to make is own outline of reform. The Commission's principal recommendation was that the members of the Indian Administrative Service must specialize; a functional field must be carved out for the IAS. This should consist of land revenue administration, exercise of magisterial function and regulatory work in the states in fields other than those looked after by other functional services. All posts in a functional area, whether in the field or in the Secretariat, should be staffed by members of the corresponding functional services. There should be clearly defined schemes for staffing the middle and higher levels in each functional area. Posts of under secretary in the Secretariat and the attached offices should first be classified as falling: (a) within functional, or (b) outside the functional area. These posts should be filled by personnel of the corresponding functional service. The tenure for the post of an under secretary should be three years and for that of deputy secretary four years. Finally, posts at the level of deputy secretary at the central headquarters which do not fall within a particular functional area, should be demarcated into the following eight areas of specialization, selection to them being made from among all class I officers on the basis of a written emanation: (1) economic administration, (2) industrial administration, (3) agricultural and rural administration, (4) social and educational administration, (5) personnel administration, (6) financial administration, (7) defence administration and internal security, and (8) planning. The senior administrative posts in functional areas should be filled by members of the respective functional services but the posts falling outside the functional areas should be filled by personnel who have had experience in one of the eight specializations. Although the ARC made this recommendation in 1969, no action on it has followed.

A durable solution perhaps lies in the split system manning policy-making positions in the headquarters organization of the government—a model of organization designed by France to ensure harmonious relationship between the generalists, and the specialists. In France, the higher civil servants comprise the administrative generalists and the scientific generalists; they are recruited differently and the reason for separate methods in understandable. The pressing requirement for engineers and technicians made France create the Ecole Polytechnic located near Paris—an engineering college set up by Napoleon and placed under the military as early as in 1794, that is, after the French Revolution. The railways were under state control and management for a long time in France, forcing the state to ensure an adequate and regular supply of engineers. In France, the recruitment of scientific and technical including engineering personnel is made by the Ecole Polytechnic. Originally, it was preparing engineering personnel exclusively for the military. The military is not the only employer of the products of this Polytechnic today: its graduates man civilian positions in the government as well as in the private sector. The Ecole Polytechnic thus is the recruitment and initial training agency of scientific generalists in France. The recruitment takes place through a most rigorous written competitive examination in which only the brightest boys and girls can expect to succeed. After passing the secondary school examination (baccalaureate) an aspiring candidate spends two to three years in intensive preparation for admission to the Polytechnic. For this intensive preparation eventually the student generally joins some prestigious lycee (state secondary school). This special preparation normally takes place in the same lycee to ensure the same style of instruction to brighten one's prospects for admission to the Ecole Polytechnic. This polytechnic has nearly 300 seats. The selected candidates have to study in the polytechnic for a period of three years of which the first year is compulsorily spent in military service. The remaining two years are for teaching; and instruction imparted in mathematics, physics, economics, and public administration. At the end of the third year, there is a final examination and the candidates are placed in order of marks obtained. Who would go where is determined according to the total marks obtained. A candidate obtaining the highest marks is the first to opt for the corps, and in this way one goes according to diminishing marks. Generally, there is a pattern in the selection of the category or branch of service. The best ones opt for prestigious corps like the Corps des Mines and Corps des Ponts et Chaussees. There are the *Grands Corps* where they undergo two years' further training. India would be advised to produce specialist administrators out of engineers, medical doctors, scientists, etc.

Specialists joining the government complain against their lower salary positions and exclusion from policy-making areas of government. The generalist service is designed to occupy high-salary positions in the government while most of the specialists spend their life in the lower pay-range, which is detrimental to their morale and motivation. The specialists' contribution as asset-builders of the nation must be duly acknowledged and no valid reason exists for paying them less than the generalists: rather they should be paid more. It would perhaps be short-sightedness to indiscriminately encourage the specialists to migrate on a very large scale to administrative positions in the Secretariat except under the split system discussed earlier. It may perhaps be a more prudent national policy to deploy the admittedly scarce specialist human resources on the urgent tasks for which society has subsidized the specialists education and this should be secured by making these posts attractive in terms of emoluments, advancement and status. The administrative positions in the specialist organizations (for example, executive organizations) must, of course, be filled as a rule from amongst the specialist personnel themselves and the practice, though of course not very regular or widespread, of appointing members of the IAS as heads of executive organizations must be discontinued. Lateral entrants to the civil service are generally scientific, technical, and specialized personnel and this mode of recruitment deserves to be more widely invoked. Mention deserves to be made of another practice. Pandit Jawaharlal Nehru, India's first prime minister made an innovation by appointing a specialist as the Secretary of the newly-established department of atomic energy, and he became the minister-in-charge. Since then, more such scientific departments have been set up in the government. Such departments are invariably headed by headed by Secretaries who are well-known scientists in the field, they being put under the political charge of the prime minister.

The society of the future would be increasingly complex and intricate, leading to the emergence of new and novel specialisions. The specialist thus has come to stay. By the same token, it is ideal to expect that the generalist is to wither away in the future. As society grows more and more complex, the integrating role in relationships is bound to become more and more pressing. This makes the stay of the generalist urgent. It would be more correct to say that society needs both the specialist and the generalist. What is more, the specialist is called upon to generalize and the generalist must specialize. Being a late arrival on the administrative scenario, the specialist is yet groping for a place in the administrative space appropriate to his role and status. Equally appropriate is the sufficient delegation of powers from the Secretariat to the specialist agencies so that specialists do not have to run to the generalists needlessly.

/

NOTES

1. *Reader's Digest Universal Dictionary.*
2. The Report has been reproduced in the *Report of the Committee on the Civil Service* (Lord Fulton), London: H.M.S.O., 1968, pp. 108–18.
3. *Report of Enquiry on Emoluments and Conditions of Service of Central Government Employees*, New Delhi: Ministry of Finance, 1959, p. 111.

CHAPTER 13

In-service Training

Training of civil servants has assumed special significance in all countries and India is no exception. Recruitment is a general process while training is more subject-specific. With the expanding machinery of government necessitating the constitution of new services and the change in the nature of governmental work in the wake of independence, it has become imperative for the government to plan suitable training and educational courses in public administration. It is well to recall the following observation of the Planning Commission in this respect: 'Next to recruitment, the training of personnel has considerable bearing on administrative efficiency. Each type of work in the government requires a programme of training suited to it. In general, in all branches of administration, it is necessary to provide for the training of personnel at the commencement of service as well as at appropriate intervals. In this connection, we would emphasize the importance of careful grounding in revenue and development administration for recruits to the Indian Administrative Service and the state administrative services.'[1] Training for civil servants in India must be attuned to the following goals in addition to making its recipients functionally competent and efficient.

(1) Training must inculcate in the recruits respect for the traditions of parliamentary democracy which India has adopted. This point needs emphasis in view of the authoritarian basis of the Indian administration in the colonial past. A seasoned administrator has rightly pointed out: 'For a country like India, with a tradition of thousands of years of authoritative paternal administration, the transition to Parliamentary Democracy has evolved a revolutionary change in the physiology of the body politic. It calls for a radical adjustment of attitude on the parts of its operative

organs, namely, the higher administrative personnel.[2] To recall the relevant part of the German Civil Service Act 1953, 'By the entire conduct the civil servant must profess his attachment to the free democratic order in the sense of the Basic Law and exert himself for its preservation.'

(2) India's destiny is linked with the successful implementation of the successive Five Year Plans. It should be an important aim of training to make the employees 'programme-oriented'. It must inculcate knowledge of managerial skills

(3) Training should aim at fostering an essentially national outlook, combating, in the process, the feelings of regionalism, communalism, casteism, etc. It should foster emotional integration with the people. This point is of enormous importance in view of the wide gulf between the 'governors' and the 'governed'.

(4) As civil services are mostly manned by urban people, having little knowledge and appreciation of rural life and problems, training programmes should take special note of this factor, so that the employees may not ignore the realities of the situation in rural areas. Training must provide a rural bias to the employees.

The British thinking on public administration largely conditioned the Indian approach to the problem of training of civil servants. This approach has been to make the young official learn the job by doing it under the supervision of a superior officer. This approach did not look apparently deficient, as the functions of the government were limited to the maintenance of law and order, and the collection of revenue. This view, however, looked dated and untenable when the Indian administration was, after 1947, attuned to newer goals and objectives, and rapid expansion of governmental activities followed. Training of civil servants, is, thus, essentially a post-independence phenomenon. Not only is it receiving greater attention but attempts are also being made to make it broad-based and wide-ranging. The Planning Commission recognized its need when it recommended the conversion of the IAS Training School into a sort of staff college for a combined training of officers of different services. The commission also proposed the appointment of a director of training charged with the responsibility of 'organizing systematic training programmes and refresher courses for different grades of employees in the Government.' The observations of A.K. Chanda, commissioned to look into the question, are noteworthy:

The best training in any service is provided by the actual doing of the jobs for which the services exist. Much time and wastage can, however, be saved by providing a certain amount of basic training to shorten and facilitate the process of learning by doing. Such basic training has to be both 'general' (i.e., applicable to all higher public servants), and 'special' (i.e., relevant to the needs of particular services). The 'general' part comprises the basic knowledge, which all higher public servants should possess, e.g., the main principles of the Constitution, the role of public servants in a Parliamentary Democracy, the organization of the machinery of Government at the Centre and the States, the principles of public Administration and personnel management and the techniques of public relations. It should also include a knowledge of Economics in general and Indian Economics in particular, and an appreciation of India's social and economic problems.

The 'special' part of the basic training would cover studying the Acts and Rules relating to the particluar service, departmental procedures, etc. The course of training in the I. A. S. Training School covers both the general and the special parts of the basic training needed by the I. A. S. officers. Arrangements for training of the Audit Service officers, Income Tax, Railways, etc., have been made by the Ministries concerned, but these are confined largely to the 'special' part of the training. It would be of great advantage if, each year, the recruits of the higher services are brought together in some Central Government institution for about six months to receive the 'general' part of the training. This will also enable officers coming from different parts of India to benefit by close contact with each other and lead to elimination of service consciousness. It may also help in reallotting the few officers, who, by temperamental or other reasons, prove unsuitable for the service to which they were originally assigned.

The Home Ministry agreed with Chanda's suggestion regarding the 'general training' that should be given to the members of specialized services, and, early in 1956, it addressed all the state governments suggesting refresher courses to officers of all-India services and central services (Class 1), invited them to participate in the proposed scheme and discussion of the subject proposed for inclusion in the syllabus for the refresher course. A beginning in this direction was made in 1957 by starting a refresher course at the IAS Staff College, Shimla for IAS officers with a service of 6 to 10 years. Later, in a statement in the Lok Sabha on 15 April 1958, the Home Minister announced the government's decision to set up 'a national academy of training so that the services, wherever they may function, whether as administrative officers, or as accountants, or as revenue officers, might imbibe the true spirit and discharge their duties in a manner which will raise their efficiency and establish concord between them and the public completely.' The various ministries were then invited to participate in the scheme to set up an academy for the training of officers of the various services. The ministries agreed in principle, and from July 1959, commenced a combined course at IAS Training School, Delhi (Metcalfe House), with the following categories of officers:

(i)   Indian Administrative Service,
(ii)   Indian Foreign Service,
(iii)   Indian Audit and Accounts Service,

(iv)   Indian Defence Accounts Service,
(v)   Indian Postal Service,
(vi)   Indian Income Tax Service, and
(vii)   Indian Customs and Excise Service.

Immediately after the commencement of the foundation course, the Ministry of Home Affairs decided to amalgamate the two sister institutions, IAS Training School, Delhi, and IAS Staff College, Shimla, and start a national academy of administration—now (since 1972) called the Lal Bahadur Shastri National Academy of Administration—at Mussoorie. The Academy started functioning at Mussoorie from 1 September 1959. The first foundation course ended in November 1959. On the basis of experience gained during this course it was suggested to the Ministry of Home Affairs that future courses should (i) begin at the same time for all services; (ii) last for five months; and (iii) include recruits to the Indian police service also who could not join the first course. All these suggestions were accepted by the Ministry of Home Affairs. Each organized service has today its own training institution to impart training to the new recruits. Recruits to the all-India and central services are given a five months' foundation course at the Lal Bahadur Shastri National Academy of Administration, Mussoorie, and then they go to the training institutions for their respective services. 'The idea underlying the (foundation) course is that officers of the higher services should acquire an understanding of the constitutional, economic, and social framework within which they have to function as these largely determine the policies and programmes towards the framing and execution of which they will have to make their contribution. They should, further, acquaint themselves with the machinery of the government and the broad principles of public administration .... The foundation course is also intended to cover such matters as aims and obligations of the civil service, and the ethics of the profession-objectivity, integrity, thoroughness, impartiality, etc.'[3] Foundation courses also develop among recruits to different services a feeling of belonging to a common civil service and a broadly common outlook. After completing this five months' foundation course, the probationers of the services other than the IAS, leave for their respective training institutions for institutional training, but the IAS probationers stay on at the Academy to undergo a further course of institutional training. From 1969, the Government has introduced a new pattern of training called the 'sandwich course' for the Indian Administrative Service. New entrants to the IAS undergo two spells of training at the Academy with an interval of about a year which is utilized for the foundation course. After completion of the foundation course and spell of institutional training, the probationer, as he is called, is sent to the state (to which he has been allotted) for practical training. During 'district training', the probationers spend some time at the state training institute, and thus acquire knowledge of the various aspects of life in the state of their destiny. They learn the language of the state. They are attached to districts where they obtain knowledge of various areas and levels of administration. They undertake socio-economic surveys of villages and this exposure is particularly emphasized as they would be spending the initial period of their career in rural areas. During the period of district training, probationers remain in touch with the Academy as they have to report regularly to a faculty member. At the end of this training, the probationer comes to the Academy for a second and concluding spell of training, where emphasis is placed on the discussion of live administrative problems the probationer has either encountered or observed in the state. This part of the training is thus more problem-oriented. At the end, the probationers appear at an examination conducted by the Academy on behalf of the Union Public Service Commission and final ranking in the service is determined on the basis of the grand total of marks obtained.

The Academy may also organize short courses, seminars, conferences, etc., for the benefit of more senior officers— ordinarily those having about 15 years of service. The course may deal with the higher problems of government or with special subjects, for instance, social security, fiscal policy, planning interdepartmental coordination, etc. Both subject as well as administrative officers might be invited to this course.

The Academy offers three types of courses as mentioned below:

(1) A one-year course for IAS officers to cover the syllabus prescribed under the All-India Services Probationers Final Examinations.

(2) A six-week refresher course for officers of the seniority of 10 to 15 years. To start with, it is proposed to run this course for IAS officers and, in due course, to throw it open for senior officers of the other services also.

(3) A combined course of five months for the all-India services and the central services, class I, for training in foundational subjects.

The purport of these courses is to widen the outlook of the trainees. The course is general in nature, and imparts general education in liberal arts to personnel recruited for posts of a specialized nature. This fills a big gap which previously existed and is a step in right direction.

The Lal Bahadur Shastri National Academy of Administration continues to be located at Mussoorie although some time ago the Government of India decided to shift it to Delhi. When the Academy was about to be taken shifted, the Government cancelled its earlier decision and resolved to keep it at Mussoorie—much to the chagrin of the civil servants. As there has always been considerable bureaucratic pressure in favour of bringing the Academy to Delhi, comments about its location seem necessary. Delhi is already a crowded metropolis and the governmental policy, in this context, should be to disperse its establishments situated in Delhi to other places, certainly not to lure them from outside.

There are higher reasons which point to the need for locating the Academy away from Delhi. In the first place, a stay of the new entrants to civil services in Delhi is apt to involve them in the not wholesome part of the life and activities in the Central Secretariat, exposing them to the existing factions and lobbies in the administration, and tempting them to evince interest in matters of postings, transfers, etc. All this is bound to have an adverse impact on their impressionable minds. Most importantly, imparting training to members of the all-India services at the seat of the central government is psychologically unfair and unwise. The all-India services are basically designed for the states. An initial stay of the new entrants at Delhi is apt to induce in them a feeling of being the employees of the central government, thus causing grave perceptual distortions. The training of the new recruits in Delhi, and not in the states is, thus, undesirable as well as improper.

TRAINING FOR INDIAN POLICE SERVICE (IPS)

Entrants to the IPS are trained at the Sardar Patel National Police Academy which was earlier located at Mount Abu (Rajasthan), but was shifted to Hyderabad during the internal emergency (25 June 1975–21 March 1977). The subjects of study and the training in drill, handling of weapons, etc., have a direct bearing on the normal work of a police officer. The syllabus of training includes studies of crime psychology, scientific aids in detection of crime, methods of combating corruption and fire and emergency relief. After completing a year's training, the probationer passes an examination conducted by the UPSC. He is, then, appointed as an assistant superintendent of police. But, before this appointment he has to undergo a year's programme of training; he is given practical training by requiring him to do the work of various subordinate officers under guidance. It is only after this that he is appointed an assistant superintendent of police. Institutional training is offered to all the members of organized services. It is natural that the content of training, quality of instruction, training methodology etc. differs from training institution to training institution.

INDIAN FOREIGN SERVICE

The Indian Foreign Service has an annual intake of 16 members. Its members receive their functional training at the Indian Foreign Service Institute at New Delhi. Since 2003, probationers attend a six-week course at the Indian Institute of Management, Bangalore, which among others provides for corporate attachment for the newly recruited members of the IFS. Since the nineties, economic diplomacy is of growing in importance to India foreign policy making it is necessary for its newly recruited members to spend time with corporate houses before they go for a foreign posting. The probationers are sent for a three-four week attachment to selected corporate houses for hands-on experience of corporate and business issues. This deputation is preceded by a six-week training course at IIM, Banglore where they are taught about trade disputes, economic negotiations, and deal with issues like attracting foreign investment, organizing trade fairs and marketing Indian companies abroad. The attachment it is expected, will bridge the gap between the thinking of Indian diplomats and corporate houses.

India is steadily becoming training-conscious. Institutional training programmes are expanding in number, scope and nature. Training institutions are established at the state level. Greater emphasis is being laid on refresher and orientation courses. Seminars, workshops, conferences, etc., are becoming increasingly popular. What is more, retraining of civil servants is likely to become an area of increasing significance in the foreseeable future. Study leave is now more liberally granted, particularly to scientific, technical, and administrative staff, and in suitable cases the staff should even be encouraged or advised to take such leave. The purposes for which study leave may be granted may also include studies which may not be closely and directly linked with a government servant's work, but which are capable of widening his knowledge in a manner likely to improve his abilities as a civil servant and equip him to collaborate better with those employed in other branches of the civil service. Study leave may also be granted for a course of learning or study tour in which a government servant may not attend a regular academic or semi-academic course, if the course of training or study tour is certified to be of definite advantage to the government from the point of view of public interest, and is related to the sphere of duties of the government servant. Study leave may also be granted for purposes of studies connected with the framework or background of public administration. All this is calculated to make the civil servant diversify his experience and broaden his vision. Every civil servant is likely to run into a groove, rust, and lose the capacity to expand his vision unless he makes deliberate efforts to keep alert and familiar with developments in his professional field. Even on the job, one must find time to study, bring to it the best current thinking on the subject. But on the job, howsoever much he might try, he is likely to be overwhelmed by the pressure of urgent routine business. An opportunity to look at oneself while away from the daily routine and one's usual surroundings is, therefore, valuable. Indeed, it is suggested here that civil servants should be attached in mid-career to universities/institutes for higher study while on study leave. They will be away from work and yet not divorced from thinking about it.

Yet the training programmes that are being organized for civil servants are not without many weaknesses. Although the number and variety of training courses have been on the increase, the government does not appear as yet to take training with sufficient professionalism. The individuals sent to the training courses are not always selected very carefully; often only the 'sparable' are spared by the government. Secondly, the content of training courses is not always relevant and meaningful to the tasks being performed or likely to be performed by civil servants and the challenges encountered. Thirdly, training has not yet become linked with other processes of personnel administration, with the result that inconsiderable amount of effort is wasted in this area. Indeed, if one were to see the amount of unrealism obtaining in the government, one has only to examine the relationship (or, the absence of it) between training and placement of civil servants! Efficiency in administration demands that training must be viewed as part of the career planning of civil servants. The Fifth Central Pay Commission has rightly observed: 'There has to be a direct relationship between the career plan of an employee and the training imparted to him. Although the present performance appraisal form has a column for training undergone and future training needs, not much importance is attached to it.' Presently, training is being treated as an isolate; it has not been integrated with other processes of personnel administration. No less worrying is the problem relating to the ready availability of sufficient training literature based on Indian setting and experiences.

Institutional training of civil servants has existed since the dawn of independence. But it received tremendous impetus since the mid-eighties. Since then, institutional training has come to cover all levels in the administrative hierarchy. Rajiv Gandhi even made institutional training for the top-level secretaries obligatory. Today, therefore one sees impressive expansion of training activities in public administration. However,

many training efforts are neither well-led nor well-fed. A general defi-
ciency of relevant, indigenous teaching material marks many such efforts.
Nor is the teaching faculty well qualified or inclined to impart training
seriously. Participants in training courses suffer from low motivation and
see training as an opportunity to wrest a measure of relaxation in their
otherwise busy official life. But perhaps the most serious limitation of
training is its lack of integration with other processes of personnel administration. The post-training posting is not related to the area in which the
officer received his training. The latter is viewed as a futile exercise not
immediately relevant to postings and promotions, the result thus being a
lot of wasted effort. Finally, training of civil servants in a basically colonial
administration inevitably cries for administrative reform but in practice
reform of the existing administration is a non-event in India. Therefore,
civil servants return to the same administration which was the subject of
criticism in training. In short, training ought to be viewed as an essential
component of administration, which view is singularly missing in the
present-day public administration.

NOTES

1. *Planning Commission, Administration and Public Cooperation*, Delhi: Manager
of Publications, 1954, p. 121.

2. Bapat, S.B. 'Training of the Indian Administrative Services,' *Indian Journal of
Public Administration*, Vol. I, No. 2, April–June 1955, p. 123.

3. *Report on Indian and State Administrative Services and Problems of District
Administration* (Chairman: V.T. Krishnamachari), New Delhi: Planning Commission, 1962, p. 14.

CHAPTER 14

Promotion

An employee joins a service in the hope of a satisfactory career of progression. An important factor contributing to the attractiveness of service is the prospect of promotion. The dictionary meaning of promotion is 'the action of raising to higher position or rank or the fact being so raised'. Promotion entails a higher level of responsibility and is accompanied by a higher compensation plan. To recap, the civil service in India falls into four classes—class I, class II, class III, and class IV—corresponding to differences in the responsibility of the work performed and the qualifications required. The Third Pay Commission (1970–3) changed these terms to group A, group B, group C, and group D, but the basic underlying concept remained the same. The highest category of functionaries are placed in group A, which includes the all-India services and higher central services. Group B comprises functionaries who are engaged in jobs of first line supervisors. Group C includes clerical personnel in the government, while group D comprises messengers, peons, car drivers, cleaners etc. Each service contains both the elements—direct recruitment and promotion—though the proportion of each mode differs from service to service. The Indian Administrative Service is directly recruited but a percentage of the vacancies is filled through promotion from the state civil service. Indeed, the general rule in each all-India service is that it is linked with a corresponding state level service which then acts as the feeder to it. Thus, a certain percentage of members of the state level police service is annually promoted in the Indian Police Service. Generally, promotion to the extent of 25 to 33 ½ per cent of the posts or vacancies in a year is a normal practice. This acts as incentive to the lower services. The Indian Civil Service of the colonial era had no feeder service linked to it: at the most the members of the provincial civil service (PCS) could be appointed to 'Listed Posts' but could not write after their name the coveted designation of 'ICS'.

As India observes the 'rank-in-man' method of job classification, a civil servant joins a service, swimming with his service all his life. He starts his career at the bottom level and moves upward with the passage of time. His career and promotional prospects are determined by the rules, regulations, and operating practices governing his service career at the bottom level and moves upward with the passage of time. The grades available to him for upward mobility are the following in ascending order: under secretary, deputy secretary, director, joint secretary, additional secretary and secretary.

In class II, the proportion of direct recruitment is less and more posts are filled through promotion. Broadly, nearly 65 per cent of the posts in class II, are filled by class III personnel. Generally speaking, direct recruitment in class II is confined to the scientific, medical, and engineering personnel. Class III assumes a different level of importance in the civil service in the sense that class II staff is small in size while class III runs into lakhs, which adds to the significance of promotion in the members' life. In contrast, there is very little provision of promotion made from class IV to class III. Indeed, in departments other than the Railways and Posts and Telegraphs no provision for promotion from class III exists.

One would see from the foregoing discussion the promotional opportunities in the civil service are rather restrictive. Large disparities are thus presently observed in career prospects not only in different classes but also within the same class. The position varies from department to department and level to level. The Third Pay Commission found them patently inadequate and sought to ensure atleast two promotions in one's career. Promotional opportunities to those holding isolated posts (India has not totally abandoned the 'rank-in-the-post' method of job classification) are nearly non-existent: the incumbents of these posts generally retire in the same post to which they were appointed. The nature of duties assigned to such isolated posts are very often similar to those of a cadre post. It is good if such isolated posts in government are not created as a rule. Posts created should always be a part of some organized cadre. What is more where creation of isolated posts is indispensable, two higher scales must be give to their holders in a time-bound manner. As the Fifth Central Pay Commission recommended: 'The dynamic assured career progression scheme shall apply to isolated posts.'[1]

One may thus see that promotion is also a method of filling positions in the civil service. This leads us to the question of the principles of promotion.

These are (i) seniority, (ii) merit, and (iii) a mixture of the two such as merit-cum-seniority or seniority-cum-merit. The principle of seniority determines promotion at the lower levels while merit is emphasized at the higher and middle levels of administration. Although formal rules prescribe for the removal of the unfit, so long as one does not commit glaring wrongs, one continues to survive in the civil service. Whatever be the formal claim, the principle of seniority governs promotion in the civil service at least upto the level of joint secretaries in the government. All members of the Indian Administrative Service sail smoothly up to this level without any special effort. The administrative pyramid, however, narrows down considerably as one moves above this level and the element of competitiveness becomes quite marked. Indeed, many heads inevitably fall while others march ahead and move to the next level of additional secretary. Competition becomes even more severe in the onward march from additional secretaryship to secretaryship.

Merit is the basis of initial recruitment in the civil service though nearly half of the posts are today filled through the reservation system. Once recruited, a tendency is seen in the civil service to grow lax as promotion becomes automatic. No surprise that an inconsiderable amount of deadwood has accumulated in the civil service , which needs to be weeded out. Provisions relating to the weeding out of these inefficient elements have been made in the civil service in the form of the voluntary retirement scheme (VRS) and compulsory retirement, but the problem has not been overcome. In 2002, the Supreme Court of India held the Government's right to compulsorily retire a public servant if his conduct becomes untenable to public interest or obstructs the efficiency of public service. The Supreme Court emphasized that 'it cannot be disputed that the deadwood needs to be removed to maintain efficiency in the service'.

The established mechanism to identify merit and fitness in the civil service is performance appraisal or the annual confidential report (ACR), as it is more popularly known. Even where the principle of seniority governs promotion, performance appraisal is necessary as it is the proven tool of control by management. The principle of seniority must not be blindly viewed as a culprit and a sinner in the civil service, more so when the basis of initial recruitment itself is merit, thus making seniority a 'merit plus' concept. Reckless projection of the principle of merit in this context runs the risk of entailing suffering and humiliation resulting from supercessions. Merit is presently discerned through the annual confidential character roles; the latter, therefore, must be completely free from biases and prejudices. This demands utmost care in the designing and writing of annual confidential reports. Many measures have been taken to make them fool-proof and reliable. The introduction of the self-appraisal system since the seventies is a check on subjectivity. The format of the annual character rolls is split into smaller items, the detailed enumeration itself being conducive to impartiality in evaluation. The ACR is written by the immediate boss (the reporting officer), it is commented upon by the grand father—the reviewing officer—and the endorsing officer. Involvement of a number of functionaries in the task of character assessment is designed to contribute to fair play and objectivity. The provisions for showing the character roll to the reported officer (only adverse remarks are presently shown) as well as of representation to the higher hierarchy in case of wrong doing are additional checks on subjectivity. An aggrieved officer enjoys access to the Central Administrative Tribunal and to the regular judiciary, which further safeguards fair play and objectivity.

Despite all such measures, the performance appraisal system has not yet become fool-proof and reliable. So long as one human being evaluates another human being, an element of subjectivity is inevitable. The fact that adverse remarks get communicated to the 'reported' official, makes the 'boss' timid in his comments. Even otherwise, at present, most reports tend to be too vague, cryptic, and non-committed to reveal the true personality-profile of the reported employee. For performance assessment, the bureaucracy will have to spend more time and attention to the job of performance evaluation. It is imperative for a truly meaningful performance appraisal by objective to introduce in the civil service the wholesome features of management by objectives and evaluate a functionary on the basis of his pre-serialized tastes. Equally, the functionary must stay in his job for a minimum period in order to show results. In other words, the transfer practices in the civil service have to be rationalized.

One criticism of the present day annual confidential reports is their general colourlessness. This is in contrast to the practice during the British rule. A complete personality profile of the civil servant could be made out from the reports during the Raj. A few excerpts from that past are given below to enlighten a reader.

A very good officer in every way and easily the best all-round census superintendent. A cool head, sound judgment and general imperturbability added to intellectual qualities above the average produce an excellent amalgam. He had much the most difficult job of any superintendent. Quite apart from the size of the province, he had to cope with the extreme difficulties caused by communal tension and the astonishing activities of persons in public position. Although no pusher of himself personally, he is an officer of strong character and in my opinion of outstanding ability. Mr. Dutch spent some time in hospital and was one of the four if not five officers who contracted, as I did myself in the 1931 Census, amoebic dysentery as a consequence of incessant and frequently rough touring.[2] And the somewhat more colourful:

- This officer has talents but has kept them well hidden.
- Can express a sentence in two paragraphs at any time.
- A thorough gentleman. That is all I can say about him.
- He is very much under the thumb of his wife who goes throwing her weight about.
- He has a towering personality but is a dwarf in his work.
- He is neither clear about the ends and is even more unsure about the means.
- It is idle to expect a person to run when he cannot walk.
- Is given to experiments with truth.
- In the absence of a higher grading, I rank him as outstanding.
- It is a sad thing that we are losing this officer. However, all I can say is, our loss is their loss.
- Maintains good relations unilaterally.
- But that God gave him powers to see himself as others see him.
- He is a social climber and his wife is a very good mixer.

SURENDRA NATH COMMITTEE ON BUREAUCRACY

In 2003, the Government of India appointed a committee on bureaucracy under the chairmanship of Lt Gen. Surendra Nath, its other members being one retired and two serving civil servants and one IIT academic. The major recommendations of the Surendra Nath committee reporting in July 2003 were the following:

1. Presently five-point grading system (outstanding, very good, good, average, poor) for the civil service should be replaced by a ten-point numerical system, the aim being to bring about greater efficiency and objectivity in the performance evaluation system.

2. Promotion should not be based in pre-determined bench mark level of performance or seniority but must be competitive and allow for supersession.

3. Empanelment for joint secretary-level posts and above in the central government should be based strictly on the merit system with equal weightage to performance and preparation for policy formulation.

4. The committee felt the imperative of specialization in the civil service and to this end recommended that the officials may be streamed into three out of 11 domains of specialization it worked out to harmonize the concept of generalist civil servant with the imperative of specialization.

5. At the age of 50 or on completion of service of 20 years of service, 'dead wood' in the civil service—reference being to non-performing, corrupt or seriously ill officers—would be identified and told to voluntary

retire. If they do not agree to voluntarily retire, their performance would be reviewed after five years at the cabinet secretary level and those who do not show an improvement in the grace period, should be compulsorily retired.

The main thrust of the Surendra Nath committee is on competitiveness and supersession in the civil service and allows a functionary a say in his/her posting.

A welcoming feature of the committee on bureaucracy chaired by Lt Gen. Surendra Nath is that it addresses itself to the challenge of performance, which is the need of the hour. India, unfortunately, is saddled with a non-performing bureaucracy, and its persistent obstinacy has defined most efforts to stir it to action. A hallmark of the Indian administration, the supremacy of the generalist, must undergo modifications. The committee has recognized its need and recommended that civil servants should pick three areas of specialization and their postings and transfers should only be in these three areas.

Most officers join the civil service in their mid to late 20s. It must not take two-decades plus in any job to identify no hopers. A critical review of performance should preferably be undertaken at the end of the first decade in service, why to wait till an officer reaches 50 before declaring him 'deadwood'? It is, of course, assumed that seniors should be doing honest gradings. This demands a definite change in the bureaucratic attitude, for at present 9 out of 10 annual confidential reports presently grade bureaucrats as outstanding! If senior officers do not change their attitude, nothing significant can be affected.

NOTES

1. *Report of the Fifth Central Pay Commission*, 1997, p. 199.
2. Government of India. Home Department, F-45/26/41.

CHAPTER 15

Salary Fixation of the Higher Civil Service

A modern government necessarily employs a large number of people who possess different educational qualifications and carry different levels of responsibility. Salary fixation of these employees becomes an important concern of the State. Not only is the wage bill to be kept under reasonable control: it should also faithfully reflect differing levels of responsibility and authority. The salary bill of public employees requires careful and cautious management.

Salary fixation is the responsibility of Pay Commissions in India, which the government sets up from time to time although they have been established only after Independence. During the British period, the basic structure of salaries conformed to the principle recommended by the Royal Commission on the Public Services in India (1912–15), presided over by Lord Islington. The Islington principle of salary fixation was as follows.

The only safe criterion is that Government should pay so much and so much only to their employees as is necessary to obtain recruits of the right stamp, and to maintain them in such a degree of comfort and dignity as will shield them from temptation and keep them efficient for the term of their service. Whilst, therefore, we have noted the rise in prices which has taken place, we have not based on this any general recommendation. Where we have advised changes of salary it has been to meet inequalities of remuneration prejudicial to efficiency, to fulfil expectations reasonably founded on formal announcements made by Government, and to improve recruitment, where the existing terms have been shown to be insufficient to obtain a satisfactory personnel.

The Royal Commission on the Superior Civil Services in India (1923–4), commonly known as the Lee Commission after the name of its chairman, expressed full agreement with this principle. The First Central Pay Commission—the Varadachariar Commission—endorsed the Islington formula, asserting that 'the test formulated by the Islington Commission has only to be liberally interpreted to suit the conditions of the present day and to be qualified by the condition that in no case should a man's pay be less than a living wage'. Until 1947, the Islington and Lee Commission Reports formed the cornerstone of pay policy in British India. The question of motivation was not studied by them and the middle and lower levels of the civil service were hardly mentioned. The Islington formula is repeatedly invoked by successive pay commissions though with varying ranges of modifications.

Several principles are propounded to govern pay fixation, the more prominent among them being the 'model employer' principle and the fair comparison principle. Superficially very attractive, the 'model employer' principle is too utopian, begging the question: the public employees should first become model employees before expecting the state to be the model employer. Similarly, the principle of fair comparison evokes the question: comparison with which sector of the national economy? No single principle of salary fixation can satisfactorily govern public pay fixation. In reality, pay fixation in public personnel administration of a country is based on a wide mix of principles—historical, social, cultural, economic, etc.

A sound pay plan must comprise the following features:

1. The 'floor' should be founded on a livable rate of wages.
2. The ceiling should be a socially and culturally acceptable multiple of the 'floor'.
3. The different (tiers)of the administration should be constituted by frictionally distinguishable levels of responsibility and duty.
4. The process of social reproduction of skills prevailing in the country should also determine the compensation tiers and differentials.

Salaries as a rule are related to units of time—a year, a month, a week, a day or an hour. In highly advanced countries, the period tends to be reduced to the smallest time unit. In the past, salaries were often related to a year or one crop season in feudal societies. In most countries at present, salary of a public employee is paid on a monthly basis and the lower level functionaries may be paid on weekly basis.

A discussion of salary fixation would be incomplete without a mention, though brief, of fringe benefits. The term fringe benefits connotes those facilities and benefits which an employees gets from his employer in addition to his salary for the job done. 'Fringe' benefits include accommodation or housing rent allowance, free transport or conveyance allowance, medical benefits, city allowance, children's education allowance, washing allowance and the like. Such benefits do contribute towards the improvement of 'environmental' facilities of an employee. The fringe benefits contribute towards the attractiveness of the job and constitute an integral part of the compensation plan.

The principle of salary fixation claims interest and consideration. But one must note, the pay system in public administration is complex and intricate and has evolved over a long period of time; no pay commission can alter it radically, thus remaining more an exercise in continuity than bold change. The Pay Commission is content to observe the incrementalist approach to pay fixation. It operates within a given framework of pay structure with its bottom and ceiling. The existing pay system cannot completely be overlooked. Generally speaking, biology fixes the bottom salary and the top salary is determined by ideology which a country espouses. By biology is meant the basic requirements of an individual worker multiplied by four (the size of the family), converted into monetary terms. The highest salary is ten times the bottom salary, which is a move towards an egalitarianism ideology.

The pay scales were too many in the past: the numbers have been progressively reduced over the years. In 2004 the entire civil service was compensated according to 35 pay scales. The annual increments range from 1.64 to 3.44 per cent of the lowest of the scale. Following the report of the Fifth Central Pay Commission the maximum monthly pay is fixed at Rs 30,000, the disparity ratio between the maximum and minimum pay and dearness allowance being 11.76. The incrementalist rate thus developed is then applied to all pay levels and categories. This approach is practically sound: it has something to offer to every one and does not satisfy any group completely.

Each of these principles has a modicum of relevance to pay determination. But the Fifth Central Pay Commission (1994–7) enumerated a few more principles to supplement them, such as the intrinsic value of the job, the need to link smaller entities to larger entities, the need to delink pay from position in the hierarchy, and the need to be even-handed in justice towards the lowest and the highest paid employees.

In addition to salary and dearness allowance, the other major benefits available to civil servants are house rent and city compensatory allowance, hardship allowance for different areas, group insurance, low interest loans for housing and conveyance and a host of allowances in individual departments.

Before the present discussion is completed, one should be treated to the following:

1. 'Pay so much and so much only as is necessary to obtain recruits of the right stamp and maintain them in such a degree of comfort and category to shield them from temptation and keep them efficient for the term service' (Islington Commission).

2. 'The lowest rate of remuneration should not be lower than the "living wage" and the highest salaries should be kept down as far as possible consistent with the essential requirements of recruitment and efficacy' (Varadhachariar Commission),

3. 'The highest and the lowest salaries should be determined on social and economic considerations and the disparity between the two in the public service should be much smaller and the lowest rate of remuneration should not be lower than a "living wage"' (Second Pay Commission).

4. 'Sound and equitable internal relativities in the determination of salaries intermediate between the highest and the lowest' (Second Pay Commission).

5. 'Pay what other responsible employers pay for comparable work' (Priestley Commission, UK).

6. 'The state should be a model employer' (MacDonnell Commission, UK (1912–15)).

CHAPTER 16

Conditions of Service

The conditions of service governing the civil services are determined by the periodically appointed Central Pay Commission. The pay commission has a recommendatory status but its recommendations receive serious attention of the Government of India. When choosing a job as a career it is reasonable for the employee to take into account not merely the initial salary given to him and other benefits available during service and on retirement but also opportunities for promotion and security of tenure. In addition to the basic pay, civil servants are entitled to a number of allowances and benefits. They are paid dearness allowance which is in the nature of compensatory payment for erosion in the real value of salaries resulting from price rise. The practice of dearness allowance originated in the Second World War to protect employees against the fall in real wages during the period of rising prices. It is a part of the regular wage structure though this practice is unique to India and does not operate in other countries of the world except Pakistan. Housing is perhaps the most pressing need of civil servants, transferred as they are from one place to another. Allowances are therefore given to government employees for hiring residential accommodation. They are also provided assistance for the education of their children. Provision has equally been made for medical facilities, city compensatory allowance, leave travel concession etc. The granting of city compensatory allowance to central government employees which seeks to compensate for the high cost of living in larger cities dates back to the first quarter of the twentieth century. Similarly, house rent allowance is granted to employees to compensate them partly for the specially high rents that they have to pay for hiring residential accommodation.

All these add to the attractiveness of the civil service. Conditions of service also restrict or prohibit certain activities of civil servants or prescribe standards of conduct related to the nature of their calling. The civil society expects from public servants particular standards of integrity, efficiency, and behaviour as laid down in the conduct rules for the civil service. In the end, one must not forget that civil service in India carries a high social status, which makes it a coveted profession in the country. A member of the Indian Administrative Service may get many things done by merely asking, for which an executive in the corporate sector will have to shell out heavy cash! In other words, what is being stressed is that the conditions of service are an important determinant of attractiveness of a service, besides the salary. Some of these matters are discussed in the following pages.

FORMAL COMPONENTS OF ADMINISTRATIVE BEHAVIOUR

India has formulated a formal and elaborate code of moral conduct for its public servants and has even laid down definite penalties for its violation. The rules of administrative ethics have evolved over a long period of time, many of them dating back to the early days of the East India Company. They are a pragmatic, piecemeal response to the ethical problems occurring from time to time, and even now new rules are being added and existing ones modified. The state governments have their own codes of moral conduct, very similar to those of the central government.

The code of conduct for civil servants is a long list of do's and don'ts and identifies actions which are either prescribed (or preferred) or prohibited. A civil servant, for example, is asked to maintain absolute devotion to duty. He must be not only honest and impartial in the discharge of his official duties but also have the reputation of being so. Even in his private life he is expected to maintain a responsible and decent standard of conduct and not to bring discredit to his service by misdemeanours. The formally prescribed morality thus regulates his private life also. He is, for instance, liable to action if he neglects his wife and family and acts in an unbecoming manner. The code of ethical behaviour was enforced equally strongly. Surendra Nath Banerjee entered the Indian Civil Service but was dismissed for his delinquencies.

A civil servant is expected to practise certain standards of decency and morality in his official life no less than in his private life. The Supreme Court observed in 1967 in the case of *Govind Menon* versus *Union of India*:

If Government were to sit back and permit its officials to commit any outrage in their private life provided it falls short of a criminal offence the result may very well be a catastrophic fall in the moral prestige of the administration. If the contention that a government servant is not answerable for the misconduct committed in his private life is correct, the result would be that, however reprehensible or abominable a government servant's conduct in his life may be, the Government would be powerless to dispense with his services unless and until he commits a criminal offence or commits an act which is specifically prohibited by Government Servants' Conduct Rules. This would clothe the government servant with an impunity which would place the Government in a position worse than that of a private employer. Nothing in the Constitution restricts the power of the State to dispense with the services of any government servant which it considered to be unbecoming of unworthy of the official of the State nor has it fettered the discretion of the State as to what type of conduct it shall consider sufficiently blameworthy to merit dismissal or removal. The State had been vested with absolute discretion in this respect. It could demand a certain standard of conduct from government servants not only while performing their official duties but in their private life as well. For example, the State has the power to require its, officials not to drink liquor at official functions or to lead an immoral life.[1]

The rules that seek to keep a civil servant to the straight and narrow path of virtue are particularly detailed as regards the acceptance of gifts, hospitality, and other inducements. He must forbear accepting lavish or frequent hospitality from any individual having official dealings with him or from industrial or commercial houses. From this point of view the usual distinction between economic and other ministries is superfluous, since officers are rotated between ministries. A civil servant is urged to avoid the familiarity arising out of private hospitality. When in doubt, he is to abstain from accepting an invitation, and he must not accept invitations particularly from persons who have cases pending before him. A civil servant must also report to the government any gift worth more than Rs 500 from a near relative, and worth more than Rs 200 from personal friends having no official dealings with him. In any case, he cannot accept any gift worth more than Rs 75 without the sanction of the government.

A civil servant is also debarred from accepting any part-time employment whether under government or elsewhere. He is not to negotiate with private firms to secure commercial employment while in government service. This restriction flows from the view that 'a servant is under an obligation to devote his energies whole-heartedly to the performance of his duties and not to divide his attention and effort in search of employment elsewhere.'

The conduct codes also seek to prevent the possible abuse of the enormous discretionary powers, which the administrators enjoy, in furtherance of private goals. Such abuse amounts to corruption—or 'corrupt practices', which is how corruption is described in India. Explicit prohibition of corruption is common to all countries, whether developing or developed.

A government employee must be able to account satisfactorily for the possession by himself or by any other person on his behalf of pecuniary resources or property disproportionate to his known sources of income, failing which he is held guilty of corruption. The underlying presumption is that one who cannot account for large accretion of wealth, which he could not possibly have saved from his known sources of income, has necessarily abused his official position and indulged in corruption. There are detailed rules regulating the buying of (and addition to) immovable property. One such rule, for instance, lays down that a public servant 'shall on first appointment to government service and thereafter at intervals of twelve months, submit a return of immovable property owned, acquired or inherited by him or held by him on lease or mortgage, either in his own name or in the name of any other person.' This means, among others, that a public servant should report to, and seek the permission of, the government before commencing the construction of or addition to any building. Besides, there are detailed rules to ensure that he does not indulge in *benami* transactions or ostensible transfers and acquisitions of secret assets illegally earned.

The conduct rules also give attention to conflict of interest. The service rules applying to the all-India services lay down: 'No member of the services shall, except with the previous sanction of the Government, permit his son, daughter or dependant to accept employment with private firms with which he has official dealings, or with other firms having official dealings with Government.' The same logic applies to the prohibition on retired High Court judges practising before the same court, the Supreme Court judges from practising before any court, or the Comptroller and Auditor-General of India on accepting any government post after retirement. Conditions of service for civil service also include explicit provisions restricting or prohibiting particular aspects of administrative behaviour some of which are discussed in this chapter.

EMPLOYER–EMPLOYEE RELATIONS IN INDIA

Public organizations provide for machinery to redress grievances of their employees. Great Britain has set up the Whitley machinery comprising a National Whitley Council for the general classes of the civil service and separate departmental councils for staff peculiar to a department. The USA does not have machinery analogous to the Whitley Councils of Great Britain. India did not have any regular machinery to examine the grievances of government servants. The First Pay Commission (1946) looked into the matter and recommended that some machinery should be kept in operation to 'secure cooperation, consultation, discussion and negotiation between staff and Government'. It felt that the Whitley system could not be usefully introduced in India. Instead, it recommended the setting up of joint councils for government employees on the lines of the Whitley bodies. In 1954, the Government of India set up staff committees in the ministries. The Second Pay Commission, 1957 found them ineffective and recommended a machinery which fully in spirit and largely in form followed the Whitley machinery in Great Britain.

Since the 1960s, the Indian public administration has in operation the Joint Consultative Machinery as a grievance redressal mechanism. In October 1960, the Government of India published a scheme to bring the staff in line with the Whitley Councils. The main features of the committee scheme are as follows: A three-tier machinery is proposed to be set up consisting of local or regional councils, departmental councils, and the national council. The local or regional councils shall deal with matters pertaining to all government offices in the particular region. The department councils shall deal with matters concerning a particular department, and each ministry shall have a council. The national council shall consider the matter relating to the working conditions of the employees with special reference to schemes for their general welfare. There will be an arbitration committee consisting of one representative each of the government and the employees. The members are to be chosen from a panel of five names submitted by the two parties. Any dispute, which the National Council is not able to settle, will be referred to the committee. In September 1963, the government announced its decision to establish these bodies on a non-statutory basis on the condition that the employees' organizations abjure strike. The scheme covers all regular civil employees of the central government, non-industrial and industrial, except class I services, class II services other than the Central Secretariat services, and other comparable services where duties are purely ministerial, and the managerial, administrative, and supervisory staff in the industrial establishments. The police and Railway Protection Force have also been excluded. The scheme for Joint Consultative Machinery and Compulsory Arbitration for central government employees was inaugurated in October 1966. Its objectives are (i) to promote harmonious relations between the government and its employees, (ii) to secure cooperation between the government and the general body of its employees in matters of common concern, and (iii) to increase the efficiency of the public service.

The Joint Consultative Machinery (JCM) discusses matters relating to conditions of service and work, welfare of the employees and improvement of efficiency and standards of work and general principles in regard to recruitment, promotion, and discipline. It is strictly precluded from discussing individual cases. The Joint Consultative Machinery is a three-tiered one, but each tier is completely independent of the others in its composition as well as in functioning. The three-tiered machinery is as follows: the National Council as the apex body, the Departmental Council at the level of individual ministries/departments including their attached and subordinate offices, and Regional/Office Councils at each individual office to deal with local problems.

The Joint Consultative Machinery includes all civil servants except (i) Class I (now called Grade A) Services, (ii) Class II (Grade B) Services other than the Central Secretariat Service, (iii) persons in industrial establishments employed mainly in managerial or administrative capacity and those employed in supervisory capacity, (iv) employees of Union Territories, and (v) police personnel.

The National Council. The National Council is the apex level body consisting of the official side and the staff side. The Cabinet Secretary is the Chairman of the National Council. The official side consists of 25 members who are appointed by the central government. The staff side has a maximum membership of 60 who are nominated by the recognized staff associations, the distribution of seats fixed by the Chairman of the council in consultation with them. The staff side elects a leader from among its members.

The National Council deals with matters generally affecting the government employees, such as minimum remuneration, dearness allowance and pay to certain common categories, for instance, office clerks, peons and the lower grades of workshop staff and matters relating to categories of staff common to two or more departments and not grouped together in a single departmental council. The National Council does not deal with matters of interest to employees of a single department. The Council holds meetings at least once in four months. A matter once disposed of by it cannot be taken up for discussion during the following 12 months.

The Departmental Council. The Joint Consultative Machinery scheme provides for departmental councils for each department, but there can be a single council for two or more small departments under a ministry. The Ministry of Personnel and Administrative Reforms has a council to deal with matters affecting the personnel of the Central Secretariat Services. The departmental councils are concerned with the problems of employees who are working in a ministry/department and the subordinate and attached offices of the department. The secretary of the ministry concerned represents the official side which is nominated by the government and may not have more than 10 members. The staff side has membership ranging between 20 and 30, the exact number depending upon the total strength of the staff and the number of grades and services in the department. The staff side is elected by the staff associations for a term of three years. A departmental council may meet not less than once in three or four months.

Regional and/or Office Councils. Such councils deal with only regional or local matters relating to conditions of work, welfare, improvement of efficiency and standards of work, and are set up only where the structure of a department permits such a course. The office council consists of not more than five members on the official side and eight members on the staff side.

If should be pointed out that these various tiers are distinct and separate ones with no formally designed links between them. They are in no way hierarchically integrated bodies and thus, do not impinge on the concept of ministerial responsibility, which is a hallmark of the parliamentary system of government.

The Joint Consultative Machinery scheme provides for compulsory arbitration in the event of a disagreement between the two sides. But the compulsory arbitration is limited to (i) pay and allowances, (ii) weekly hours of work, and (iii) leave of a class or grade of employees. The awards of the Board of Arbitration are binding on both sides subject to the overriding authority of Parliament. Till 1993, the Board of Arbitration has given 201 awards out of which 148 decisions went in favour of the staff side. In no case has Parliament shown an inclination to intervene.

The National Council has held 38 ordinary meetings and two special meetings since the inception of the scheme in 1966. Besides, its standing committee and other committees also meet from time to time.

A discussion of the Joint Consultative Machinery is apt to remain incomplete without a mention of the negotiating arrangement in the railways Industrial peace in the railways is critically important, and the government is fully aware of it. As early as in 1951, therefore, the railways set up in addition to JCM a Permanent Negotiating Machinery (PNM) in which two most powerful employees' associations in India, namely the All-India Railwaymens Federation and National Federation of Indian Railwaymen, participate. The scheme seeks to settle disputes and disagreements between railwaymen and government at three levels. When no agreement is reached between the federations and the Railway Board, the matter is referred to an ad hoc railway tribunal composed of representatives of labour and railway administration presided over by a neutral chairman. The government takes the PNM very seriously because its utmost concern is to maintain industrial peace in the railways. It fully knows that a strike by the railwaymen is apt to paralyse organized life in the society.

The Fourth Pay Commission (1986) gave a clean chit to the JCM and found its functioning satisfactory. The Fifth Pay Commission (1994) asserted: 'Overall, the scheme of JCM has functioned well and been able to provide a viable platform for sorting out problems through consultation between employees and the government'. The scheme is functioning satisfactorily (*Report of the Fifth Pay Commission*, vol. 3, p. 1743). These views are superficial and not true. The Joint Consultative Machinery has not been very effective in India. The essence of Whitleyism lies in an enduring spirit of give and take, and it is this spirit which is lacking in the machinery of joint consultation in India. The government has not always taken the staff side into consultation with the result that unimportant matters are seen to crowd the agenda of the councils whereas momentous subjects get excluded from discussion. Nor is the staff side serious and responsible enough in making its demands. The councils meet irregularly and the agenda for discussion is compiled in a somewhat casual way. The Joint Consultative Machinery scheme has not been fully implemented; so far only 14 departmental councils have been set up whereas the government had promised to establish 21. Moreover, the present machinery does not seek to redress the grievances of what are called 'officers'—the incumbents of grade A and grade B.

POLITICAL RIGHTS OF CIVIL SERVANTS

In a democracy, the political executive is temporary, its continuance in power being subject to the verdict of the voter in periodically held elections. Its tool, namely the civil service, should also be temporary. This is logical so that the new political executive enjoys the freedom to choose its own instrument to execute its policies. Indeed, there was a time when the newly elected political executive brought its own civil servants whose stay in the government depended on the life of the executive. Permanent tenure of the civil servants demands that government functionaries must enjoy the absolute trust and confidence of the party in power. Political neutrality is the price which the civil service had to pay in order to secure a life-term employment. In other words, political neutrality, the hall-mark of a modern civil service, obliges its members to be politically impartial in regard to political views, having a mind untinged by political pre-disposition. This is imperative so that a civil servant may enjoy the complete trust and confidence of the political masters.

Political neutrality gave permanence of tenure to the civil servants. The system which earlier prevailed in the USA was the 'spoils system' deriving its name from the saying 'to the victor belong the spoils'. Its best spokesman in the USA was President Andrew Jackson who declared that the duties of all public offices are plain and simple and that any man of intelligence can perform them. He therefore argued that a system of rotation would give healthy action to the system. The USA was the home of the spoils system till 1882 while the system of patronage prevailed in Great Britain. A subtle difference marks these two terms. The 'spoils system' regulates both entry and exit on grounds of political considerations whereas in 'patronage', the initial appointment is made on the basis of jobbery and nepotism but once appointed, the appointee continues in his job till retirement. The merit principle was adopted in the USA in 1883 consequent to the enactment of the Civil Service Act of 1883 (the Pendleton Act) which set up the Civil Service Commission, the immediate provocation coming from President Garfield's assassination by a disappointed job seeker. In India, the civil service conduct rules prohibit civil servants from active participation in political activities. For example, Rule 4 of the Central Civil Service (Conduct) Rules, 1955, debars a government servant from being a member of any political organization and from participating in any political movement or activity or subscribing to it or assisting it in any way. He is also prohibited from taking part in any election of the legislature or local authority. The only exception to this sweeping restriction is that he can vote in an election. Rules 5 and 6 deny to the civil servant even the right of freedom of expression on all matters except those of a purely literary, artistic, or scientific character. Identical provisions exist in the Railway Service (Conduct) Rules, 1966 and the All India Service (Conduct) Rules, 1954. State governments and even local bodies follow the central government pattern. Of late, many local bodies and even educational institutions, like the universities, have made rules forbidding their employees from standing for any legislature. As regards public undertakings, the government's policy is to treat their employees on par with officials in this respect. Thus, except for the limited right of voting in secret, a government employee cannot participate in any way in any political movement or activity, including election campaigns. He cannot join a political party even as an inactive member or contribute financially to its funds; he cannot express any opinion on political issues; and he cannot stand for election to any legislature. There is, however, a provision for an official to contest elections to a local authority with the prior permission of the government. This provision, in practice, has remained a dead letter.

There is no uniform pattern regarding the political rights of public employees. Some countries, like France and Germany are very liberal and hardly put any restriction, while others, like the USA, deny any political right except the exercise of franchise. India falls in the latter category. The major arguments in favour of liberal grant of political rights including the right to contest elections are two. In the first place, the appeal is made to the right of every citizen in a democracy to take part in political activities. The question is asked: is it in consonance with democracy to deny this right to an ever-expanding number of public servants? To deny public employees the right of freedom of speech and expression is to treat them as less than full citizens. Further weight is added to this argument by the fast expansion of public services. For instance, there are today about 40 lakh government servants employed by the Government of India alone. If we add to this the employees of state governments, local bodies and state undertakings, the total will mount up to many million. Is it fair to cut these millions away from the mainstream of public life? Secondly, such restrictions may also harm the interests of the country. It will be readily admitted that civil servants in India constitute a highly intelligent section of the community. Can we afford to keep them out of public life, particularly when there is an acute dearth of citizen leadership?

The arguments on the other side are equally forceful. In the first place, no thinking person can underestimate the need for, and the importance of maintaining the political neutrality and impartiality of the civil servant. The Masterman Committee, which is generally quoted in support of the case against the existing restriction, admits:

Public opinion is a sensitive barometer reacting sharply to any breaches of the traditional impartiality of the civil service. The importance of these considerations can hardly be exaggerated today when vital decisions or claims for social benefits, assessment of taxes, liability to various forms of national service, entitlement to certain rationed commodities, and many other aspects of daily life are being taken by officials, often of humble rank. Whether we consider the man-in-the-street seeking employment, the professional man applying for a supplementary allowance of petroleum or the member of the business community dealing with the various economic controls now operated by the civil service, the life of every citizen is being directly and acutely affected by all grades of hierarchy. In these circumstances, public faith in the non-political and impartial attitude of the civil service as a whole would be quickly shaken if individual civil servants were known or even suspected, rightly or wrongly, to be not in fact detached from party allegiance.[2]

Secondly, it has been pointed out that the restrictions are largely in the interest of the public service itself. The American pattern is defended on the ground that the Civil Service Act of 1883 and the Hatch Act of 1939 have 'the effect of insulating the federal career employee against the effects of political considerations that might damage his job tenure. They are a protection to the employee against political "reprisals" ... because they eliminate grounds for such reprisals.' It is on this ground that both the American Federation of Government Employees and the National Federation of Federal Employees opposed any change in the Hatch Act.[3] The Masterman Committee too emphasized this point:

There is finally to be considered the harmful effect upon the services itself if the political allegiance of individual civil servants became generally known to their superior officers and colleagues: If a minister began to consider whether "A", on account of his party views, might be more capable of carrying out his policy than "B", the usefulness of "B" would be limited and the opportunities of "A" would be unfairly improved. This would become known, and a tendency to trim the sails to the prevailing wind would be one consequence. Another would be a cynicism about the reasons for promotion which would be very damaging to morale. If it be thought that we have exaggerated this risk, we would point to the experience of those countries which are suffering from the consequences of taking a course different from our own. The danger is, we believe, a real one. It may result from only a small beginning, but, once begun, it produces a snowball effect, which is difficult, if not impossible, to check. Once a doubt is cast upon the loyalty of certain individuals or upon the equity of the promotion machinery, an atmosphere of distrust may rapidly pervade an office and affect the arrangement of the work and damage the efficiency of the organizations.

Thirdly, it is argued that entry to the civil service is purely voluntary, and a person who chooses to enter it should not grudge certain restrictions on his conduct. One cannot have roses without thorns. Public service has privileges as well as disabilities. In the words of the Masterman Committee Report, 'Entry into the Civil Service is a voluntary act, and there can be no reasonable complaint if the conditions of service include some restrictions.' Certain restrictions exist in the case of other professions and employment too. The Second Pay Commission, after giving full consideration to all the relevant factors, came to this conclusion: 'What may be sound and feasible in a homogeneous community like that in the United Kingdom, with a long-established tradition of democratic Government, may not necessarily be sound and feasible in India. There will be a serious danger to the merit system and the service interests of those staff if they became partisan in political controversies, (any) change or relaxation in the existing restrictions on the political right of civil servants would not be in the public interest, or in the interest of the employees themselves.' The Commission, however, did recommend liberalization of the right of free expression: 'A general freedom of intellectual expression should be recognized and only such restrictions should be imposed as are necessary to meet the requirements of the public service.'

The question of conferring political rights on civil servants—on par with other citizens—came alive, in 1973, when a petition was presented to the Committee on Petitions (Rajya Sabha), pleading for the grant of political rights to civil servants. The committee considered this petition in its Fifty-First Report, presented to the Rajya Sabha in June 1977. It stood against the grant of political rights to civil servants on the ground that this measure 'would have an adverse effect on the objective and non-partisan approach expected of a government servant.' An extension to civil servants of equal political rights as are available to other citizens is apt to 'impair the efficiency in the administration. The rule against permitting government employees to partake in political activity was indeed a salutary rule and it was essential in the interest of the employees themselves. The Committee would find the situation rather unhappy where a government employee committed to a certain political ideology is hounded by his superior officer with a different political commitment.'4 The Committee, however, observed that civil servants should continue to enjoy the political right of exercising their franchise. It also recommended that the rules governing the right to form trade unions and staff associations by government employees should be liberalized to make these bodies effective instruments functioning on healthy lines. The Committee argued that this would provide civil servants with adequate channels for redressing their grievances. To conclude this part of the discussion, civil servants in India do not enjoy political rights except the right to vote.

WORKING HOURS

Hours of work to be put in by public functionaries have evolved over the years to suit the functional requirements and the nature of work. Hours of work were 33 ½ hours per week before Independence, which increased to 40 hours per week. Historically, India had a six-day week enjoying a weekly off. A weekly break is necessary for preventing physical and mental fatigue, for enabling the employee to attend to his domestic and social obligations and for pursuit of his cultural interests. In India, Sunday is observed as a 'weekly off'. Punjab was the first state in India to depart from this practice: in the early 1960s it switched over to a five-day week with eight hours of duty per day. At the time of Independence India provided for 6 ½ hours of actual work on each week day after allowing half-an-hour for lunch and 3½ hours of work on Saturdays: office-attendance was fixed at 38½ hours a week.

The Second Pay Commission (1957–9) looked into the employees' demand for a five-day week but rejected it. Giving reasons, it observed 'A five-day week is a highly expensive arrangement, and wasteful of manpower whose uninterrupted service has to be provided'.[5] A shorter working week is possible with longer daily hours, which is not acceptable to the employees who want both shorter daily hours and a shorter working week.

Rajiv Gandhi became the prime minister of India in 1984 and one of the earliest actions of his government was the introduction of the five-day week in the Government of India. The argument in favour of this move was that employees having sufficient rest and leisure would be more energetic and efficient on working days, which would add to productivity in administration. The results however, have belied these expectations. In practice, the work output has not improved. An increase in the daily working hours has made punctuality a casualty, work culture in the government being so slow. The Fifth Pay Commission observes: 'The five-day week also tended to get converted into a four-day week, as the employees tried to go out on extended weekends, leaving early on Friday and returning late on Monday. If there were one or two holidays in the middle of the week, the entire week could be written off, as far as serious work was concerned.'[6] The pay body was against the five-day week and recommended reversion to the older six-day working pattern. The government did not accept the recommendation in view of the employees' opposition. Benefits once conferred upon the employees may not be easily withdrawn more so by coalition governments given to unbridled populism. The five-day week seems to have become a normal pattern today in India. State governments have a shorter working week. So do many corporate organizations.

OUTSIDE EMPLOYMENT FOR CIVIL SERVANTS

A question has been raised recently that civil servants ought to be allowed flexibility in their service conditions to enable them to move more freely to foreign governments, international agencies, and even the private sector. Mobility would be facilitated if their conditions of service, particularly those relating to forwarding of applications, retention of lien on the parent department while working in other organizations, transfer of pensionary benefits in case permanent absorption, etc. have been liberalized but the extent of mobility at present is insubstantial.

An important agenda of reform of the civil service is right-sizing which, in the case of present-day public administration means down-sizing. The policy of liberalization underway since the 1990s demands a slimmer bureaucracy, which calls for conscious encouragement to exit from the government to the private sector and foreign governments, with the aim of restricting of the size of government agencies. Examples in this respect have already been set up by states like Kerala. Kerala government employees are permitted to avail of leave without pay for a total period of 15 years to accept alternate employment either within the country or abroad. At the national level, there is the example of the National Hydroelectric Power Corporation Limited which permits its employees, declared surplus, to retain their lien for two years to enable them to accept alternate employment either within the country or abroad. Similarly, the Himachal Pradesh State Electricity Board allows its employees to accept employment in selected private sector companies, the normal period being two years.

But these examples of adopting a more liberal policy in regard to mobility between government and other sectors are exceptions in India. The central fact is that the civil service in India does not encourage inter-sector migration of personnel. By the same token, it does not encourage lateral entry to its ranks: recruitment takes place at the lowest level of a service. Even the Fifth Central Pay Commission did not take a very positive view on the matter of inter-sectoral mobility, observing 'it may not be desirable, as a general principle, to permit all government employees to accept employment' in the private sector or abroad while retaining their connections with the Government.'[7] Its specific recommendation was that on an experimental basis, certain specified categories of civil servants could be permitted to retain their lien in their posts in government for, say, two years, while being employed in the private sector or abroad.[8]

A related question is part-time outside employment of civil servants. It is suggested that civil servants should be permitted part-time work after office hours. They should be allowed to take up jobs on Saturdays, Sundays, and holidays. This would thus enable the employees to supplement their income. The suggestion is calculated to ease the pressure on the government to raise the employee's emoluments.

If civil servants are permitted to take up part-time jobs elsewhere, they will not be able to give undivided attention to their office work nor will they get sufficient time for rest and recreation, resulting in deterioration in both health and efficiency. Part-time outside employment will also reduce the job-market. The Fifth Central Pay Commission examined this question but firmly rejected it. It observed 'We do not support the idea of allowing the Government servants to undertake part-time employment beyond office hours or accepting private employment during spells of extra-ordinary leave'.[9]

CONTRACT EMPLOYMENT

The most coveted career in India, it is worth repetition, is the civil service, for entry into it means life term employment, security of job, time-bound promotion, and an assured comfortable existence. Even when a job is temporary and employees are recruited on a purely temporary basis to begin with, the job prolongs itself and ultimately the employee becomes a permanent and regular one. The current labour laws and the general attitude of the law courts are honestly very sympathetic to employees and are even pro-labour. For temporary jobs in the civil service, temporary hands are employees. These persons are shifted to another project or jobs of temporary nature and sooner or later they got absorbed in the permanent work force. The Fifth Pay Commission has rightly emphasized: 'Providing security in employment thus assumes greater importance than ensuring that the work of the Government is done at the minimum possible cost.'[10]

Contract employment is an alternative path of recruitment where the work is of a purely temporary, time-bound nature. Absence of provisions of lateral entry system in the civil service may be partly compensated by contract employment. Very close to contract employment is the scheme for consultants in operation in India since 1993. Definite terms and conditions of employment have been laid down which must be observed by ministries while appointing consultants. The work for which consultants are to be hired must not be of the regular nature and they are not to be appointed for more than two years. They are basically preferred for temporary work. The scheme applies to senior level functionaries only.

Future scenario of society is likely to be more tumultuous, more prone to change, inducing many thinkers to predict the advent of ad hocism in human organizations. Such a situation is admirably suited to contract employment. It is therefore, not surprising that the Fifth Central Pay Commission has recommended a much wider use of contract employment in the country's public administration. It recommended: employment on contract basis in the government needs to be recognized as one of the legitimate forms of employment and should be resorted to more frequently in certain situations like (i) replacement for temporarily absent personnel for a considerable duration ranging from one to five years (ii) specialized jobs not normally required and (iii) for the purpose of maintaining a certain flexibility in staffing both for the purpose of lateral entry of experts, moderating the numbers deployment depending on the exigencies of work and ensuring availability of most competent and committed personnel for certain sensitive/specialized jobs.'[11]

PENSION AND GRATUITY

Just as recruitment and selection is an inevitable process in the civil service so is retirement or superannuation. The physical and mental energy of human beings do not remain at the same level always: they tend to decline after a certain age. On reaching such an age, the active association of the person with the government ceases to make way for the latter to hire the services of a younger person. But the individual so superannuated continues to have his physical, social, and cultural needs. Adequate financial provision must therefore be made for his old age. This is done through pension. The age of retirement in the civil service was 55 during the colonial rule. As most of the officers were Englishmen they preferred early retirement from service in India so that they could go to their homeland and peacefully settle down. The age of retirement was raised to 58 on the recommendation of the Second Pay Commission (1959). It is 60 years since the mid-nineties, the recommendation to this effect having been made by the Fifth Central Pay Commission (1997). The retiring age was re-fixed at a higher level in view of its criticism. With improved health care facilities life expectancy in India has increased which keeps the. employees fit and efficient even after they have crossed the age of 58. Social norms are also changing. Late marriages are becoming a normal pattern in India with the result that the employees have not settled their children by the age of 58. Also, scientific and technical personnel are in short supply, warranting maximum use of such personnel. Such professionals start their career at a higher age and thus must stay in the service for a longer period.

Pension is defined in the Oxford English Dictionary as 'an annuity or other periodical payment ... esp. by a government, a company or an employer of labour, in consideration of past services or of the rights, claims or emoluments.' It continues: 'Such pensions are provided in most civilized countries by the state or other public body, for its officers and servants on retirement from active service ...'

Two theories govern the pension system. According to the state, pension is awarded by the employer for the loyalty of service on the part of the employee: pension is the recognition of good work on the part of the employee. Thus, pension is discretionary, certainly not a right of the employee. The other theory which is the employees' view point is that the pension is the deferred wage and thus the employee's right. The country's judiciary is of late inclined towards the latter viewpoint. In the case of *Dr Uma Aggarwal* vs *State of U.P.* dated 22 March 1999, the Supreme

Court of India said 'grant of pension is not a bounty but a right of the government servant.'

In another case, namely, *D.S. Nakara and others vs Union of India* (AIR 1983; SC130) the Supreme Court held: Any pension scheme consistent with available resources must provide that the pensioner would be able to live (i) free from want, with decency, independence and self-respect, and (ii) at a standard equivalent to the pre-retirement level'. The Court held that pension is neither a bounty nor a matter of grace depending upon the sweet will of the employer. The Fifth Central Pay Commission emphatically observed: 'The senior citizens need to be treated with dignity and courtesy befitting their age. Pension is their statutory, inalienable, legally enforceable right and it has been earned by the sweat of their brow. As such it should be fixed, revised, modified and changed in ways not entirely dissimilar to the salaries granted to serving employees.'

Until recently the quantum of pension was 50 per cent of the last pay drawn. The Fifth Central Pay Commission recommended: 'We realize that it would not be possible for Government to fund this sudden increase in the quantum of pension from 50 per cent to 67 per cent. It is, therefore being suggested that, while retaining the Government's contribution at 50 per cent, the balance should be funded by employee's contributions. Even so, the figure of 67 per cent cannot be reached overnight for those retiring within the next few years.'

Mention in the end needs to be made of the new pension scheme announced by the Government of India in August 2003. Under the scheme, all central government employees who joined service after October 2002, excluding the defence forces, would be covered under a contributory pension scheme. Under this scheme, the employees and the government would make a matching monthly contribution of 10 per cent of their salary and dearness allowance and the pension contributions and accumulations would be accorded tax preferences up to a certain limit. While existing bank branches and post offices would be used to collect contributions and interact with participants, the scheme provides for a central record keeping and accounting infrastructure and several pension fund managers.

The employees would have three options for investment, the first being where 60 per cent of the investments would be in government securities, 30 per cent in investment grade corporate bonds, and 10 per cent in the equity market. Under the second option, the investment would be around 40 per cent each in government securities and investment grade corporate bonds and 20 per cent in equity. The third option provides for 10 per cent each in government securities and corporate bonds and 50 per cent in equity.

Another significant clause is that the pension fund managers would be free to make investments in international markets, subject to regulatory restrictions and supervisory provisions. For overseeing the pension sector, an independent Pension Fund Regulatory and Development Authority (PFRDA) would be set up and till that is done, an interim regulator would be appointed through an executive order. The interim PFRDA would have as chairman a person of status not less than that of Secretary to the Government of India and would function under the overall administrative control of the Ministry of Finance.

By utilizing the various investment options, the government estimates that an individual employee would build up a pension wealth providing for 56 per cent of the last emoluments (basic pay and dearness allowance) for group 'A' employees, around 58 per cent for group 'B', around 59 per cent for group 'C' and around 68 per cent for group 'D' employees.

The new scheme provides for an individual to normally exit from it at or after the age of 60 but at the time of exit, it would be mandatory for the individual to invest 40 per cent of the pension wealth to purchase an annuity from a life insurance company approved by the Insurance Regulatory and Development Authority (IRDA).

The option of joining the new system is available to the state governments as and when they decide to do so. Explaining the rationale for switching from the current system where the government provides pension out of its own resources to the contributory system, official sources said that while only about 11 per cent of the working population currently enjoyed retirement benefits, the financial burden of the deferred pension benefit was rising to unsustainable levels.

The total pension liability of the central government employees rose to 1.66 per cent of the gross domestic product in 2002–3 and the actual outgo estimated at Rs 23.158 crore (excluding telecom) for 2003–4. This expenditure rose from Rs 15,346 crore in 1998–9 to Rs 21,172 crore (excluding telecom since the Department of Telecom has been corporatized) in 2002–3.

NOTES

1. *Govind Menon* vs *Union of India*, (AIR 1967 SC 1274).

2. *Report of the Committee of the Political Activities of Civil Servants* (Chairman: J.C. Masterman), C.M.D., 7718, London: H.M.S.O., 1949, pp. 15–16.

3. Vide the evidence given by their spokesman in 1957 before a Committee of the Congress considering changes in the Hatch Act.

4. *The Hindu*, 13 June 1977.

5 *Report of the Commission of Enquiry on the Emoluments and Conditions of Service of Central Government Employees*, 1959, p. 403.

6. The Fifth Central Pay Commission, vol. III, p. 1703.

7. Report, p. 171.

8. Ibid.

9. *Report of the Fifth Central Pay Commission*, p. 172.

10. *Report of the Fifth Central Pay Commission*, p. 173.

11. *Report of the Fifth Central Pay Commission*, 1997, p. 175.

CHAPTER 17

Civil Service Ethics

Civil service has, over the years, taken upon itself a variety of tasks of different magnitude. The functions of a modern civil service take it to almost every nook and cranny of society, thereby draping it with unprecedented power. Power carries an innate risk of its abuse, which is why civil servants must not only be competent but also possess unabridged integrity. Public officials not only administer but also make policy. Not only do they advise on policy-making but also make policy by enunciating rules and regulations and by making precedent-setting decisions in the course of administering.

The citizens' dependence on the civil servants in developing societies is of a degree that people in the developed world may not easily understand. The citizen who approaches a civil servant is, more often that not, poor, resourceless, and a supplicant. His relationship with the civil servant is one of dependence—a feature characteristic of the Riggsian prismatic society. Where so many look to civil servants for so much it becomes of paramount importance that they observe the highest standards of moral conduct in their actions and behaviour. Public administration is a profession—and must be seen as such by its practitioners. It is an essential attribute of a profession to evolve—and enforce—a code of normal conduct for its members.

The official rules which require a civil servant to avoid impropriety or unbecoming behaviour are, in a sense, elliptic. Behaviour is indivisible, and runs through the general course of life—in conduct, in deportment, in manners no less than in speech and in one's associations. The existing administrative codes are, for this very reason not very exhaustive, entailing as they invariably do an 'unwritten' code of conduct which everyone in the public service is expected ceaselessly to uphold. A complete compliance with the 'implied' orders is a part of the latter code: a public servant must also honour the implications of the various conduct governing rules taken as a whole.

Upholding this line of reasoning that a public servant is expected to practice certain standards of decency and morality in his official life no less than in his private life, the Supreme Court observed in 1967 in the case of *Govind Menon* versus *Union of India*:

If Government were to sit back and permit its officials to commit any outrage in their private life provided it falls short of a criminal offence the result may very well be a catastrophic fall in the moral prestige of the administration. If the contention that a government servant is not answerable for the misconduct committed in his private life is correct, the result would be that, however reprehensible or abominable a government servant's conduct in his life may be, the Government would be powerless to dispense with his services unless and until he commits a criminal offence or commits an act which is specifically prohibited by Government Servants' Conduct Rules. This would clothe the government servant with an impunity which would place the Government in a position worse than that of a private employer. Nothing in the Constitution restricts the power of the State to dispense with the services of any government servant which it considered to be unbecoming or unworthy of the official of the State nor has it fettered the discretion of the State as to what type of conduct it shall consider sufficiently blameworthy to merit dismissal or removal. The State had been vested with absolute discretion in this respect. It could demand a certain standard of conduct from government servants not only while performing their official duties but in their private life as well. For example, the State has the power to require its officials not to drink liquors at official functions or to lead an immoral life.[1]

The manualized code of ethics has been discussed in the chapter. Its absence manifested by corruption is discussed in what follows.

The Second Five-Year Plan (1956–61) released for the first time, in an organized manner, regular forces causing distortion in the country's political and bureaucratic orientation and behaviour. The Plan, with its relatively large public expenditure and self-reliant industrial growth, had the effect of generating large-scale politico-administrative corruption in the country. The mixed economy pattern of development, based on an extensive network of regulation and control, brought the industrialist, the politician, and the civil servant closer to each other in a wide variety of matters: the industrialist wanted a licence, permit or quota or some such favour which the politician-minister alone could grant. Processing of papers is the responsibility·of the civil servant, and his collaboration, willing or grudging, was also essential for the deal to materialize.

In the 1960s, the environment became charged with talk about corruption in government. Two committees were set up in 1964 to look into the matter—the S.R. Das Commission of Inquiry against Pratap Singh Kairon, the Chief Minister of Punjab, and the K. Santhanam Committee on Prevention of Corruption. The reports of both these committees confirmed the popular misgivings about the presence of large-scale politico-administrative corruption in India. The Santhanam Committee observed:

The sudden extension of the economic activities of the Government with a large armoury of regulations, controls, licences and permits provided new and large opportunities. The quest for political power at different levels made successful achievement of the objective more important than the means adopted. Complaints against the highly placed in public life were not dealt with in the manner that they should have been dealt with if public confidence had to be maintained. Weakness in this respect created cynicism and the growth of the belief that while governments were against corruption they were not against corrupt individuals, if such individuals had the requisite amount of power, influence and protection.[2]

The committee made as many as 137 recommendations including that for the immediate establishment of the Central Vigilance Commission. Many of these recommendations were carried out, including the setting up of the Central Vigilance Commission, but corruption far from getting checked, has become even more pernicious. Commissions of enquiry, if at all they are instituted, are set up selectively by the executive at its discretion, generally on political motivation. Even so, the 23 commissions of inquiry set up by the central and state governments since 1947 to examine, among others, charges of corruption against political leaders have all generally confirmed in varying ways the veracity of such charges. And what they have disclosed is but the tip of the iceberg.

Corruption in India is basically politico-administrative—it pervades both the political and the administrative levels in government. It runs deep, is well-organized, and systematic. Secondly, it often emanates at the top political and administrative levels, unlike corruption of the traditional variety, which is confined generally to lower level public functionaries in certain areas of administration. This top-level involvement makes its eradication nearly impossible. Thirdly, present-day corruption involves astronomical figures. Fourthly, it has become multi-hued: there are more ways than through money alone of pandering to the moral weakness of the public functionary. Fifthly, interlinkages of corruption have grown between the businessman, the politician, and the civil servant—with many of the latter two having sold themselves to the former. Indeed, many politicians, exploiting their power and position, have themselves set up businesses, especially in areas where a fast buck is assured such as entertainment industry, land and building, government contracting, etc. Sixthly, corruption is not a monopoly of any political party.

However, one should not assume that corruption in administration only involves scams. Corruption is fairly ubiquitous in India, penetrating into almost every nook and cranny. There is the story of an income tax consultant who having been approached by a rich industrialist client with the request to show the funeral expenses on his recently deceased father under company account readily agreed, saying: 'We will show them under packaging and forwarding'. What is more, corruption is growing, showing no signs of abatement. It is getting legitimized also by its apologists, who claim that corruption redistributes wealth in the society, thus emerging as a tool of socialist transformation in the society or those who view it as aid to development by speeding up decision-making in administration. It is therefore imperative to initiate some broad steps aimed at the political and administrative establishments to ensure transparency and improve efficiency.

1. *Electoral reforms.* Elections should be made substantially less expensive than at present. For society to generate a politician with a different orientation electoral reform is essential.

2. *Reform in the management of political parties.* This is tied up with electoral reform. Political parties must be brought under a measure of public discipline. They must be obliged to maintain their accounts which must be audited and made public.

3. *De-glamourizing politics.* Some gloss must be taken off politics. Elections are currently fought at a strident pitch because the stakes are too high: the winner at once shoots into a charmed world of almost unlimited facilities and perks, of unmatched power and pelf—more so if he has no scruples.

4. *Allowing market forces to prevail in place of licence permit raj.* A clean public life would demand that the state should restrict the area of permits and licences. Increasingly, the governmental power of regulation and control of granting permits and licences is being used for plainly partisan purposes, The discretionary powers of the minister and the style cultivated by Abdul Rahman Antulay, the former Chief Minister of Maharashtra, should be an eye-opener.[3]

5. *Raising productivity.* Shortages breed corruption. The national effort therefore ought to be to raise productivity. The electricity boards in India, which are guilty of under-production, are, for instance, encouraging corruption by their slack habits alone and should reorient their ways. Besides, government itself, where feasible, could sell certain categories of goods and services at a premium, thus channelling to the public treasury the money that at present flows into private pockets.

6. *Enforcement of the laws of the land, especially taxation laws, with uniform strictness.* Tax morality must be restored.

7. *Trimming the flab off government*. India suffers from an excess of government. Over-legislation is itself an important cause of delay, harassment, and corruption. Many laws and regulations are antiquated and have no business to be in the rule book. They only provide a handle to the public servants to harass the citizens they are supposed to serve. A process of de-regulation and de-legislation is an integral part of a well-designed battle against corruption.

8. *A strong and effective vigilance machinery which can act independently of the executive*. The Central Vigilance Commission, while it has autonomy, does not possess its own investigative machinery. This is provided by the Central Bureau of Investigation, which itself functions under the executive. Also, the Vigilance Commission cannot launch a probe against a politician, its jurisdiction being narrowly demarcated. It is astounding that not a single politician has been convicted since Independence on grounds of corruption. What is important, therefore, is to establish powerful ombudsmanic institutions charged with the responsibility of identifying the black sheep wherever they operate. As the overall tone in regard to public service morality is set by the political leadership of the land, the latter must be brought under public surveillance and control.

THE HIGHER CIVIL SERVICE IN INDIA:
ITS EMERGING POLITICIZATION

The British colonial rulers gave to India a public administration that was well-knit, reliable, and possessing a very high level of integrity. Notwithstanding the many shortcomings of the colonial bureaucracy—such as insensitivity, rigidity, inflexibility, procrastination, subordination of national interests to metropolitan ones, etc.—the civil service evolved during the course of the colonial rule a code of rectitude and uprightness and imposed it on all its members without fail. When the country emerged to statehood, almost at the same time it began showing concern for planning and, under the twin impacts of democracy and development, the civil service of the country expanded considerably. In addition, its impact on the life and happiness of people became increasingly pervasive and close. Viewed in this background, the original standards began showing signs of wear and tear, and new equations were emerging. Justice M.C. Chagla remarked in the LIC Inquiry Commission[4] involving T. T. K. Krishnamachari (politician), H.M. Patel (civil servant), H.V. Iyengar (civil servant), etc., made as early as in 1958, that such senior persons occupying very responsible positions under the Government were withholding information and offering naïve explanations. The LIC Inquiry was then viewed as an aberration, and it was believed that such actions constituted an exception and were not to be repeated in future. The second inquiry constituted by the Centre was against Punjab's controversial Chief Minister Pratap Singh Kairon, initiated in 1963, that is, during Jawaharlal Nehru's lifetime. The S.R. Das Commission of Inquiry against Kairon reported in June 1964—shortly after Nehru's passing away. Observing strict judicial standards, Justice S.R. Das indicted Kairon on several points and found several cases of abuse of authority on the part of the chief minister. The broad profile which emerges from the Report is as follows: The Punjab Chief Minister Pratap Singh Kairon influenced even the high-ranking civil servants in Punjab to decide cases beneficial to the members of his family. What is more, even senior civil servants did not show the independence and objectivity expected of them and got wilted and tilted. The Report proved the emerging culture of collusion between the politician and the higher civil service of the land. It cites numerous instances of special undue favours shown by civil servants when dealing with the chief minister's son and relatives. A district collector, who is a fairly senior official, illegally granted sanctions to the chief minister's son without making the normal inquiries and even before the report of the executive engineer from the public works department had been received.[5]

The S.R. Das Report cites case after case to prove that the civil servants of Punjab under Pratap Singh Kairon gave short shrift to established rules and proprieties and came under the complete control of the Kairon family.

In 1965, a commission of inquiry was set up against Jammu-Kashmir's Chief Minister Bakshi Ghulam Mohammed, its chairman being N. Rajagopala Ayyangar. The commission reported in 1967. Bakshi Ghulam Mohammed and his relatives were of fairly modest means in 1947, but acquired vast assets and pecuniary resources by abuse of official position or through exploitation by his family and other relatives. Citizens were coerced into selling their properties against their will at very low prices and the official hierarchy changed the entries in revenue records under the influence of Bakshi Ghulam Mohammed. Civil servants were going out of their way to seek postponement of judicial cases launched against Bakshi Ghulam Mohammed in order to delay justice. Cases of malpractices committed by Bakshi Ghulam Mohammed and his relatives are numerous, but the following observation made by Justice Rajagopala Ayyangar is revealing:

... when abuse starts from the top, demoralization sets in the permanent services, and even officers who by virtue of their status and position could normally be expected to take an objective view of matters coming up before them, succumb to the temptation of becoming subservient and willing tools for furthering the interests of those under whom they serve.[6]

Justice Rajagopala Ayyangar writes:

The most saddening and depressing of the materials placed before me were the affidavits of the officials who confessed to have knowingly done improper acts extending even to tampering with official records to the prejudice of the state and state property and monies in carrying out the desires or orders of the respondent (Bakshi Ghulam Mohammed) to benefit himself or his relations.[7]

The Commission's verdict was that civil servants were 'lacking in character',[8] were 'very unreliable persons'[9] and were 'willing tools of the government in power'. It felt anguished at such a sordid level of affairs and argued that an 'honest and public spirited civil service' was among the pre-requisites of high political morality in the society.[10]

The Aiyer Commission of Inquiry 1967–70

The United Front Government, which came into power in Bihar after the elections of 1967, appointed a commission of inquiry, under T.L. Venkatarama Aiyer, against certain ex-ministers who had held office at different times during 1943 to 1967 (that is, during Congress rule). The Venkatarama Aiyer Commission, reporting in 1970, discovered many instances of ministries and senior civil servants colluding with each other in getting things done to the neglect of public interest. It commented upon ministers operating through their 'favourites' in the government departments and civil servants going out of their way to please them, and considered this kind of a mutually supportive relationship to be a truly 'depressing state of affairs'.[11] It went on to add: 'It is hardly necessary to emphasize that the existence of an independent, strong and able secretariat is the *sine que non* of any good government … . It is undoubtedly the duty of the officers to carry out truly and faithfully the orders of the ministers, but at the same time it is also their duty to advise them clearly and firmly whenever the actions of the ministers are not in accordance with the well-recognised and established principles, of administration. Nothing can be more disastrous to a state than that the heads of administration should, instead of advising the ministers properly, take to humouring them and toeing their line.'[12]

The Mudholkar Commission of Inquiry (1968–9)

Being a very loosely knit coalition, Bihar's United Front Government, under the chief ministership of Mahamaya Prasad Sinha, fell early in 1968. The new ministry, which replaced it, lost no time in retaliating against its predecessor and in March 1968 appointed what is called the

Mudholkar Commission of Inquiry (J.R. Mudholkar being its chairman). This commission submitted its report in 1969. The United Front consisting of eight non-Congress parties had taken over the reins of government on 5 March 1966. The spectacle of the Congress party, which was uninterruptedly in power since 1946, losing and the erstwhile opposition parties coming into power was too novel, and the implications of the political change were apparently not fully understood and absorbed by the civil service.

The Mudholkar Report briefly refers to the bureaucratic behaviour based on less than complete cooperation with the new political masters, many of whom were till the other day sitting in the opposition. It observed: '... I have come across at least one case where a secretary to the government failed in his duty to give his own opinion even when it was sought by the minister. Similarly, I found that in several cases, local officials just sat tight on the orders of the secretariat requiring them to submit their reports immediately on matters such as withdrawal of criminal cases and revocation of orders of detention under the Preventive Detention Act. It is this remissness which exasperates ministers and makes them dispense with the reports of officials and leaves them no option but to pass orders on the basis of the material on record though inadequate or on the basis of their own views or information received by them from unofficial sources. Perhaps because of this some orders passed by a minister may have turned out to be wrong or to be prejudicial to public interest. The larger share of blame should in such cases, rest on the official who neglected to perform his duty and allowed matters to tarry on leisurely.'[13] The Commission further observed: 'Perhaps also where a minister deliberately declines to obtain advice on matters from officials as required by rules or when obtained rejects it without giving any reasons, there may have been a lurking suspicion in his mind that he may not get disinterested advice'.[14]

These observations though brief and unelaborated, are not without significance providing as they do sure cues for further meaningful research by social scientists. The civil service, accustomed to the rule by the Congress party since 1946, appeared to have been less than fully prepared to work loyally and with zeal under a different ministry, at least initially. One party rule for a long time tended to erode the professionalism in the civil service, more so when it came to serving those who till sometime ago were sitting on the opposition benches. Also, the new leadership appeared to have begun its political career with a measure of distrust of the state level civil service, as was evidenced by it not consulting the latter sometimes. Or, maybe, it was ignorant of the procedures of work in vogue in the

Government. At any rate, these are only the hypotheses, and need to be further tested.

The A.N. Mulla Commission of Inquiry (1969–71)

The A.N. Mulla Commission of Inquiry against Govindan Nair and T.V. Thomas observed a distinct pattern of bureaucratic behaviour which deserves a mention. The Commission narrates a case in which a senior civil servant had at one time recommended compulsory retirement of a delinquent functionary but, when a new ministry came into power in the state, the same person changed his tune and even the chief secretary, who had earlier endorsed his colleague's recommendation, saw no contradiction or compunction in agreeing with him again. The upshot was that the guilty officer, originally slated for compulsory retirement from civil service, was reinstated. This was not an isolated example. It appeared to be a regular practice with quite an appreciable number of civil servants to look to the local political climate for designing their individual strategy of action. The Commission's Report also invites attention to an emerging alliance between the civil servants, the ministers and the industrialists, much to the detriment of public interest. ... In my opinion the mistake committed by Govindan Nair (the Minister for Agriculture and Electricity against whom the inquiry was launched) was that he should not have shown any interest in Toshiba Anand Ltd. Or if he considered it desirable to promote local industries, he should have kept a stricter watch on the activities of the Board (that is, the Kerala State Electricity Board, a state-owned departmental undertaking) and seen to it that the Board did not transgress the rule and let him down... .'[15] A.N. Mulla says elsewhere: 'I have no hesitation in coming to the conclusion that C.L. Anand (of Toshiba Anand) succeeded in creating a strong lobby in his favour both in the Board and the secretariat and this is how he secured his ends'.[16] The report concludes:

If the files of KSIDC (Kerala State Industrial Development Corporation) and Toshiba Anand Lamps Ltd., are read together, it would be quite apparent that there existed an undesirable intimacy between C.L. Anand and some officers of the KSIDC. I want to focus the attention of the Kerala Government on the question whether the way it has been nursing this firm is really in the interest of the industrial development of the state. Is it not a fact that under this garb C.L. Anand with his lobby everywhere is having everything his own way and the state is not getting that return which it should receive? C.L. Anand got away with a highly questionable deal with KSEB (Kerala State Electricity Board) also. It is the tribe of C.L. Anand's and C.N. George's (another favorite of KSEB) whose steps must be watched if the Government intends to purify these autonomous boards.[17]

The G.K. Mitter Commission of Inquiry (1973–4)

In 1973, the Government of Orissa appointed a Commission of Inquiry in 1973 to look into charges of favour shown to tendu leaf merchants, G.K. Mitter being its chairman. The report, which was published in 1974, directed its attention to some highly placed civil servants. What the report says about the conduct of one of the civil servants is quite revealing:

The Commission feels constrained to remark that the attitude of Shri Sundararajan and his conduct were throughout not such as dare to be expected from a Secretary of Department. It is not for a Secretary to follow the lead of subordinate officer or anticipate what would please the ministers and shape his opinion accordingly. He should take a detached and objective view of the facts of a case and place all matters fairly before the minister, pointing out the pros and cons of the case. ... Shri Sundararajan's conduct falls far below that standard. Shri Sundararajan's appears throughout to have ignored the interest of the state and to have adopted a policy which was likely to be favoured by the minister.[18]

In the affidavit of the State in the case of Shri Satpathy (Under Secretary), reference was made to the matter of grants of rebates, concessions, and exemptions in the figure of stipulation as also the renewal of the agreement in September 1971. The report observes:

Shri Satpathy changed his views with regard to grant of concessions after Shri Sahu became the minister even though he had at first recommended their rejection. In forming the policy decisions, he appeared to have played a more important role than that of the Secretary Shri Sundararajan. It would appear that he could foresee the views which would be to the liking of the minister and shaped his own views accordingly. In more than one instance, he received instructions directly from the minister Shri Sahu without prior reference to the Secretary and followed the instructions. In all this, however, it was the minister, who was principally to blame. The Under Secretary had no direct responsibility in any of the matters and his duty, if any, was to collect facts and figures and place the same before the Secretary to enable him to advise the minister properly. It was none of his duty to advise on the policy to be adopted by the minister not was it his business to suggest that action should be taken in terms of the report of I.C. Mishra Probe Committee. Neither under the rules of business nor under the instructions under the said rules did he occupy any official position which enabled him to make such recommendation or try to formulate the policy to be adopted by the Minister.[19]

Commission of Inquiry against Prakash Singh Badal
and Others (1977)

Justice D.S. Dave, in his Report of the Commission of Inquiry into the allegations against certain former ministers of Punjab (1977), made the following observation:

I would like to point out that having regard to the prevailing condition about the laxity in the political life of the country to which a reference has been made which discussing the guiding principles, I am constrained to observe that Shri Prakash Singh Badal had certainly acted in a manner which has exposed him to criticism.[20]

The period of internal emergency, though spanning only two years, was (in India's post-1947 political history) highly crowded with events covering a wide range of bureaucratic behaviour. The characteristic democratic processes remained in abeyance during internal emergency and the public administration of the land came under a new leadership. As the Shah Commission of Inquiry pointed out, the government began to post on vital public positions persons who were willing to further the interests of the 'centre of power' and these appointments were made in gross violation of established administrative norms and practices.[21] What is more, there was wider acceptance of civil servants indulging in 'short-circuiting of administrative procedures, level jumping in chains of command, and non-conformity to standard administrative norms and value'.[22] 'The attitude of the general run of the public functionaries was largely characterised by a paralysis of the will to do the right and proper thing'.[23] Even highly placed public functionaries were not prepared to speak the truth before the Shah Commission: They were 'withholding the information'. This is but a sample of the politico-bureaucratic behaviour portrayed by the Shah Commission on Internal Emergency.

The above discussed case studies, brief though, eloquently prove the closing or at least reducing of the traditional distance between the politician and the civil servant. Both these players have been suitably 'motivated' by individual selfish desires. A nexus has thus developed between the civil servant and the politician. The civil servant has forsaken his truly professional traits and is increasingly inclined to seek personal favours. A civil servant, enjoying permanence of tenure is expected to be professional in his conduct and advise the politician-minister impartially, and objectively. Also, he must implement programmes and plans according to established laws, rules, and procedures, without showing any favours. Today, a civil servant has become a seeker of favours. These favours can under the established rules be conferred by the politician-minister who possesses the triple prerogatives of posting and transfer, of promotion, and of suspension. He needs the civil servant to process the papers to accommodate the political master. The civil servant seeks personal favours and both the players have adjusted to each other in a wide range of situations—of course, at the expense of public interest. Both have as a result forfeited society's confidence.

The civil servants are perceived by society to be arrogant, self-opinionated, inaccessible, career-minded, and power-hungry. They indulge in manipulation and singularly lack unity. They are technical worshippers of prescribed rules and regulations and are procedure-focussed rather than performance-oriented. In contrast, the self-perception of the administrators is radically different. The administrators show a high level of self-confidence and are confident that they are capable of solving any problem confronting society and demanding administrative action. They on the whole carry a low image of the politician who under the system happens to be their political boss. They feel psychologically insecure—in the sense that if they made even a bonafide mistake they may not be supported by their superiors, both bureaucratic and political. The civil service presently suffers from over-staffing, wastefulness, corruption, politicization, and excessive generalism. It must be made accountable, ethical and sensitive to the citizens. T.S.R. Subramanian, who retired as a cabinet secretary in the Government of India, writes in his *Journeys Through Babudom* and *Netaland*[24]: 'They (civil servants) contribute very little, rarely perform any useful function, are arrogant and rude to general public, and at the same time subservient and sycophantic to seniors and their political masters. A civil servant generally creates and lives in his own make-believe world unrelated to reality—that is why most of them have a faraway look when you see them—they will not meet you in the eye.' Such is his portrayal of the 'netas' (politician). 'In my four decades of public service, I have come across thousands of politicians, small and large, operating at the district or village or state or national level. I have worked closely with hundreds of them in one context or another. I am saddened to say that I have come across only a handful of honest politicians.' And how does the 'neta' himself view the 'babu'? He quotes the Uttar Pradesh chief minister, Mulayam Singh Yadav addressing a conclave of IAS officers, 'you all have such excellent minds and education; some of you are scholars; some of you have Nobel Prize minds; you will all succeed in any walk of life, wherever you turn your attention to; you have good jobs; you can educate your children well; and you are all respected by society;—(and then, the clincher, raising his voice)—why do you come and touch my feet? Why do you come and lick my shoes? Why do you come to me for personal favours? I will do as you desire and then extract my price from you.' Subramanian adds, 'it was an amazing statement because it succinctly summed up the situation and pinpointed the reason for the collapse of the steel frame.'

Certain erosion of values is painfully visible in all sectors and levels of life in India. Indeed, today, by and large, India's behaviour—social, political, and administrative—is getting increasingly governed by normlessness, and even amorality. The moral deterioration first began at the lower levels

of government and travelled upwards. Normlessness in politico-administrative behaviour first made its appearance at the level of the locality and
later surfaced itself at the state level. It is only later that dimness of ethical
values began to characterize the orientation and behaviour at the central
level. Today, however, this historical evolution has become substantially
irrelevant and the line of demarcation between the Centre and the states
in the matter of ethical norms has become increasingly blurred. Though
both the politicians and the civil servants privately accuse each other of
moral deviation, the fact is that, today, both have accommodated each
other in a large number of matters and are thus ungrudging partners in
shady deals. Who tempts whom is now not very relevant: it seems, every
one is apparently trying to make hay while the sun shines. In other words,
the line separating politics and administration is becoming more unreal.
The interface between the two being so close and intimate that it is more
relevant to refer to India's politico-administrative culture. Also, both the
country's contemporary politics and public administration generally show
little sensitivity to the larger public interest, each being engrossed in its
own little world of selfish pursuit of career, wealth, and power. Finally, the
politico-administrative culture is characterized more than anything else
by a high level of tolerance of deviant behaviour. Wrong-doers have rarely
been punished and thus isolated. India's higher civil service is presently
politicized with some exceptions. A growing nexus can be seen between
the civil servant, the politician, and the don. Many politicians are former
criminals. This is well documented in the Vohra Committee Report.

Another area where politicization is most manifest is of administrative
transfers, postings, and transfers which are ordinarily routine processes in
public administration, hardly inviting public comment or discussion. But
when public officials are changed too fast or when their shifting is
revengeful they become a topic of public concern and debate in civil
society. Of late, administrative transfers have been assuming disturbing
proportions that send alarming signals calling for appropriate remedial
action. Indeed, transfers and postings of bureaucrats appear to be the only
'creative' activity in states like Uttar Pradesh and Bihar, and the evil is
fast spreading.

Conceptually speaking, postings and transfers are a normal feature in
personnel administration. Transfers reinforce the Weberian concept of
separation of the incumbent from the office he is holding. A planned
system of transfers broadens one's administrative experience, which is an
essential preparation for upward mobility. Being inherent in a career
service, they are so routine that they are ordinarily handled by middle
level functionaries in the government. Indeed, well-defined rules and

practices have in the past governed personnel practices, and their individual application hardly constituted news. The governing rules and practices ensure observance of the principle of continuity with change: officials must stay in their jobs for a reasonably long term to show performance and, on their transfer, they should as far as possible be given a posting in which they can usefully utilize their previous experience.

These practices did not gain willing acceptance by the new rulers. Administrative transfers in India began to cause public concern since the early seventies, with the emergence of non-Congress governments in the states. The long continuance of single party dominance in India put the time-honoured concept of civil service neutrality under a lot of stress: many civil servants began to be viewed as being partisan to the party in power. When non-Congress governments came to power in some states in the seventies they began to change such functionaries. Since then, the practice has grown that a new government more often than not brings new officers though drawn from the regular bureaucracy.

In the later part of the 19th century merit was recognized as the basis of public recruitment. India adopted merit in 1854 and the first competitive examination for recruitment to the legendary Indian Civil Service was held in 1855, its hallmarks being permanence of tenure, anonymity, and political neutrality. Civil servants enjoyed life-term employment, retiring from service at a prefixed age, thus holding office unaffected by the fluctuating fortunes of political parties. Thus, while ministers come and go, civil servants continue in employment rather indefinitely, serving whoever be their political masters with equal respect—or, as a wag put it, with equal contempt! As civil servants are appointed for a life term they are obliged to serve their ministers with the best of their professional ability. It is implicit in the arrangement that they ever remain in the background never making public their political and ideological beliefs. They are legally prohibited from joining political parties and contesting elections. They enjoy only one right—namely the right of casting their vote passively and silently. These limitations and prohibitions are mandatory so that they enjoy the full confidence of the political masters even when the government changes after an election and new personalities come to power. The advantages of such personnel practices and arrangements are, one may note, reaped by the political executives themselves.

Civil servants, as a rule, are endowed with two roles in a democracy. They implement the policies, programmes, and decisions of the government of the day. In addition, they advise the political executive on policy making by supplying the necessary data and performing other related services. Of course, they perform these two functions silently, never deviating from the conventionally prescribed professional cult of neutrality and anonymity—the traits that ensure the political masters' unquestioned control of the instrument of administration, including the civil service, which constitutes the political executive's strength. Civil service, as a norm, possesses an instrumental value, but is an undoubted asset to the party in power. The credit for good governance—or its opposite—thus goes to the government of the day, the full benefit of which it reaps at the time of the next election. But the civil service is a highly sensitive agency of administration and care must be taken not to demoralize or weaken it. Yet the truth is that nothing demoralizes the civil servants more than arbitrary transfers and postings.

This power is one of the three prerogatives of the political executive, the other two being the minister's right of suspension and of promotion of officials. But it is a well understood practice that a civil servant must stay in his post at least for two or three years to enable him to show his performance as related to the goals of the organization. When a civil servant is transferred to a new post, he necessarily requires a minimum time to become familiar with the new job. He must then stay in the new post for a minimum period to show results, which is the direct concern and has meaning for the minister. Mindless transfers negate these benefits. When one joins the civil service one has to take in one's stride the posts that are offered. It is exactly this which many civil servants are not mentally prepared to accept, and it is precisely here that the minister intervenes—most effectively.

Many civil servants are inordinately choosy in this regard and, what is more, the resourceful among them even succeed in getting plum posts in administration. The politician-minister exploits the civil servant's weakness to promote his own political and personal ends. The minister obliges the civil servant by giving him postings of his liking, and, as quid pro quo, the latter too learns to reciprocate. The cult of political neutrality and anonymity is in the process fast getting eroded. The politician is in search of pliable civil servants, many of whom are today becoming a marketable commodity. Transfers and postings are a lucrative source of revenue both to the seeker and the giver of the job. Field posts in the police are alleged to be sold, the amount being fixed by how much the post yields to the incumbent. Public administration, vast as it is, offers ample room for such 'patronage'.

A district collector in Uttar Pradesh has an average tenure of 60 days and a superintendent of police serves a district for an average of 35 days according to the *Hindustan Times* which published the research findings in

2003. This may not be exactly true but yet is not way off the mark. The government has been changing but the pattern of civil service transfers remains more or less the same. Over 7000 higher civil servants have been transferred in the state of Uttar Pradesh during the period 1992–2000 though the combined strength of the IAS and the IPS in the state (including Uttaranchal) is nearly 960, of whom nearly 30 to 35 per cent remain on central deputation. At the back of most such transfers are extra administrative factors such as political affiliations, personal obligations, and castes.

One must not blame the entire tribe of civil servants. There are even today many who are highly conscientious, applying the laws of the land in an evenhanded way. It is natural that they would some time or the other harm certain local vested interests which, thus provoked, mobilize their resources to get them transferred out and posted at far-off and inhospitable places. This has an extremely demoralizing effect on the bureaucracy. In short, administrative transfers and postings are no longer the function of the personnel agency in the government designed as a tool for career development; they have become devices available to the manipulating politician to domesticate the civil service servants. They are increasingly viewed as a tool for controlling and taming the bureaucracy. The malady is restricted to the higher levels of administration and mostly affects the Indian Administrative Service and the Indian Police Service, the two elitist services of the land, common to both the levels of government. It has also been seen that officials holding powerful posts are directly affected. Stay in the posts is becoming shorter. Honest and professionally oriented civil servants are being gradually eased out and posted at the administrative periphery while the pliable and the pliant ones find themselves planted at all strategic positions. The result is poor governance all over the administrative space. The kitchen is bound to serve unsavoury food when the instrument has become blunt. A demoralized civil service hurts most a popularly elected government. Civil service placement must be depoliticized. The institutional remedy lies in entrusting postings and transfers to an independent civil service board—one at the Centre and one in each state. The civil service board should be presided over by the cabinet secretary at the Centre and the chief secretary in the state.

CRITIQUE OF MANUALIZED ADMINISTRATIVE ETHICS

Ethics connotes much more than a mere absence of corruption. It is a child of a particular time and place. Values differ not only among societies, but in the same society at different times. Codes of conduct in black and white therefore have limited applicability. People with a flexible conscience may even consider themselves free of all constraint in areas of conduct not covered by the written code of conduct. The threat is not of immorality, but amorality.

Unsaid even in the most comprehensive code of conduct is much that covers the conduct of civil servants. It does not, for instance, take into account lackadaisical performance. It is silent on the need for a public servant to identify himself with his work. Nor does it cover aspects like intellectual honesty, citizen-oriented disposition, moral qualities like initiative, risk-taking, fearlessness, truthfulness, etc. A public servant may strictly abide by the rules of conduct as laid down, but if he is deficient in these qualities of head and heart he is no true public servant. A public servant's conduct is shaped, besides the code of conduct, by the cumulative ethos of the profession itself, which articulates and upholds certain norms of conduct and action, and above all, certain personal beliefs and values which are unique to him but which project themselves forcefully in his actions.

The second aspect of the ethics of civil servants is in terms of their place as a subsystem in a wider society. If there is no reinforcing or supportive structure of values in other subsystems of society, the bureaucracy's own articulation would be wanting. It is asking for the moon to expect that the civil servant must be cast in the heroic mould while other groups in society function without any moral curbs. It is vain to expect him to hold the banner of rectitude aloft when all around people are chipping at the integrity of the system. If in present-day India a not too small segment of the bureaucracy observes this codes more in the breach than observance, and there is an agonizing discrepancy between the behaviour preferred by the bureaucracy and that prescribed by the government, the blame must go, in no small measure, to other subsystems of society. Ethical behaviour is indivisible. At a time when the political leadership itself discounts integrity in public life, and public opinion is tolerant of assaults on integrity, it is no wonder that the civil servant gets affected by the polluted atmosphere around him. The various commissions of inquiry set up since independence to examine certain allegedly shady deals confirm the existence of linkage between politics and public administration in the growth of corruption in India and often the civil servant and the politician have learnt to accommodate each other in a wide variety of ways.

The impact of society on bureaucracy tells in another way. When the society around is reverberating with a revolution of rising expectations based on consumeristic culture, the standards of ethical behaviour codified in rules and manuals for public servants are themselves too austere and become largely inoperable. Compounding this problem is the phenomenon of hypocrisy in public life. The Indian political culture emphasizes, even if only at the level of rhetoric, the putting up of saintly postures in public life. This was first introduced—and practiced—by Mahatma Gandhi, but his successors have found the austerity mode too impracticable. Over the years, they discovered devices to circumvent them in practice. This perhaps explains the widespread prevalence of hypocrisy in Indian political life, of which public administration is an integral part. India has an elaborate morality code, scattered over several laws, rules and regulations enjoining upon civil servants how to conduct themselves both in public and private life, leaving almost nothing to chance, but accepts behaviour which is in violation of them.

Civil service ethics is at a dangerously low ebb in India, which is a serious cause of concern. Nor are the all-India services notable for maintaining high standards of integrity among their members. The extent of corruption among them is subject to speculation but the widely shared view is that it is high and, what is more, is not on the decline. Corruption in the politico-administrative system of the country, indeed in nearly all walks of life, is rampant and there is no sign or assurance of its getting curbed in the immediate future. Corruption must be combated urgently and professionally. To this end a well-planned strategy must be devised and enforced, which should include effective punishment of corrupt officials, confiscation of ill-gotten wealth, freedom of information, greater use of information technology, accountability, and transparency in the civil service. Nothing less than the moral resurgence of the entire society can bring about this change. Of foremost importance in this respect is the commitment at the highest political level to uphold, at any cost, a certain level of morality and not to permit anyone, howsoever exalted, to lower it. It is equally necessary for public administration to wholeheartedly simplify its procedures at all levels, especially those which concern the common citizens. Many such procedures have over the years grown very complicated, even mystifying. The hapless citizens, unable to understand or comply with them, consider it safer to bribe the officials concerned in order to purchase their peace. A third aspect that needs attention is the present all-pervasive official secrecy, which makes information a prized commodity. To access it, the interested individuals have no option but to offer appropriate inducements to those who hold the key to this information. A measure of *glasnost* in public administration is overdue for cleaner, citizen-oriented administration. In other words, administrative reform is a prerequisite for public service ethics. Public officials being placed in fixed salary groups, a firm control of inflation is very necessary to protect their purchasing power, to enable them to remain above easy temptation. This would be part of a larger concern towards the curbing of consumerism currently permeating society. No less important, when all has been said, is the existence of supportive structures in the other professions in society. It is utterly futile to expect a corruption-free public service when other professions—medical, legal, teaching, business, etc., evince total or substantial unconcern towards it in their own individual jurisdiction. A society, in a sense, is like a grid and there is a lot of 'buying' and 'selling', in the psychological sense at least, between them, thereby producing effects with far-reaching sweep

A last word before concluding, on the impact of training on ethics building in the civil service. While there is no discounting the overall importance of training, the impact of training with emphasis on civil service ethics would at best be minimal in improving professional conduct. The pressures on individual public officials are generally overwhelming, and they are expected to respond to them in some measure at least. There is no escape from such pressures unless the larger society is itself prepared for a transformation in its opinions regarding responsibility and accountability. This demands change at a much earlier stage—in the family and in the school—with full understanding of the cultural dispositions of the society. When all is said and done, the surest way out is the self-ethicization of the individual.

NOTES

1. *Govind Menon* vs *Union of India*, (AIR 1967 SC 1274).
2. *Report of the Committee on Prevention of Corruption*, New Delhi: Ministry of Home Affairs, Government of India, 1964, pp. 7–8.
3. Antulay had founded a few public trusts named after India's then prime minister Indira Gandhi. For allocating controlled items of goods to individuals he would collect donations, apparently for the trust. How much of it went into the trust and how much remained in private pockets is anybody's guess.
4. *Report of the Commission of Inquiry to Inquire into the Transactions of the LIC* (Chairman: M.C. Chagla), New Delhi: Government of India, 1958.
5. *Report of the Commission of Inquiry Against Pratap Singh Kairon* (Chairman: S.R. Das), New Delhi, Government of India, 1964, see chapter XXXIII and XXXIV, pp. 277–88.
6. *Report of the Commission of Inquiry Against Bakshi Ghulam Mohammed* (Chairman: N. Rajagopala Ayyangar), Srinagar: Government Jammu & Kashmir, 1967, p. 720.
7. Ibid.
8. Ibid.
9. Ibid.

10. Ibid.

11. *Report of the T.L. Venkatarama Aiyer Commission of Inquiry*, Patna: Government of Bihar, 1970, p. 476.

12. Ibid.

13. *Report of the Mudholkar Commission of Inquiry on the Charges Against Fourteen United Front Ministers*, Patna: Secretariat Press, Government of Bihar, 1970, p. 373.

14. Ibid.

15. *Report of the Commission of Inquiry Against M.N. Govindan Nair and T.V. Thomas* (Chairman, Mulla A.N.), Trivandrum: Government Press, 1971, p.44.

16. Ibid., p. 43.

17. Ibid., pp. 155–68.

18. *Report of the Commission of Inquiry to Look into Tendu Leaf Purchases* (Chairman: Mitter, G.K.) Bhubaneswar: Home Department, Government of Orissa, 1974.

19. Ibid., pp. 202–3.

20. *Report of the Commission of Inquiry into the Allegations against Certain Former Ministers of Punjab*, New Delhi: Department of Personnel and Administrative Reforms, 1977, p. 303.

21. Shah Commission of Inquiry on Internal Emergency, 1978, Interim Report II, New Delhi: Government of India, p. 142.

22. Ibid., p. 143.

23. Ibid., p. 140.

24. T.S.R. Subramanian, *Journeys Through Babudom* and *Netaland*, 2004, Delhi: Rupa & Co.

CHAPTER 18

Making the Civil Service
Accountable

To keep the civil service tuned to the right perspective, including goals, society needs to have at its disposal definite ways of holding the mandarins accountable. The need for accountability grows as the variety and multiplicity of the functions handled by the civil service grows, and is all the greater in a developing country like India, with its overwhelming majority of people mired in poverty and ignorance. On the one hand, sensitivity and care is called for in handling their demands on public service; on the other, they lack the kind of assertiveness, much less aggressiveness, that a more sophisticated society would evince to keep the civil service on its toes. Unless India's civil service is called to strict account, the many maladies afflicting it—chief among which are corruption and unresponsiveness towards even the people's genuine needs—are bound to get worse.

Ironically, the greater the need for accountability, the greater is the difficulty of its enforcement. Bureaucracy tends to monopolize within itself awesome power, which is not necessarily used for the citizen's welfare. Bureaucracy is a social institution, and its members, like other human beings, do not shrink from exercising this power in their own favour, unconcerned about, or to the detriment of, the people whom they profess to serve.

No government, of whatever complexion, can evade the need for accountability. Accountability is at the heart of every government. What the nature of that accountability, and how it is articulated, however, depends upon the kind of polity a country has. In a democracy, accountability inevitably assumes a pre-eminent position as it derives its legitimacy from the people at large.

Accountability in India has two facets, somewhat separate but interrelated. The first is political, founded on its parliamentary system of government of the Westminster model. In this system the executive is accountable to Parliament, which has many devices and instrumentalities for keeping tabs on the executive. The second facet is primarily administrative, where the (political) executive holds the civil servants accountable for how they carry out their responsibilities.

In India's parliamentary form of government, where Parliament is elected by the people on the basis of universal adult franchise, the political party commanding a majority in the lower house, called the Lok Sabha, constitutes the government. The term of government, as of the Lok Sabha, cannot go beyond five years. Constitutionally, the supreme executive authority is vested in the President of India, and government is conducted in his name. But the President is under a firm constitutional obligation[1] to act in accordance with the 'aid and advice' given by the Council of Ministers, with the Prime Minister at its head. It follows that the Council of Ministers alone may be called to account.[2]

The executive's accountability to Parliament is total and unabridged, which the latter reasserts in many ways and on many occasions. Since the executive is obliged to attend to people's grievances, the redress of people's grievances precedes the grant of 'supply', that is, taxation. Before it grants funds to the executive, Parliament must be satisfied that the purpose for which the funds are needed are worthwhile and that the funds will not be misused. In calling the executive to account, Parliament has at its command numerous tools and opportunities, such as parliamentary questions, adjournment motions, vote of no-confidence, discussion on demands for grants, calling attention notice, half-an-hour discussion, zero-hour discussion, etc.

COLLECTIVE RESPONSIBILITY

Collective responsibility is the kingpin of the parliamentary system of government. It implies that the Council of Ministers is collectively accountable to the lower house of Parliament. The logic of the concept is as follows: In a parliamentary government, the party commanding a majority of seats in the Lok Sabha enjoys the prerogative of forming and running the government. Each member of the Council of Ministers is therefore required to ensure that his policies command the agreement of his colleagues. If an important issue affecting any minister gets rejected by the

Lok Sabha, the whole Council of Ministers has to resign. Within the Council of Ministers he persuades his colleagues to accept his proposals. Whether he carries the day depends upon his ability to persuade. If he fails to obtain the agreement of his colleagues on a policy which he considers to be very important, or he does not agree with a policy made in the Cabinet and which he cannot publicly defend, he must resign.

MINISTERIAL RESPONSIBILITY

Matters that pertain to collective responsibility are clearly laid down in rules of business and must be compulsorily brought before the Cabinet. The remaining items remain under the care of individual ministers concerned. A minister's personal accountability to Parliament extends to all matters within his competence, which is as basic a principle of the Constitution as is the rule of law. A minister is accountable to Parliament (the Lok Sabha, to be precise) for his own action pertaining to his ministry—or inaction—and also for all those of the civil servants serving in his ministry. The civil servants are protected by the well-known principle of anonymity. Parliament holds the minister responsible if something in his ministry goes wrong, even if he did not have knowledge of it or did not even approve of it. The minister's responsibility to Parliament, without any qualification or modification, is the essence of ministerial responsibility.

It does not follow, however, that the concept of ministerial responsibility leaves the civil servant unscathed at all times. A mistake may be one of four kinds. First, if a civil servant carries out an explicit order of the minister, the latter must protect him and take the entire responsibility when questioned in Parliament. So also if a civil servant acts properly in accordance with the policy laid down by the minister. The third kind of mistake is where a civil servant commits a mistake or causes some delay but not on an important issue of policy and not where a serious claim to individual rights is involved. In this case the minister must acknowledge the mistake and own up the responsibility, although he is not personally involved.

It is only in the fourth category of actions that the erring civil servant earns, at his minister's hand, and what is more, publicly, the blame. This is where action has been taken by the civil servant of which the minister disapproves and has no prior knowledge, and the official's conduct is plainly reprehensible. Although the minister is still accountable to Parliament, he is not obliged to endorse the action. Herbert Morrison even permits public naming of the erring official. He writes:

There is a circumstance in which I think a considerable degree of frankness is warranted. If a minister has given a specific order within the department on a matter of public interest and his instructions have not been carried out, then, if he is challenged in the parliament and if he is so minded he has a perfect right to reveal the facts and to assure the house that be has taken suitable action. Even so, he must still take the responsibility. It is, I think legitimate in such a case that disregard of an instruction should be made known even if it involves some humiliation for the officer concerned and his colleagues knowing that he was the one who disobeyed: for the civil service should at all times note that the lawful orders of the minister are carried out.[3]

A classic case of the fourth category of error by the civil servant and its implications for the minister was the Life Insurance Corporation affair in 1958, in the wake of which T.T. Krishnamachari, Finance Minister in the Nehru Cabinet, had to resign. His defence was: It would be impossible for any minister to accept the dictum that he must take full responsibility for the acts of his subordinate without being permitted to say that his subordinate did not reflect his policy or acted contrary to his wishes and directions.[4] But Jawaharlal Nehru observed, while accepting his resignation: 'You very rightly say that according to our convention the minister has to assume responsibility even though he might have very little knowledge of what others did and was not directly responsible for anyone of these steps.'[5] Justice M.C. Chagla, who had been constituted as a one-man commission to investigate into the LIC affair, observed in his report: The doctrine of ministerial responsibility has two facets. The minister has complete autonomy within his sphere of authority. As a necessary corollary, he must take full responsibility for the actions of his servants.'[6]

This concept needs to be further clarified, particularly in the context of the emergence of the party system in general and party discipline in particular. If the concept is applied rigorously, the minister himself should appear before the parliamentary committees, to give an account of the functioning of departments under his charge. Also, he should resign even if a petty official anywhere in the country errs. This would indeed be like opening a Pandora's Box. In turn, it would cramp the functioning of the ministry, since the minister may be excessively cautious and demand that all or most matters in the ministry be compulsorily referred to him. Also, the civil servants, aware that the matters might be discussed in the legislature would feel stymied in their initiative and get into the habit of checking the smallest detail with the minister.

The minister, therefore, must soon learn, in order to survive, how much to do himself and where to stop. He must, in other words, concentrate on major matters of policy and leave tasks of day-to-day administration to the career civil servants. As Sir Warren Fisher has stated:

Determination of policy is the function of the minister and once a policy is determined, it is the unquestioned and unquestionable business of the civil servant to carry out that policy with precisely the same goodwill whether he agrees with it or not.[7]

No hard and fast rules can be laid down about matters which need compulsorily be referred to the minister for his decisions: the secretary, the administrative head of the ministry, should know well his minister's mind and devise the reference-schedule accordingly. Every minister has his own style of work. But it may, perhaps, be safely observed that he should generally shape and formulate policy, leaving day-to-day administration to the civil servants under him. He should ensure accountability, among others, by selecting and scrutinizing cases on a random basis and by invoking the managerial principle of rule by exception.

As far as theorizing goes, political accountability is fine. But how many ministers resign when there is proven mismanagement of affairs under them? The political fact is that so long as the minister enjoys the support of his political party, in general, and of the prime minister, in particular, he cannot be dislodged from ministership, no matter if his ministry is seriously mismanaged.

Theoretically and practically, then, ministerial accountability has obvious limitations:

1. It is just a convention, without any legal sanction behind it. It is essentially a matter of conscience, a moral principle.
2. It is limited by sheer common sense. If some railway station master has misbehaved with the public, there will be no demand for the railway minister's resignation. Similarly, if there is drought, the minister of agriculture is not asked to resign.
3. A minister continues in his office so long as he enjoys the confidence of the prime minister.
4. If the minister is an important leader of his party and commands its wide support, he is always sought, never sacked.

PARLIAMENTARY CONTROL

A passing reference was made earlier to the tools which Parliament has at its command to make the executive account for its actions and behaviour. It is time to discuss these in some detail. The various tools and mechanisms that Parliament has of enforcing accountability on the executive are broadly of two types. The first type is concurrent and contemporaneous and, thus, are of day-to-day application. They exercise the function of control. What can be called tools of accountability, strictly speaking, are the second type of tools, which are basically *post facto* in nature. These are activated after some action has already taken place, by way of evaluation of the work under scrutiny. Audit and the various committees of Parliament hold the administration accountable after the event has occurred, and the thrust of this category of investigation is to find out why and how a particular work has been done.

This classification has another angle too. The control mechanism is basically directed against the political executive and is political in nature. In contrast, the tools of accountability make the career bureaucracy their target and are, so to say, administrative in nature. They are non-partisan, uninfluenced by those political considerations which weigh when, for instance, an adjournment motion is moved in the legislature.

Let us now consider the various devices of parliamentary control to ascertain their effectiveness.

Question Hour

The first hour of each House in reserved for putting up of questions by members and their answering by the ministers concerned. A maximum of twenty questions may be admitted for answers. Ordinarily not more than half of them get answered on the floor within the allotted time. The question hour is easily the liveliest—and perhaps the noisiest—time of the legislature; not only are members in full attendance in the House but the public galleries also are generally packed.

The device of question hour has certain features either unique to itself or in its effect. It gives members of Parliament perhaps the fullest freedom to question the government's functioning. Even members of the party in power may, and do, put questions and thus subject the members of the Treasury benches to a sort of cross-examination. It is not the question, one must note, which the minister dreads: a question put to him is but a leaked out question! But it is the right to put supplementaries which keeps the minister on his toes. He really cannot foresee what thunderbolt the backbenchers may hurl after the main question is answered! This is its second remarkable feature. Thirdly, the parliamentary question is addressed to a particular minister. When handling it, he is specifically being sized up not only by the opposition parties but also by his own party members, including his ministerial colleagues. It is for these reasons that the question hour is an exceptionally sharp and sensitive device of control. It is not deadly—a minister remains in office so long as the prime minister wants him—but it may show him up as inept.

Adjournment Motions

Members of Parliament can move adjournment motions to discuss matters which, according to them, are urgent and of public importance. An adjournment motion has an element of drama in it. It is an intervention in the regular work of the House whose attention is desired to be focused on the subject of the motion. Adjournment motions need not necessarily pertain to subjects under the federal government's direct responsibility. Even matters which are the states' direct concern may be discussed. The adjournment motion has an obvious publicity value. The general motive of the questioner is to censure the executive of the day for its acts of omission or commission and he seeks to turn public opinion against the executive. After the discussion is over the motion is either withdrawn by the mover or negated by voting, thanks to the majority behind the government.

Vote of No-Confidence

By initiating a vote of no-confidence the Lok Sabha arraigns the executive for its sins of omission or commission and threatens to withdraw its confidence, compelling it to resign unless on hearing the executive on the preferred charges Parliament renews its confidence in it. It is a solemn event, challenging as it does the claim of the government to stay in power. A definite time is allotted for the discussion on the vote of no-confidence; the opposition censures the government which at the end gives its reply followed by voting on the move.

The first time a no-confidence motion was discussed in Indian parliamentary history was in the 1963 monsoon session of the Lok Sabha. It was then defeated. The frequency of no-confidence motions has increased in the post-Nehru era, but with no better result. The 'no-confidence' vote is more symbolic and does not ordinarily cause the defeat of the government if it has a safe majority parliamentary support. But where the ruling party commands only a thin majority and party cohesiveness is low, the result may prove fatal—as happened with Morarji Desai's Janata government (1977–9). Because of factionalism in the ruling party, Morarji Desai, then Prime Minister, tendered his resignation to the President on the eve of the crucial voting. Of late, the vote of no-confidence has become rather ritualized.

Discussion on Demands for Grants

The executive is obliged to come to Parliament seeking funds. Before Parliament grants money it insists on articulating the people's grievances against the executive and seeking the latter's assurance for their redress. The discussion on Budget offers an apparently limitless opportunity to members of Parliament to expose the government to public gaze and keep it under a measure of surveillance and control. The time allotted for discussion on demands for grants is nearly 100 hours and over 200 Members of Parliament (out of a total of over 520) participate in the discussion.

Calling Attention Notice

The calling attention notice, like the adjournment motion, is meant to pertain to matters of urgent public importance; but unlike the latter, it does not have an element of censure of the government. It is therefore moved more uninhibitedly by members of the ruling party as well. The time allotted to this notice is thirty minutes.

Half an-hour Discussion

Members can ask for an half-an-hour discussion on a matter of sufficient public importance which has been the subject of a recent question, and the answer to which needs elucidation on a matter of fact. This occasion is also used by members to keep the executive actions under surveillance and control.

Zero Hour Discussion

'Zero hour', India's innovation in the field of parliamentary practices, has emerged, since 1962, as a tool of control over the executive though it is not a formally prescribed device available to members of Parliament. It is extra-constitutional and is so called because it is invoked in the House immediately after the question hour but before the items on the order paper of the House (that is, the agenda for the day) are taken up for discussion and disposal. As Parliament meets at 11.00 a.m. and the question hour is over at 12.00 p.m. what follows is the zero hour. In this hour Members of Parliament can raise, subject to the permission of the presiding officer, matters which in their eyes are of public importance even if not listed in the day's order paper. Zero hour has come to assume parliamentary status since 1962 because so many questions of great public urgency have begun to crop up, which could not be raised in accordance with the earlier parliamentary practices. The opposition parties somehow broke their earlier patience with the set parliamentary agenda paper, thanks to the advent of Dr Ram Manohar Lohia's open pressures against the agenda-bound 'order, order' and persistent demands for attention to be paid to specific, recent public calamities such as strikes, hunger-strikes, sudden sufferings caused by natural calamities, awful accidents resulting in deaths, etc. MPs succeeded over one or two sessions in familiarizing

Parliament with the emergence of what has come to be the 'zero hour'—a parliamentary weapon with which the government has to contend with and the presiding officers have to live with and moderate their 'order order' in a suitable manner, without the loss of face to the chair.[8]

Zero hour discussion has evolved bit by bit but became prominent during Neelam Sanjeeva Reddy's first term of speakership of the Lok Sabha. Since 1977 the 'Zero hour' has undergone a subtle change in the sense that up to five members are allowed by the Speaker to raise, soon after the question hour is over, matters of public importance under rule 377 of the Rules of Parliamentary Procedure. 'Zero hour' discussion has the virtue of surprise and, moreover, being on a specific topic it is usually directed against individual ministers, which has the possible effect of embarrassing them and sometimes also tripping them.

AUDIT

Parliament's control over the budget is apt to remain superficial, even incomplete, until it provides for an independent examination of the public accounts to make sure that money granted by it has been spent strictly in accordance with the parliamentary behests. In India, the audit of govern- ment expenditure is conducted by the Comptroller and Auditor-General, a functionary provided for in the Constitution and endowed with powers and status which make him independent of the executive and effective in the matter of his functioning. As audit reports are, as a rule, made available to Parliament and, moreover, become the chewing fodder for the Public Accounts Committee, it is a tool of direct parliamentary control over the executive in addition to providing data indicative of how tasks and affairs in public administration are managed. The provision for audit of government expenditure has an anticipatory effect: the hindsight of the auditor becomes the foresight of the civil servant. Secondly, audit brings to the notice of Parliament (and of the larger public) cases of financial irregularities and other transgressions so that that august body is enabled to identify the public servants responsible for them. When the audit has unearthed certain irregularities the civil servants responsible for them are censured by the political executive. Thus viewed, audit is an aid to the assuring of administrative accountability .

COMMITTEES OF PARLIAMENT

Parliament is a busy body and does not have the necessary time for detailed examination of specified matters. Nor can such tasks, which are of a technical nature, be efficiently performed in the whole House, whose proceedings are guided by unconcealed political considerations. To relieve it of such detailed exercises and also to enable their undertaking in a non-partisan spirit, Parliament has set up committees composed of members drawn from amongst its own ranks. These are: the Public Accounts Committee, Estimates Committee, Committee on Subordinate Legislation, and Committee on Public Undertakings. A parliamentary committee summons civil servants to give evidence before it, and in the process subjects them to a cross-examination on matters being examined by it. The civil servants may refuse to disclose information in public interest or for national security, but there do not appear to be any firm guidelines in India governing bureaucratic behaviour vis-à-vis these committees.

Each parliamentary committee undertakes a detailed and thorough examination of issues within its terms of reference and submits its report to the House. The report is not formally discussed—a convention which avoids any possible controversies in Parliament. Members may, however, refer to the report in the course of debates and discussions. A well-defined convention is that—(a) a parliamentary committee reports on behalf of the House; (b) the report straightaway goes to the executive for action; and (c) the latter must report to Parliament on action taken. A parliamentary committee, thus, not only examines matters but also has a kind of follow-up programme.

The Public Accounts Committee has 22 members, seven of them from the Upper House. It examines the accounts of the executive departments to ascertain whether money granted by Parliament has been spent according to authorization, and with 'wisdom, faithfulness and economy'. The examination, it is formally laid down, does not extend to questions of policy; it is concerned with methods of expenditure and in particular whether sound financial principles and the prescribed procedures had been observed. In practice, the committee has consistently interpreted its charter in liberal terms.

The Estimates Committee consists of 30 members, all belonging to the Lower House. The committee suggests how the accepted policies can be carried out with the maximum economy. The Speaker of the Lok Sabha defined this committee's functions as follows:

The fundamental objectives of the (Estimates) Committee are economy, efficiency in administration and ensuring that money is well laid out; but if on close examination it is revealed that large sums are going to waste because a certain policy is followed, the Committee may point out the defects and reasons for the change in the policy for the consideration of the House.

This committee, too, has thus defined its tasks in inhibited terms and has even been discussing issues and problems which cut across departmental jurisdictions.

The Committee on Public Undertakings and the Committee on Subordinate Legislation examine, respectively, the functioning of (specified) public undertakings and the practice of subordinate or delegated legislation.

All these committees, it may be recalled, scrutinize actions after they have taken place, thus being in the nature of post-mortems. The object of the examination is the bureaucratic conduct of public affairs and in the process acts of misadministration and malpractices have been exposed. The Public Accounts Committee, in its 50th report (1966), referred to certain transactions by the Ministry of Iron and Steel in 1959–62 which involved wrongful issuance of pre-import licences to the Amin Chand Peareylal group of firms, resulting in a loss of foreign exchange earnings of about Rs 24 million. As a result of this exposure, the career of the then Secretary of the Ministry, S. Boothalingam came to an abrupt end. This is not an isolated case. These committees keep the machinery of public administration under parliamentary scrutiny, which exercises a wholesome influence over the executive. By highlighting the shortcomings and mistakes of public organizations they enforce accountability on them. The very fear that the arms of these committees reach the wrongdoers and their names and deeds get publicized tends to keep the bureaucracy fair and just.

CRITIQUE OF PARLIAMENTARY CONTROL

Present-day government is not a minimal one, addressing itself only to tasks oriented to regulation and maintenance. It is taking up an unprecedented array of functions both in the traditional and new fields which impinge heavily on people's welfare. The need, therefore, is all the greater that such government is kept accountable for its acts of omission and commission. Most devices of parliamentary control seek to exercise control over the political executive. It is only audit and parliamentary committees which are directed towards an examination of bureaucratic action. What do the several tools of parliamentary control add up to?

First of all, the word 'control' for the kind of work done by Parliament is not very apt. These devices do not enable Parliament to control the executive. They merely help in pressing attention on selected aspects and features of administration and serve the purpose of building public opinion on the matters raised. The executive, however, is not necessarily deterred from action, secure behind its majority.

For various reasons Parliament, with all its devices and opportunities, is unable to exercise sustained and effective control over the executive. For one thing, parliamentary democracy has long since yielded supremacy to the Cabinet; and it is the latter which has in reality come to control and commandeer it. The party system, by ensuring majority support for the executive of the day, ensconces it in safety no matter what may be said on the legislative floor. The party system has also seriously compromised the members' freedom of expression. MPs enjoy freedom of speech in Parliament only to the extent and so long as the political parties to which they belong permit it. The device of whips, which parties impose on their members, mobilizes majority support for the party in power. Individual MPs' dependence on the party has also decisively increased over the years, for the latter provides the resources indispensable for fighting today's elections.

Also, as membership of Parliament has today become the source of livelihood for the politician, he would not let Parliament be dissolved prematurely. He knows that if Parliament does not behave to the prime minister's liking, he can advise the President to dissolve the House, thus exposing its members to the risks and uncertainties of an electoral contest. Moreover, Parliament's functioning itself is far from ideal. It was better in the time of Jawaharlal Nehru (1947–64), India's first prime minister. Even though the Congress party enjoyed a massive legislative majority, Nehru made sincere efforts to nurture parliamentary democracy and was responsive to the criticism made in Parliament. His successors, however, have not always had the same amount of regard for Parliament. The decline of Parliament became pronounced by the early 1970s, and worsened ever since. M. Ruthnaswamy, himself an MP, has correctly emphasized:

The minds of members (of Parliament) are already made up before the debate begins and they vote accordingly in spite of the arguments that have been urged on the other side. In fact, it is the avowed practice of the ruling party to have the issues to be raised in Parliament to be discussed and decided upon before hand at the meetings of the Congress Parliamentary Party, and its members go into Parliament and vote according to the decisions taken at the meetings of the Parliamentary Party. Decision, therefore, comes before discussion in Parliament. Thus the debates of the Indian Parliament have become a form of ritual exercises that have little or no effect on the final result and the debates have been robbed of their meaning and purpose. This accounts for the sparse attendance of members during the debates, the members trooping in at voting time especially when a vote of confidence is imminent.[9]

Exceptions apart, the present-day Parliament has persons of average and sub-average intelligence with much weaker parliamentary knowledge and interest than in the past. Many members' indifference towards their parliamentary duties is obvious to an observer. On an average day, a large

number of MPs ritualistically troop out once the question time is over. The
attendance in the afternoon is still thinner. Quite often, the quorum bell
has to be rung to get the honourable members into the House. Even the
members whose questions appear on the day's list may not be present in
the House when the Speaker calls them formally to ask the questions![10]
Attendance on Friday, the day set for the discussion of Private Members'
Bills, which is thus truly the members' event, is, ironically, often the
lowest! Besides, Parliamentary sessions are shrinking over a period of
time. In 1956, the Lok Sabha sat for 205 days; in 1987 the count was but
152 days. In 1986 and 1987 the Lower House took 29 and 26 days
respectively to pass the Union Budget. The legislative slackness persists
over time.

OTHER TOOLS AND MECHANISMS

Reference so far has been made to the external aspect of accountability.
Accountability has an internal aspect as well. All civil servants working in
a ministry are accountable to the minister. As the minister is responsible to
the legislature for actions (and inaction) of the civil servants, the latter
must obviously be held accountable to him. This boils down to the
following:

1. The civil servants must know well their minister's mind and seek
    faithfully to project it in what they do.
2. They must observe, in all their official transactions with citizens, due
    process of law and laws of natural justice.
3. They must remain alive to the sensitivities of the legislature and must
    abjure from doing things which might embarrass the minister, par-
    ticularly in his relationship with the former.
4. They must be responsive to the larger public opinion.

Accountability is made more specific and is ensured by a complex of
organizational and procedural devices. Hierarchy is itself an accountabil-
ity-fixation exercise.[11] Therefore, without adequate control and supervision over the actions of the lower levels, accountability can hardly be
enforced. Span of control, unity of command, inspection, supervision, etc.,
are other well-known devices facilitating accountability. Noting is also a
mechanism of accountability. Devices like the memorandum of
understanding call for wider application. To ensure financial accountability, a financial advisory system with the use of zero-based budgeting is
now apart of each ministry. Lateral agencies like the ministry of Home
Affairs, ministry of Finance, etc., are other accountability mechanisms.

Audit is another powerful tool of accountability, so powerful that the Comptroller and Auditor-General is one of the topmost constitutional functionaries and is independent of the executive.

CONCLUDING OBSERVATIONS

For the sound health of the state system, its three organs—the executive, the legislature, and the judiciary—must remain in a state of dynamic equilibrium, for any disturbance in their equation subjects the political system to stress, which does not augur well for the continued health of the polity. In present-day Indian polity the classical mechanisms to keep the executive accountable are sadly found to be insufficient and inadequate. The power of the executive has expanded enormously, largely by design but partly also by accident. Parliament's control over the executive is inadequate, the two bodies being ill-matched. Consequently, the controlling authority of Parliament is also ineffective. The executive is not compelled to take action even against a civil servant censured by Parliament.

The control of the political executive cannot be qualitatively different in its impact from parliamentary control. The political executive is but a microcosm of Parliament. If Parliament cannot even remotely touch the public servant, it is too much to expect the political executive to consistently keep the civil service accountable.

Effective control should not be confused with exercising terror. Control must not in the least be inhibitive of managerial initiative and risk taking—qualities which are vital for growth and development. But terror tactics, through arbitrary actions, may totally demoralize the bureaucracy. Adequate control on the executive, and thereby the public administration, calls for an alert judiciary, a vigilant Parliament, a fearless and watchful press, and powerful watchdog organizations. It is vital, therefore, that these institutions move forward to restructure themselves, redesign their business practices, and thus reinforce themselves. The emergence of the administrative state is inevitable in modern times but its abuses and dangers posed must be countered by strengthening extra-administrative state institutions and processes. The unwieldy size of present-day bureaucracy itself makes it difficult to bring it to account. Civil service must be pruned; and the surviving part should, as far as possible, be brought under social audit.

It is universally acknowledged that the civil service in most countries is much larger than the need. It must be pruned. The civil service is much more costly than a country can afford; this calls for strong cost containment programmers aimed at reforming public pay and employment systems.

The issue of civil service pay and employment poses three major problems demanding urgent reform. First, excessive public wage bills, confirmed by a high ratio of personnel expenditure to government revenue must be brought down. Secondly, there is a need for wage compression. This means that the ratio between the highest and the lowest civil service salary must be brought down. Also, the present practice of proliferation of non-wage benefits for civil servants must be discouraged if not totally neutralized. Reform is equally called for to improve morale and productivity in the civil service. Similarly, attention needs to be given to introduce modern management skills in the civil service. Career development and merit-based promotion should be energized. What is emphasized is that civil service is in need of wide-ranging, multi-prong reform, and no single item can be an effective cure. Also, accountability would have greater meaning if common citizens are given the right to sue a public functionary for damages caused by negligence. The law of torts needs to be developed by effective judicial interventions and interpretations. No amount of external accountability, however, matches in quality the pride in one's work and in one's worth. The ultimate endeavour, therefore, must be to humanize and professionalize the bureaucracy.

NOTES

1. This has been done explicitly under the Forty-Second Amendment to the Constitution, passed in 1975.

2. Yet, the President of India enjoys one effective power—that of inviting the leader of the party commanding a majority in the Lok Sabha to form the ministry. When no party has a clear majority, the President has to use his discretion, which confers on him real power. To keep the President within bounds the Constitution lays down a procedure of his impeachment.

3. Herbert Morrison, *Government and Parliament*, London: Oxford University Press, 1964, p. 332.

4. *Lok Sabha Debates*, Vol. XI, No. 7, 18 February 1958, Col. 1283.

5. *Times of India*, 14 February 1958.

6. *Report of Inquiry into the Affairs of Life Insurance Corporation of India* (Chairman; M.C. Chagla), p. 23.

7. Sir Warren Fisher made this observation while giving evidence before the Tomlin Commission on the Civil Service in Britain (1929–31). See *Royal Commission on the Civil Service: Minutes of Evidence*, London: HMSO, 1931, p. 1268.

8. N. C. Ranga,: 'Parliamentary Armoury of Democracy: Old and New Weapons', in S.L. Shakdher (ed.), *The Constitution and the Parliament in India*, Delhi: National, 1976, p. 271.

9. M. Ruthnaswamy, 'The Manner of Members in Parliament, in S.L. Shakdher (ed.), *The Constitution and the Parliament in India*, p. 336.

10 As an example see *Lok Sabha Debates*, 13 March 1979.

11. Paul H. Appleby, *Policy and Administration*, Alabama: University of Alabama Press, 1949, p. 72.

CHAPTER 19

Road Map to the Future
The Fifth Central Pay Commission and Beyond

A discussion on the higher civil service in India is apt to be considered incomplete and insufficient without a peep into its future role and shape, which compels a careful study of the Fifth Central Pay Commission. Though not exactly in the category of pay commissions, important in their own right are the other committees appointed around this time. The opening of the twenty-first century witnessed a revival of interest in the country's civil service. Leadership in this respect has been provided by the following three committees: (1) The Surendra Nath Committee on Performance-Oriented Appraisal System (2) The B.N. Yugandhar Committee on Upgrading Civil Service Skills, and (3) The P.C. Hota Committee on Civil Service Reforms.

The Fifth Central Pay Commission under the chairmanship of S. Ratnavel Pandian was appointed in 1994 and reported in September 1997, taking over three years to complete its task. It examined matters relating to the pay of civil servants but in addition it looked into questions of civil service reform. The pay body looked at the task of governance in the twenty-first century. Civil service by its definition as an agency of the state to subserve its goals, its being of instrumental value. In India, civil service is presently obliged to find its true role within the established framework of economic liberalization, free market, and globalization. Inevitable under the new dispensation, the state reduces its role as manufacturer of goods and services. It has instead to ensure that a level playing field is provided to both domestic and international players. At the same time, it has to play a major part in promoting infrastructural and social services as also in combating poverty and unemployment. The new challenges call for a sea-change in the role and place of the civil service. From mere controller and regulator, it is obliged to get converted into a catalyst, promoter, and facilitator. The emerging parameters within which the country's civil service would be obliged to operate must need to be carefully understood. The civil service must concentrate on the core duties of government and ensure that non-core functions be off loaded on to the non-governmental sector. This entails downsizing (or right-sizing) of the public bureaucracy and reduction in its flab, which would involve bold measures of privatization or corporatization and contracting out. Downsizing calls for re-engineering of the entire administrative set-up to make it functional, efficient, productive, cost-effective, and service-oriented. At the same time, the civil service must evolve and enforce performance standards, promote transparency in public administration, emphasize productivity, quality, courtesy, and customer satisfaction. Above all, accountability must be enforced and rewards and punishments must be closely related to performance.

Under the above dispensation the future civil service would be a facilitator of economic activity and builder of the infrastructure. Equally, it is to promote its role as investor in social services as well as in poverty alleviation programmes. It follows from the foregoing that the civil service needs to be right-sized and an officer-orientation brought about. Government itself needs to be restructured by closing down departments or amalgamating them by transferring subjects and institutions to the state government and Panchayati raj bodies, by converting departmental undertakings into public sector undertakings and by encouraging cooperatives, autonomous bodies and non-governmental organizations to take over some of the functions of the state. In other words, reliance is to be put on civil society. Simultaneously, the government office needs to be reinvented. Large, unwieldy sections have to give way to small, business-like desks, the vast army of ministerial staff may be gradually replaced by executive assistants, with the group 'D' personnel being trained as multi-skilled functionaries. Automation and computerization should be brought in wholesale, so as to cut down paper-work. Employees could be seated in large ergonomically designed halls with furniture of modular design in an aesthetically pleasing environment. Their productivity can be increased remarkably by cutting down on holidays, keeping a check on punctuality by adopting the time-clock system and asking canteens to serve tea right on their tables. In India, the work of the government is shrouded in mystery and the Official Secrets Act gives the prevalent furtiveness a legal sanction. What is required is a Right to Information Act, under which citizens enjoy a right to find out exactly what is going on, at least immediately after a decision is taken. Transparency also means that all decisions are reasoned ones and contain an innate justifying logic.

India needs a reformed civil service to fit this new role. For the present, there is no alternative to the competitive exanimations held by the Union Public Service Commission, the Staff Selection Commission, the Railway Recruitment Board, etc. to get the best talent. But these bodies need not be bothered if recruitment to less than 15 jobs is involved. Employment on contract basis should as a policy be encouraged. Government employees should have the right to retain their lien for two years in case they wish to migrate to the private sector. Several steps have been suggested by the Fifth Pay Commission to make performance appraisal more effective. The Annual Confidential Report (ACR) format should follow the rating system based on a 10-point scale as in the armed forces. Any performance below the benchmark laid down for promotion should be treated as adverse. The final grading should be communicated to the employees. An important suggestion of the pay body is that of a quinquennial appraisal of group A officers, so that a fuller picture of the personality emerges after every five years. Remarks about integrity would be allowed in such periodical reviews by a knowledgeable group and could lead to compulsory premature retirement of the officer in a manner that would be upheld by the courts.

Many solutions have been tried out in the past to remedy stagnation. The Pay Commission suggested an Assured Career Progression scheme (ACP), under which two guaranteed financial upgradations would be given to group B, C, and D officials after 8 and 16, 10 and 20, and 12, and 24 years respectively. For group A cadres, there would be three such upgradations after completion of 4, 9, and 13 years of service. The benefit of higher pay scale, including pay fixation, would be available but not a functional promotion to the higher post.

There is also a Flexible Complementing Scheme, which had been initially designed for the group A scientists involved in research. A number of functional promotions were made under this scheme in scientific departments notified as such by the Department of Science and Technology. The Fifth Pay Commission widened the scope of the scheme so as to cover all research and development professionals, whether they are scientists, technologists or medical and computer professionals, at the same time taking out of the scheme certain non-entitled categories which had managed to get the benefit undeservedly.

In order to build the spinal chord of the bureaucracy, the Pay Commission advocated the constitution of a high-powered civil services board both at the Centre and the states. The civil services board would attend to the vexed questions of postings and transfers. Minimum tenures would have to be notified for each post. Appointments, even in the states, have been suggested through the mechanism of the civil services board and the Appointments Committee of the Cabinet. No premature transfer would be allowed except after a proper case giving detailed reasons for such transfer has been moved to the civil services board. The findings of the board are to be accepted invariably and in case of disagreement, the entire proceedings have to be laid on the Table of the House. Government employees who bring extraneous pressures to bear for their postings and transfers would have to be proceeded against departmentally.

Coming to the employment in the central government, the Pay Body first analysed the rate of growth in the size of the government machinery. Contrary to popular belief, the annual compound rate of growth in the number of civilian employees during 1984–94 was 1 per cent, while the armed forces personnel increased by an annual rate of 1.4 per cent. Among the civilians, the central police organizations multiplied very fast, showing a growth rate of 5.6 per cent. The pay body advocated a multi-pronged strategy to cut down numbers. First, the central government had a backlog of 350,000 vacant posts. These could be abolished straightway. Secondly, there could be a freeze on further employment of junior staff while a sharp cut-back in intake has been advocated for the executives. Thirdly, there is need for a perspective manpower plan under which there would be a downsizing of numbers by 30 per cent in a 10-year period. This could be achieved by the usual wastage through deaths and retirements, assisted by a greater number of retirements under the Voluntary Retirement Scheme with the golden handshake and compulsory retirement of those who are found to be incompetent or corrupt. Detailed strategies have been worked out for the optimization of the all-India and central services, scientific, engineering and medical services, and employment in the departments of railway, posts, telecommunications, central police organizations and the defence services. In each of these, a minimum cut of 30 per cent in the next 10 years was recommended.

GENERAL PRINCIPLES FOR PAY DETERMINATION

Coming to the principles of pay determination, the pay body examined the concepts of inclusiveness, comprehensibility, and adequacy, and the parameters of job evaluation, fair-comparison, equal pay for equal work and model employer. Among the parameters, the pay body felt that job evaluation cannot be applied in such a short period; it can possibly be relevant if a permanent pay body is set up. Comparisons with the public and private sector have many limitations, but these have to be necessarily made not with a view to granting parties but in order to establish some broad relativities. The central government can no longer pretend to be a model or even a good employer in the context of other sectors of the economy having forged ahead of it in the matter of compensation packages to employees. What the Pay Commission did was to apply a number of parameters simultaneously. One of the principles is the intrinsic value of a job, as shown by the skill, the drudgery, the work environment, the qualifications required, the power, the prestige, the perquisites—all the quantifiable and non-quantifiable characteristics which make a job what it is. Then there is the delinking of pay from rank in the hierarchy, which has been introduced through the Assured Career Progression scheme. A broad framework of qualification-based pay scales has also been hinted at, by trying to bring about a broad uniformity between jobs requiring a minimum qualification of middle, matric, 10+2 with 2-year diploma, 10+2 with 3-year diploma, graduate in arts, agriculture, law, science, postgraduate degree in arts/science/commerce, degree in medicine, engineering, technology, etc. An attempt has been made to merge small entities with larger ones: isolated posts have been placed in cadres and disjointed cadres combined into services. Thus, for example, a Subordinate Economic Service has been suggested to combine all the posts of junior and senior economic investigators in different ministries. So, the pay commission mooted the idea of new all-India services in the fields of medicine and engineering and central services for agriculture, veterinary science, informatics, libraries, archives, archaeology and the like.

In order to arrive at the new pay scales, the Pay Commission first tried to fix the two cardinal points of minimum and maximum salary. For minimum salary, the commission requested the country's National Productivity Council for advice. The commission arrived at a figure of Rs 2440 as the minimum salary. A figure of Rs 26,000 per month has been suggested as the maximum pay—that is, the salary to the secretaries to the Government of India. This incidentally keeps the minimum-maximum ratio stable at 1: 10.7, which was the ratio determined by the Fourth Pay Commission.

The civil services are currently classified into groups A, B, C, and D. The Commission suggested a classification into top executives (secretaries, special secretaries, additional secretaries and equivalent), senior executives (joint secretaries, DIGs and equivalent), executives (all others in group A), supervisory personnel, support personnel and auxiliary personnel. The commission also recommended that the distinction between gazetted and non-gazetted officers in the government be abolished. These two suggestions are intended to take the bureaucracy out of its feudal past into a modern present.

CIVILIAN EMPLOYEES: PAY SCALES

The Pay Commission suggested a merger of pay scales, with the result that the total of 51 pay scales which existed then were reduced to 34. Regarding all-India services pay (AIS), the Pay Commission suggested several steps to strengthen their all-India character. For direct recruits, the allotment of cadre has been recommended on the basis of 'merit-cum-option' while for promotees, 50 per cent of them are to be allotted to contiguous states in the same region. The commission also recommended that each AIS officer should mandatorily have to do at least one stint in the Government of India. The commission made several suggestions in order to stiffen the backbone of the AIS officer. The state governments should have only the power to recommend their suspension, giving full reasons, and the central government should decide the matter one way or the other within five days of the reference. The central government should have the power to change the cadre of an AIS officer if he is found to have developed too close a nexus with local elements. State governments should also follow the procedure of posting officers on the recommendations of a civil services board and through the Appointments Committee of the Cabinet. There should be prescribed minimum tenures for each post and no premature transfer should be allowed, except according to the prescribed procedure after a reference to the civil services board.

With regard to the edge in pay scales that is currently enjoyed in respect of three scales of pay by the officers of the Indian Administrative Service and the Indian Foreign Service, the commission did not find any persuasive reason to disturb the same and as such the replacement pay scales are suggested. In order to set the controversy of a single examination at rest, the restoration of the old system of examination which used to prevail before 1979 was suggested. It has also been suggested that no IAS officer should be posted as a district collector unless he has completed nine years of service. All posts of Director General of Police in the states are to be uniformly remunerated. Currently, there is no cadre post of additional DGP in the states. In fact, the Ministry of Home Affairs had made an abortive attempt to abolish these posts but had to retrace its step in view of the strong reaction from state governments. The commission has recommended that the rank of additional DGP be recognized. The demand of the IPS Association for abolition of the rank of DIG was not accepted, as it was functionally necessary at the level of the range and there was no desire to disturb the established relativities with the armed forces. There has been a long-standing demand that the Indian Forest Service should be at par with the IPS. This has been accepted.

The commission took special steps to ameliorate the conditions of all group A central services. Uniform career prospects in all services being a distant objective, the best option is to go for a model cadre structure. The distribution of posts at different levels is laid down as under:

Scale	Percentage of senior duty post	Mandatory eligibility period
Senior Time Scale	30	5th year
Junior Administrative Grade	30	9th year
Selection Grade	20	14th year
Senior Administrative grade	17	17th year
Higher Administrative grade	3	25th year

The Fifth Pay Commission rationalized cadre services. Cadre reviews are now a part of the cadre rules and they are mandatorily to be held every five years. Moreover the holding of a cadre review itself is being declared as a justiciable matter. Optimization of numbers has also been advocated, by reducing the numbers in each service by 30 per cent. The obvious solution is to target an overall cut of 30 per cent in the total numbers, but their distribution over the different pay scales has to be adjusted so as to bring it closer to the model cadre structure. While cadre control continues to be vested in the present cadre controlling authorities, it has been suggested that an officer of the particular central service in the rank of Joint Secretary/Director/Deputy Secretary be posted in the office of the cadre controlling authority, to keep an eye in the interest of the service. For the medical services, the pay commission recommended an all-India health and medical service as a long-term objective. A high-powered panel should open a dialogue with the states in order to form such a service within five years. Meanwhile, the pay body recommended that existing central health and medical posts be unified into a single central health service with common seniority. Entry into the service should be at graduate, specialist and superspecialist levels, but seniority should be integrated at each level. In case superspecialists are not available on normal terms, they could be taken on contract on negotiated terms and conditions.

Project allowance is granted when employees work on major projects in undeveloped/underdeveloped areas to compensate them for lack of basic amenities and facilities. Training allowance is currently given at the rate of 15 per cent of basic pay. The commission recommended that the percentage should remain unchanged, and the allowance be made admissible to all faculty members, including trainers on deputation from universities and other academic institutions. The Fifth Pay Commission suggested that civil servants of and above the rank of deputy secretary and equivalent should be provided with a telephone attendant at their residences. The attendant would be recruited directly by the officer and would not enjoy the status of a government employee, but the fixed salary of Rs 1500 per month for such attendants would be borne by the government. This facility will not be additionally available to officers who are already entitled to personal attendants by whatever name they may be called. In the armed forces, an entertainment allowance is admissible to certain officers who are required to entertain high-ranking guests or reciprocate such gestures. The pay commission recommended that for certain specified officers on the civilian side, both in the Centre and the states, entertainment allowance ranging from Rs 600–1000 per month be paid. There are certain allowances and facilities already available to officers of AIS and the central government posted in the North-East. These have been liberalized. The Special Duty Allowance has been retained at 12.5 per cent of the new basic pay, with no upper ceiling. Officers can retain accommodation at the place where their family is staying on payment of normal license fee and also retain a residential phone at government expense.

Hours of Work, Holidays, and Overtime Allowance

Some drastic suggestions have been made under this head, in order to increase productivity in government offices. These are:

a)   Shift from 5-day to 6-day week, with second Saturday being off day: This would mean an increase of 40 working days in a year.

b)   Gazetted holidays have been reduced from 17 to 3—namely, Republic Day, Independence Day, and Mahatma Gandhi's birthday. The reduction of 14 days here has been made up by increasing the number of restricted holidays.

c)   No holidays to be declared on the demise of any leader, except the incumbent President of India and Prime Minister.

d)   Overtime allowance should be abolished.

The Pay Commission recommended a series of measures to benefit women employees in the government. Some of these are enumerated below:

a)   The quantum of maternity leave has been enhanced from 90 to 135 days.

b)   Paternity leave of 15 days has been recommended for male employees during the confinement of their wives.

c)   Flexi-time and flexi-place has been suggested on a pilot basis.

d) Age of initial recruitment for women has been enhanced to 35 years.
e) Part-time employment on optional basis has been introduced, with the proviso that they can work half-time for 6 years connected with two child-rearing periods at half the salaries, with the period of service counting for all purpose.

The pay body recommended the age of superannuation to be 60 years for all employees, except for personnel of central police organizations and the armed forces. Voluntary retirement has been recommended under two different schemes. One is the normal scheme of voluntary retirement after a service of 20 years, which is retained. A special scheme of VRS with a golden handshake is being proposed for departments having identified surplus staff. Apart from the normal weightage of 5 years, this scheme envisages cent per cent commutation of pension and special exgratia payment.

The pay commission estimated that the additional annual financial implications for acting on its report would come to Rs 8800 crore. The total financial implications of implementing the Pay Commission's report for a period of 27 months from 1.1.1996 to 31.3.1998 is likely to the Rs 11,262 crore.

The Fifth Pay Commission recommended that pay revision should, in future, be entrusted to a permanent pay commission drawing its authority from a constitutional provision, whose recommendations should have a binding character. Pay should be revised annually as in other countries. As an alternative, it has been suggested that dearness allowance should be converted into dearness pay every time the cost of living rises by 50 per cent over the basic level. This would imply a revision of pay every four to five years. The final option is to have a decennial exercise as at present, but with fixed dates. The Commission has suggested that the date of constitution of the next pay commission should not be later than 2003 and the date of implementation of its recommendations should be 2006, irrespective of when its reports is submitted.

The foregoing narrative presents a broad blueprint of the future civil service of India. Since the 1980s, new concepts are assailing public administration, thus marking a paradigm-shift in its theory as well as practice. Further, the public bureaucracy is universally viewed as a great sinecure and society is in search of alternatives, which it sees in the market and civil society. Public administration of the land is on the retreat, the new dominating concerns being the off-loading of its functions and more and more attention to efficiency, the economy, and effectiveness. These new waves are reaching India through the report of the Fifth Central Pay

Commission. Its report continues to be India's most authentic explicit text on the shape of the country's emerging civil service. The pay body has shown ample generosity in responding to the civil service's financial expectations but will the latter return the value of the money spent on them? As said in the beginning of the chapter, three committees made their submissions in the early years of the twenty-first century. In a space of less than two years, three committees have reported on various facets of civil service reform in India. In 2003, the Government of India appointed the Surendra Nath Committee to examine the performance appraisal system for the higher civil service. Later, B.N. Yugandhar was invited to suggest ways of strengthening the administrative capabilities in the all-India services at different stages of their members' service careers. The latest report on the civil service reform is presented by the Civil Service Reform Committee headed by P.C. Hota. All the three ventures referred to have been bureaucratic exercises, manned by governmental functionaries only. The civil service of the land claims only instrumental value and it would have been very wholesome to impart to the reform exercise a broader social base. The Surendra Nath Committee stressed the need for weeding out the 'deadwood' in the civil service at the age of 50 or on completion of twenty years of an officer's service. At present, nine of ten officers get graded 'outstanding', which is puzzling. Grading of performance should be honest and realistic. If senior officers do not change their mindset, no significant reform in any sector of administration much less civil service is possible. The hallmark of the Indian Civil Service is the supremacy of the generalist, which must undergo suitable modifications. The Surendra Nath Committee has recognized the need and recommended that civil servants should pick three areas of specialization and their postings and transfers should only be in these three areas.

The B.N. Yugandhar Committee, reporting in 2003, recommended a series of measures to upgrade the skills and competencies of the all-India personnel. Its report is a sort of handbook of desirable training of the higher civil service in India.

The latest report, submitted in July 2004, is of the Civil Service Reform Committee appointed in February of the same year. One may not find in the report any grand vision or future map of the state and the role and place of its front, namely the civil service. The committee made 64 recommendations in all. This study focuses on a few of them considered to be of critical importance.

Being a career service, the civil service recruits young graduates at their college-leaving stage, and examines them in subjects of academic import. Should they fail in the competitive test, they are still young enough to start a career elsewhere. The age group, therefore, corresponds with the college-leaving age. For the first twenty-years after Independence, the age-group eligible for entry into the civil service was 21–4. Under populist pressure the upper age for entry into the public service went upwards. In the 1970s the upper age was first raised to 26 years only to be further raised to 28 later on. In December 1998, the upper age limit was fixed at 30, the lower age remaining at 21. The upper age for Scheduled Castes and the Scheduled Tribes is 35 years, and for Other Backward Classes 33 years. It is an established public policy in India to give a grace of five years to the weaker sections, the underlying idea being that such deprived people confront serious handicaps in life and complete their education much later. A candidate is allowed four chances but those coming from marginalized groups can appear as many times as they want, subject, of course, to the upper age limit. However, they do not remain in the service long enough to rise to the level of Secretary to the Government of India, for they get overtaken by the retirement age much before they are within the sight of the top positions. The Hota Committee on Civil Service Reform has recommended 21–4 years as the age of eligibility for general candidates. The proposed age-group 21–4 may be too urban-centric, even elitist, and may result in keeping out of recruitment the students in rural areas where education starts late in life and where more than seventy-five per cent of India's population lives. Society in India is not homogeneous. A lower age-group may equally hit hard the candidates coming from disadvantaged sections of the society in which education traditionally starts later in life. Equity demands fixing the upper age at 26, which was the upper age for quite some time in India.

The Hota Committee has recommended that at fifteen years of service of an official, a review must be undertaken of his performance based on the earlier quinquennial review of performance. Low performance and low integrity should be visited by punitive action.

An acute problem plaguing the civil service in India is that of constant reshuffling of officers, especially in key postings. Civil servants do not enjoy fixed tenure but the empirical reality is even more shocking. A District Collector in Uttar Pradesh, for instance, has an average tenure of 60 days and a Superintendent of Police serves a district for an average of 35 days according to a recent research study. This may not be exactly true but yet is not way off the mark.

The practice of administrative transfers must also undergo a change. An officer should enjoy a fixed tenure of three years and transfers should be announced in April–May of the year only. Some reformers even support posting for a term of five years—the time span of the country's Five-Year

Plan—for better enforcement of accountability. A posting for a period shorter than three years is apt to make a mockery of accountability. A transfer before the expiry of three years must as a rule be made with the explicit consent of the state chief minister or prime minister. It would be better to regulate the recruitment and conditions of service of civil servants under a law to be enacted by the appropriate legislature. It would be appropriate to set up the civil services boards to implement a stream-lined transfer and promotion policy to assist the political executive in effectively managing the civil service system. Such a civil service board should function under the Cabinet Secretary at the Centre and the chief secretary in the state. India must institute a statutory barrier to frequent transfers of senior officers.

The Hota Committee has also sought closer supervision of the junior officers to ensure better performance. Officials indulging in corrupt practice and found with assets disproportionate to known source of income must be summarily dismissed or removed. Functioning of government offices having large interface with the common man should be periodically assessed by independent organizations. In addition, the Civil Service Reforms Committee has made recommendations to make the civil service e-government friendly.

CHAPTER 20

Challenges for the Future

Despite seven sets of administrative reform packages and recommendations of committees, the civil service in India bears the indelible mark of
Thomas Babington Macaulay (1800–1859): his Report on the Indian Civil
Service (1853) continues to govern its supreme philosophy, notwithstanding the fact that the Report was submitted more than 150 years ago. His
recommendation for the supremacy of the generalist administrator in the
system of governance continues to be the cornerstone of the civil service in
India. How long Macaulay will continue to animate the civil service in the
future is a relevant topic of discussion. Inauguration of the policy of
economic liberalization in 1991 has put the civil service in a new trajectory, accelerating its pace of change and calling for necessary adjustments.
Under the new policy of 1991, India would get progressively integrated
into the global economic system with freer movement of goods and
capital, resulting in increased intercourse with international players. This
in turn would pose new challenges and make new demands on the
country's civil service. Higher civil servants would be called upon to
negotiate with well-established multinational corporations, testing their
communication skills and knowledge of international economics and
trade. This calls for a well-thought out departure from the prevalent
generalist culture of the civil service in India. Liberalization, already in
accelerated motion, is surely to release new forces demanding new skills
and competence. The future is likely to see the establishment of arbitrating
institutions corresponding to the USA's independent regulatory commissions, which in turn necessitates possession of in-depth knowledge of
numerous areas of social concern. Even the Fifth Central Pay Commission
noted the desirability of establishment of autonomous regulatory agencies

with quasi-judicial powers in order to ensure that the functioning of private units is regulated in the social interest'.[1] What is being contended is that the present structure of the civil service will be called upon in the near future to re-tune and redefine itself, which will compel, among others, a measure of specialization.

One must not conclude from the foregoing that the generalist administrator would become obsolete and wither away. Far from it. The civil service entry into new trajectory referred to above would demand new levels of synthesizing and coordinating skills. A rapidly differentiating society intensifies the search for more sophisticated integrating abilities. If the civil service does not initiate well thought out measures for augmenting the supply of such trained manpower, it will surely face a skills shortage in the years to come.

The presently growing disillusionment with the career bureaucracy has initiated a conscious search for non-state actors. Civil society is dynamic in India since the eighties even though the growth is uneven. What are particularly known as non-governmental organizations are already mushrooming. This third sector is emerging as an alternative to the public bureaucracy. Apart from the fact that the NGOs at the present stage of development suffer from numerous maladies calling for state regulation; they cannot and are not designed to, replace the state and its time-tested instrument, the civil service: civil society including NGOs can at best marginally take the load off the civil service, the former can never be a substitute for it, Various researches undertaken in the country lend reinforcement to this view.[2]

POLITICS-ADMINISTRATION DICHOTOMY EXAMINED

The present study may be accused of subscribing to politics-administration dichotomy under which the civil service is a passive factor and assigned a professional role in implementing public policy. Far from it. Even otherwise, this dichotomy today stands completely repudiated in the light of both theoretical researches into bureaucratic behaviour as well as local empirical realities. Theoretical literature convincingly disproves such a restrictively demarcated role of the civil service. Civil service is not a mere technical instrument: it has an inherent tendency to exceed its instrumental function and emerge as a separate force within society. Employing the generic term 'bureaucracy' for civil service, David Beetham views it as a separate power group within the state, a separate status segment within society at large.[3] Even the chief proponent of the concept, Max Weber (1864–1920) was aware of the special status the bureaucracy enjoyed in society. Weber was aware of the power of knowledge, which bureaucracy by its very definition possesses. Civil service translates political will into action: It has the necessary expertise which is deployed for the conversion. Politics, obviously, cannot do without bureaucracy which in turn makes politics dependent on it. Civil service, thus, possesses larger than life-size image! This is graphically brought out in the BBC serial *Yes Minister*.

Mrs Betty Oldham (MP on Select Committee): Look, Sir Humphrey, whatever we ask the Minister he says is an administrative question for you. And whatever we ask you, you say is a policy question for the Minister. How do you suggest we find out what's going on?

Sir Humphrey Appleby: Yes, I do think there is a real dilemma here, in that while it has been government policy to regard policy as the responsibility of ministers and administration as the responsibility of officials, question of adminis-trative policy can cause confusion between the administration of policy and policy of administration, especially when the responsibility for the administration of the policy of administration conflicts or overlaps with responsibility for the policy of the administration of policy.[4]

Since the sixties, the civil service is increasingly portrayed in a negative light with its hidden policy-agenda and not as a neutral role-payer, as supposedly depicted above, credit going to scholars, all trained econo-mists, like Gordon Tullock, Anthony Downs, William Niskanen, etc.

In his work *The Politics of Bureaucracy*, published in 1965, Gordon Tullock propounds the principal thesis that civil servants are motivated primarily by selfishness. A civil servant is motivated by the desire to enhance his promotion prospects and what is known as public interest is relegated to the periphery. The bureaucrats' pursuit of promotion, which provides them access to political power and enhanced physical comfort, depends on their capacity to please their superiors. Consequently at the top of the organization there is a concentration of officers who are self-servers and self-seekers whose motivation to contribute to formal organi-zational goals is suspect. At the root of this inefficiency lies the fact that civil servants are not subject to the disciplining influence of competition. Gordon Tullock observes :

Government agencies can follow inefficient policies for very long periods without being eliminated ... . The official is much less subject to pressure for efficiency than is the normal business manager. To the individual official, efficiency is meaningful not in terms of the organisation's goals, but in terms of his own.[5]

Tullock concludes:

Much of the modern bureaucracy is simply a mistake. ... continuing features of bureaucracy are met in part by continuing reorganisations. ...; In part, the failures are met by concealed shifts in the objectives of the organisation. ... The government bureau becomes the permanent fixtures, with the objective continually changing. Over time, the vested interests of the bureaucrats themselves become more and more important in justifying the organisation.[6]

Anthony Downs is another scholar who indicts the civil service. His *Inside Bureaucracy*, published in 1967, demonstrates that civil servants are motivated by survival instincts and thus they act in their own self-interest. Anthony Downs classifies them into five basic types: (1) climbers (2) conservers, (3) zealots, (4) advocates, and (5) statesmen. Each category possesses certain traits. 'Climbers' consider power, income, and prestige as all-important in their value system. Conservers place great value on convenience and security. In contrast to climbers, conservers seek merely to retain the amount of power, income, and prestige they already have, rather than maximize them. Zealots are loyal to relatively narrow policies or concepts such as the development of nuclear power, to which they are loyal. The fourth category of bureaucrats, namely 'advocates' are loyal to a broader set of functions or to a broader organization than zealots. They also seek power because they want to exercise significant influence over policies and action associated with the concerned functions or organizations. Statesmen are loyal to society as a whole. They desire power in order to have significant influence upon national policies and actions. They are altruistic since their loyalty is to general welfare. Statesmen thus resemble the classical bureaucrats of the textbooks. The central thesis of Anthony Downs is that a civil servant is motivated by self-interest even when acting in a purely official capacity. In business administration individual self-interest is checked and diluted by the fear of loss of sales and declining profit. But in public administration, the self-interest of the public bureaucracy is unrestrained by an absence of market discipline. The absence of a competitive environment means that bureaucratic behaviour is primarily determined by consideration of power, prestige, money, security and convenience. Anthony Downs develops from this his Law of Self-Servicing Loyalty, by which he means that all officials exhibit relative strong loyalty to the organization when job security and promotion is at stake. To serve self-interest of the bureaucrats abstract bureau-ideology, even when it undergoes a change, maintains or expands its scale of activities, as the top-level officials' utmost concern of is to justify the present size of the bureau.

The most severe criticism of the civil service, however, came from William Niskanen, an economist by training. Most studies of bureaucracy, one needs to be reminded, have been by sociologists and political scientists (or public administration experts). Niskanen's *Bureaucracy and*

Representative Government, published in 1973, is a rather unique work where economic concepts are applied to the problem of design and operation of a bureaucracy and are provided a prescription for radical changes. As is to be expected from an economist, the book bristles with data and supply and demand curves as well as equations. Niskanen's contribution marks a kind of revolution in the study of civil service. He studies important questions such as: can the responsiveness and efficiency of bureaus be significantly improved? Can some public services be efficiently supplied by other forms of organizations? Can representative government better express our demands for public service? How? *Bureaucracy and Representative Government* criticizes the career bureaucracy on many counts. Civil servants' attitude towards the consumers of their services is different from the attitude of the private sector's producer to his customers. The producer's revenue comes from his customer but in government there is no clear correlation between public revenue and expenditure: the revenue comes from the Finance Ministry. Secondly, a civil servant has little incentive to minimize costs and maximize profits. In government he does not gain financially from any such transaction. A civil servant, according to William Niskanen, is budget-maximizer. He tries to get maximum budget allocation for his bureau in order to enhance *salary*, perks, power, patronage, and public reputation. The bureaucrat's budget maximizing behaviour inevitably leads to oversupply of public service to justify expansion of the bureau, its staff, and equipment. The bureau's per-unit cost of production is surely to go up as no incentive system is in operation—the saving of the tax-payers' money is hardly an incentive. William Niskanen built a formidable case for the public choice theory, arguing that the government bureau's revenue does not depend on the customer and as such the officials are indifferent to them. The public choice theory abolishes the monopoly of the government in respect of the supply of public services: it instead introduces market. As under the public choice theory, public bureaus will get exposed to competition, there will be a continual search for improvement in service standards. This promotes decentralization also: as the service users get the choice to choose between competing service suppliers, power is decentralized. Niskanen advocates competition within the bureaucracy to ensure better supply of public services. The monopoly power of the bureaucracy must be reduced by exploring private sources of supply of public services. The increasing dissatisfaction with the performance of bureaucracy stands in sharp contrast to the success of the private sector, which should tilt our inclination towards the private sector for the supply of public services. This being the case, Niskanen recommends the following package of reforms:[7]

a)   Increase the competition among the bureau for the supply of the
     same or similar public services.
b)   Change in the incentives in the bureaucracy to induce more efficient
     behaviour by the senior bureaucrats.
c)   Increase the competition to the bureaucracy by greater use of private
     sources of supply of public services.

A mix of such mechanisms would prune the bureaucracy and enhance
its performance. Niskanen is of the firm view that 'a better government
would be a smaller government'.[8]

Also, ground level reality in India proves that civil servants are seen
more or less as policy makers, thus assuming the dubious distinction of
policy makers as well as protégés of their political masters. Various
commissions of inquiry set up since 1947 conclusively establish the nexus
between the politician and the civil servant.[9] In short, the role of the civil
service is really much larger than ordinarily supposed.

Historically, India's Civil Service combined both the roles of policy-
making and execution in itself. Such a phase ended with the commencement of the Government of India Act, 1919 when the politician for the first
time made his advent in the country's governmental system—that too in
the 'transferred' half of the provincial administration. From 1921 (when
the Act of 1919 came into force) onwards the civil service was progressively shedding policy-making responsibility. Under the constitution of
India, the civil service is the implementer of public policy, the making of
which is the province of the professional politician although it is even now
formally engaged in subordinate legislation and administrative adjudica-
tion. The civil service is formally committed to the cult of political neutrality
and anonymity but these traits began to be eroded, particularly when
India entered the sixties. 'Wet' posts in the civil service multiplied consequent upon the assumption of new functions by public administration
under the Second Five-Year Plan (1956–61). Many civil servants found
such posts very alluring, making them forget their classic behavioural
code: What maternity is to woman, transfer is to a civil servant. The civil
servant's selective interest in matters of postings and transfers had the
effect of eroding the professional boundary between the politician and the
civil servant. The minister in a democracy enjoys three prerogatives—
right to postings and transfers, right to promote, and right to suspend. A
culture of mutual accommodation was seen to emerge around this time—
a civil servant sought a particular post which the politician minister alone
could confer. Both saw an advantage in developing the unholy alliance.
The minister had the ultimate authority to finalize a questionable deal for
which he wanted a favourable processing of the case by the civil servant.

The latter was inclined to accommodate the minister in anticipation of favourable postings. This is how the process of nexus building and politicization of the civil service began. The Fifth Central Pay Commission has rightly observed: 'Integrity has never been a strong point of the bureaucracy in India and the situation has definitely worsened ill recent years'.[10]

The regrettable fact is that today the higher civil service of the land has abandoned the classical traits of neutrality, anonymity, and objectivity and become politicized. Civil servants are in possession of official files and well know the minutiae of administration, which the minister lacks. They have mastered the rules and regulations and are in a position to show the minister the course of action to achieve his immediate goal. There is a joke in the civil service saying 'you show me the man, I will quote the rule!' What is contended is that the advice given to the minister is not professional, based on public interest but partisan, suited to his personal liking. It should look natural that the whole tribe of the civil service cannot be painted with the same brush. The higher civil service in India may be said to fall into three broad categories: (i) Those who would neither wilt nor tilt; (ii) weather-report readers; and (iii) incorrigibles. The first category of civil servants are truly Weberian and are motivated by public interest, observing a high standard of ethics in their behaviour. The second category of civil servants observes the current trends and swim with the current. If the contemporary culture is of permissiveness, they too would be inclined to make hay. They would closely read the weather-reports and conduct themselves accordingly. They can be swayed either way—to the first category or the third one, depending on the climate of the times. And the third category are black sheep, using their office for purposes of personal enhancement, little caring for the public interest. At present, the number of those in the first category is perceptibly declining and such souls are seen to man peripheral posts in administration, which is not a wholesome sign.

NOTES

1. *Report of the Fifth Central Pay Commission*, p. 962.

2. See present author's *Rural Development in India: A Public Policy Approach*, New Delhi: Sage Publications, second edition, 1995, its chapter on 'Voluntary Organisation and Rural Development', pp. 235–46.

3. Beetham, David, *Max Weber and the Theory of Modern Politics*, London: Polity Press, 1985, Second Edition, p. 67.

4. Lynn, Jonathan and Antony Jay, *The Complete Yes Minister*, London: BBC Books, 1982, p. 176.

5. Gordon Tullock, *The Politics of Bureaucracy*, p. 68.

6. Ibid., p. 193.

7. Niskanen, William A., *Bureaucracy and Representative Government*, Chicago: Aldine-Atherton, 1971, p. 228.

8. Ibid., p. 227.

9. Maheshwari, S.R., *Political Development in India*, New Delhi: Concept Publishing Company, 1984, pp. 98–123.

10. *Report of the Fifth Central Pay Commission*, p. 102.

Index